Relationships and Development

Social Science Research Council

Committee on Social and Affective Development During Childhood

RELATIONSHIPS
AND
DEVELOPMENT

Edited by

WILLARD W. HARTUP
Institute of Child Development
University of Minnesota

ZICK RUBIN
Department of Psychology
Brandeis University

SPONSORED BY THE SOCIAL SCIENCE RESEARCH COUNCIL

LEA LAWRENCE ERLBAUM ASSOCIATES, PUBLISHERS
1986   Hillsdale, New Jersey   London

Lawrence Erlbaum Associates, Inc. Publishers
365 Broadway
Hillsdale, New Jersey 07642

Library of Congress Cataloging-in-Publication Data
Main entry under title:

Relationships and development.

   Based on presentations made at a conference held at
Harwichport, Mass., in June 1982.
   Includes bibliographies and indexes.
   1. Interpersonal relations in children—Congresses.
2. Attachment behavior in children—Congresses.
3. Social interaction in children—Congresses.
I. Hartup, Willard W.   II. Rubin, Zick.   III. Social
Science Research Council (U.S.)
BF723.I646R45   1986 C.2 155.4   85-20517
ISBN 0-89859-621-1

Printed in the United States of America
10 9 8 7 6 5 4 3 2 1

Contents

Preface

It has become a truism that children's social and emotional development emerges from their relationships with other people, especially parents, siblings, teachers, and friends. The central importance of these relationships has been assumed by most major theoretical approaches to child development. Psychoanalytic theory, for example, views children's early relationships with their parents as the primary determinants of personality development. Conceptions of attachment, as elaborated by John Bowlby and others, emphasize the importance of the child's early attachment to a primary caregiver. Social learning approaches focus on reinforcement, modeling, and instruction in the context of the child's social world. The importance of children's social relationships is assumed by caretakers and educators, as well. Parents and teachers are highly attuned to their children's social adjustment—or ''getting along'' or ''relating''—not only because it contributes to a peaceful home or school but also because it enriches the child's social and emotional growth.

Despite this universal acknowledgment of the central role of social relationships in children's maturation, those who research social and emotional development have applied relatively limited conceptual and methodological approaches to the study of early social interaction. There has been considerable research on the nature of parent-infant relationships, and more recently a renewal of interest in children's peer relationships, but for the most part, students of development have taken relationships for granted. They have not systematically explored the various dimensions of children's relationships: the nature and measurement of such aspects as intimacy, hierarchy, reciprocity, and loyalty; the ways in which specific encounters or interactions are organized in relationships over time; the social and emotional resources provided by these relationships; the ways in which these relationships are shaped by the physical environment and the surrounding culture; the ways in which relationships are embedded in complicated social networks; and the ways in which relationships are altered as children themselves change and develop.

Many of these issues have been examined by social scientists concerned with adult behavior but there has been relatively little contact between these scholars—in such fields as social psychology, sociology, social anthropology, ethology, and family therapy—and students of child development. Consequently, our basic knowledge of social relationships is itself undeveloped and anemic. As Robert Hinde (1979) has noted, the contributions of the various disciplines remain fragmented and unintegrated.

This volume attempts to correct the lack of fresh perspectives in the study of children's social relationships and presents a wide range of new and relevant research. The time seems right for such a volume. In recent years there has been a heightening of efforts by social psychologists and other social scientists to develop systematic frameworks within which to view social relationships (e.g., Hinde, 1979; Kelley et al., 1983). At the same time, there have been valuable methodological advances in the study of social interaction and social relationships, especially as they develop over time (e.g., Gottman, 1979). Among developmental psychologists, moreover, closer attention is being paid to the conceptualization and measurement of aspects of relationships. Thus, the ingredients for an integrative effort have been brewing.

In view of these developments, the Social Science Research Council's Committee on Social and Affective Development During Childhood sponsored an interdisciplinary conference on "Relationships: Their Role in Children's Development." The conference, organized by the editors of this volume, was held at Harwichport, Massachusetts, on Cape Cod, in June, 1982. Theorists and researchers representing a wide range of disciplines and perspectives were invited to participate. The atmosphere of the conference was one of heady intellectual exchange, with frequent foraging across disciplinary boundaries. This volume is based on ideas that were first raised and debated at that conference.

Many of the authors have been deeply involved in research on child development, from infancy through adolescence, while others have conducted their research mainly with adults. The contributors represent the disciplines of biology, developmental psychology, social psychology, clinical psychology, sociology, and social anthropology. They also have been identified with a wide range of methodological orientations, including ethology, qualitative observation and ethnography, clinical interviews, questionnaire studies, laboratory experiments, and quantitative analysis of interaction sequences. Most important, each contributor has an important perspective on social relationships that may help to advance our understanding of children's relationships as well as their social and emotional growth.

OVERVIEW OF THE CHAPTERS

In Chapter 1, Willard Hartup provides a map of the territory to be explored: the intersections between relationships and development. He enumerates the various sorts of links between children's relationships and their social and emotional development that we must come to terms with, including the ways in which relationships influence development, the ways in which development influences relationships, and the ways in which relationships influence other relationships.

In Chapter 2, Robert A. Hinde and Joan Stevenson-Hinde focus on the interplay between an individual's personality or temperament, on the one hand, and an individual's social relationships, on the other. They illustrate their conceptual framework with data obtained from detailed observations of mother-infant interaction among rhesus monkeys and of preschool-age children's social interactions at home and school. Their chapter demonstrates the value of an ethological approach to the connections between relationships and development. It reflects Hinde's (1979) position that we must devote major attention to describing dimensions of relationships before we can progress to explaining them. The chapter further emphasizes the need for students of social relationships to consider both the personal characteristics that individuals bring with them to their relationships and the social context in which these relationships take place.

In Chapter 3, L. Alan Sroufe and June Fleeson provide a current view of attachment in infancy, as a reflection not of a characteristic of the infant but of the relationship between the infant and the caregiver. They show how infant-caretaker attachments may shape the child's future relationships and argue that relationship histories are carried forward to new situations, in the form of the person's expectations and understandings about relationships. In this way patterns of relationships may be transmitted from one generation to the next. Sroufe and Fleeson's framework helps to explain the surprisingly great stability of people's patterns of relationships, even in the face of rapid individual development and change. Sroufe and Fleeson also discuss some of the clinical implications of their view of attachment and the construction of relationships, drawing some examples from cases of families with abusive parents and incest.

In Chapter 4, Gerald Patterson shows how investigations of the microdynamics of social interaction—the specific sequences of interactions between mothers and children—can help both to describe and to explain enduring patterns of mother-child relationships. In particular, Patterson is able to shed light on the relationships between parents' failure to monitor and discipline their children, children's antisocial behavior, and maternal rejection. His data also support the notion advanced by Sroufe and Fleeson that children's difficulties in parent-child relationships are likely to produce difficulties in their peer relationships as well.

Whereas the authors of Chapters 2, 3, and 4 are developmental and clinical psychologists (or, in Hinde's case, a biologist) who have focused directly on children's interactions and relationships, the authors of Chapters 5, 6, and 7 are sociologists or social psychologists whose approaches to social relationships derive mainly from studies of adults' relationships. In their chapters, they consider the implications of these approaches for children's relationships and development.

In Chapter 5, Robert S. Weiss takes up the theme of attachment from a unique vantage point. Beginning with his research on the provisions that different types of social relationships furnish to adults, he speculates about the antecedents of these bonds in childhood. In particular, the attachment of adult lovers or spouses may be traced back to the infant's attachment toward its caregiver. Weiss also considers the developmental antecedents of other sorts of social bonds—such as a sense of community—which may be quite distinct from attachment.

In Chapter 6, George Levinger and Ann Levinger summarize a comprehensive new framework for describing the qualities of relationships. This framework was put forth by Harold Kelley and his colleagues (1983), including George Levinger and Ellen Berscheid, and it begins with the premise that to understand relationships we must begin with the systematic description of interaction sequences. (This view is very much in accord with the approaches to describing relationships taken by Hinde and Stevenson-Hinde, and by Patterson.) With this background, Levinger and Levinger consider the temporal course of close relationships, from initiation to interdependence and, in some cases, to dissolution. Their framework is grounded in research with adult relationships, especially those of dating or married couples. They then consider the applicability of this framework to children's developing relationships, both with parents and with peers.

In Chapter 7, Ellen Berscheid grounds her analysis of emotional experience in close relationships in the same general framework introduced by the Levingers. From this perspective, close relationships are found to be necessary but not sufficient conditions for the experience of intense emotion. Within this framework, she goes on to analyze the impact of children's close relationships on their emotional experiences. Berscheid's approach points to the close links throughout the life-span between cognitive development, social relationships, and emotional experience.

In Chapter 8, Barrie Thorne deals with children's peer relationships from the vantage point of a sociological student of interaction. She discusses the pervasive tendency of school children's friendships and social encounters to be separated by sex, and she analyzes in detail the "gender arrangements" that govern this segregation. As a valuable counterpoint to the volume's central concern with children's social development, Thorne also emphasizes the need to understand children's social worlds and experiences in the present.

In Chapter 9, Thomas S. Weisner, a psychological anthropologist, considers some of the ecological and cultural constraints on children's socialization into particular patterns of relationships. Parents and others influence children to value particular styles of relating to others, but there is often a gap between relationship "ideals" and relationships in practice. He illustrates his thesis with observations of socialization in both "conventional" and "nonconventional" American families.

Taken together, the contributions to this volume provide a useful beginning for new considerations of the nature and dynamics of children's social relationships and of the role that these relationships play in children's development.

Willard W. Hartup
Zick Rubin

REFERENCES

Gottman, J. M. (1979). *Marital interaction*. New York: Academic Press.

Kelley, H. H., Berscheid, E., Christensen, A., Harvey, J. H., Huston, T. L., Levinger, G., McClintock, E., Peplau, L. A., & Peterson, D. R. (1983). *Close relationships*. San Francisco: W. H. Freeman.

Hinde, R. A. (1979). *Towards understanding relationships*. London: Academic Press.

Acknowledgments

In addition to the contributors to this volume, the Harwichport conference was enriched by the participation of a number of other researchers and clinicians who either presented papers or served as discussants: Elizabeth Douvan, Carol Dweck, John Gottman, Philip Guerin, Peter Read, Gerald Stechler, Beatrice Whiting, and James Youniss. We are grateful for their contributions, which are in many cases reflected in the final versions of the papers that are published here. In addition, June Fleeson and Joan Sloman prepared valuable summaries of the conference proceedings. Finally, we owe a special debt of gratitude to Peter Read. As program officer at the Social Science Research Council, Dr. Read played a central role in all aspects of this project, from the first plans for the conference to the publication of this volume. We also wish to acknowledge the financial support provided to the SSRC's Committee on Social and Affective Development During Childhood by the Foundation for Child Development.

Relationships and Development

1

On Relationships
and Development

Willard W. Hartup
University of Minnesota

Socialization involves the construction of relationships as well as the inculcation of social skills, social motives, and social norms. The study of relationships, however, is not well advanced and as yet we have an unclear appreciation of the manner in which relationships are implicated in human development. Various writers argue that until we have adequate ways to describe them, we shall be unable to gain a clear understanding of their functions and dynamics (Hinde, 1979). Certainly, relationship outcomes remain difficult to specify among both children and adults.

There are at least three ways in which relationships seem to be involved in individual development: First, relationships are the contexts in which most of socialization takes place. The child does not acquire communication skills in social isolation or in contact with random others. The regulation of emotion and the basic elements of the self-system also have their origins in relationships with significant others (Berscheid, this volume; Sullivan, 1953). We do not know whether relationships affect these acquisitions because most of the child's time is spent with significant others, or because the child's experience within relationships contains unique demands and challenges. It is widely believed, however, that the transactions that the child makes within close relationships and their fluctuations through time have special importance.

Second, relationships constitute bases or resources that enable the child to function independently in the wider world. Thus, a secure attachment between the young child and the mother promotes exploration of the environment away from the mother (Ainsworth & Bell, 1974), a sense of self-efficacy (Mahler, Pine, & Bergman, 1975), and social skill in new situations (Sroufe, 1983). Similarly, children's friendships seem to generate the security and the sense of

1

belongingness that are central to further development (Youniss, 1980). In this sense, relationships are more than mere contexts for social learning; they are gateways or channels to an ever-widening range of experiences.

Third, the relationships of childhood—both those in which the child participates and those that the child observes—serve as important templates or models that can be used in the construction of future relationships. Of course, relationships do not replicate themselves in endlessly repeated cycles over the life course; the quality of any relationship depends, in part, on the specific individual with whom the relationship is formed. But consequences of earlier relationships can frequently be detected in later ones so that, once again, the importance of relationships in development transcends their role in the inculcation of social skills and norms.

Nearly everyone who has studied children has recognized the importance of close relationships in child development. First, came notions that the nature of these relationships is closely linked to psychosexual vicissitudes and that there are critical periods for them (Freud, 1933). Next, came formulations that depicted relationships as bilateral transactions in which two individuals provide one another with a basis for continuing interaction through selective elicitors, reinforcing events, and anticipatory tendencies (Sears, 1951). Relationships have also been conceived as goal-corrected partnerships that operate as feedback systems (Bowlby, 1969) and, elsewhere, as associations based on "interdependence" and "reward and cost" in their formation and maintenance (Kelley & Thibaut, 1978). These notions have enriched the child development literature, most notably with respect to our understanding of the attachment between the infant and its caregiver. The vicissitudes of these attachments have been traced as well as some of their antecedents and sequelae (Sroufe & Fleeson, this volume). More recently, a beginning has been made in studying some of the issues involved in the emergence and maintenance of peer relationships.

But many gaps remain: For example, the central dimensions in the relationships between caregiver and child have not been identified in middle childhood and adolescence. The measurement of certain constructs is not well advanced: Intimacy, reciprocity, commitment, and disillusionment remain elusive notions. We know little about the ways in which specific encounters, interactions, or exchanges are organized in relationships that extend over time. Finally, we are just beginning to understand the resources that certain relationships (e.g., friendships) provide to the child and the ways in which one relationship impinges on another.

In the remainder of this chapter, we consider what it means to adopt a "developmental perspective" in the study of close relationships. Four assumptions must be made in order to do this: First, relationships are describable with reference to their content, qualities, structure, and patterning (Hinde & Stevenson-Hinde, this volume). It is sometimes useful to describe relationships at more than one level of analysis, as when Patterson (this volume) simultaneously measures general dimensions in family interaction (family management) and specific transactions occurring between family members (e.g., coercive exchanges).

Second, we make the assumption that relationships are not static events but dynamic ones. Whether examined in terms of "stages" that include "formation," "maintenance," and "termination" (see Levinger & Levinger, this volume) or whether described in some other manner, it is clear that relationships fluctuate with the passage of time.

Third, individuals change over time. The search for the best ways to characterize developmental change has been a centuries-long undertaking from which we have learned that many motives, affects, and cognitions have "growth functions," i.e., change with age.

Fourth, relationships are, at one and the same time, both independent and dependent variables in social experience. One can, for example, consider relationships as determinants of change in the individuals involved in them. One can also consider changes in individuals as determinants of changes in their relationships. Because these events occur simultaneously, this means that individuals are changed by relationships at the same time that changes in relationships are precipitated by changes in the individuals. Causation thus extends simultaneously from relationships to individuals as well as from individuals to relationships, making it extremely difficult to identify developmental "origins" or "sources."

In this essay, a three-fold scheme is used to examine these dialectics. First, an attempt is made to assess what we know about developmental changes in individuals as determinants of change in their relationships. In doing this, it is necessary to recognize that the developmental status of both children and their companions must be taken into account. Second, an effort is made to bring together various studies dealing with the impact of relationships on individual development. Third, consideration is given to the assessment of relationships in connection with their own future workings as well as the workings of other relationships.

These issues are just beginning to be studied in certain domains (e.g., sibling relationships) but have been examined more extensively in others (e.g., attachment relations involving the young child and the caregiver). In this essay, the contemporary literature has been examined as one would examine a stamp collection; specimens have been sought that illustrate important issues and promising research strategies, but neither a complete review of the literature nor a theoretical synthesis has been attempted. Rather, an effort has been made to provide a sampling of what the field currently has to offer and an assessment of its strengths and weaknesses.

INDIVIDUAL DEVELOPMENT AND ITS IMPACT ON RELATIONSHIPS

Changes in the psychological organization of the child precipitate changes in the child's interactions with others. In this section, some of the evidence pertaining to this assertion is examined along with evidence showing that developmental change in the child's companions has similar effects. Simultaneous consideration of developmental changes in children and in their companions is not easy but, as will be seen, essential to an understanding of the manner in which the development of individuals is associated with the development of relationships.

Changes in the Child

The young infant possesses only rudimentary capacities for coordinating its actions with the actions of other persons, cannot use words, and apparently possesses a limited sense of "self." With time, these conditions change, and the nature of the child's interactions with the caregiver change concordantly. The sources of these changes are probably to be found both within and outside these interactions. That is, certain changes may depend on substrates whose behavioral expression does not depend heavily on experience. On the other hand, the hundreds of hours spent by the child with its caregiver in the first few months of life may also engender developmental change.

Recent studies on the development of focused relationships contain examples: The visual stimuli that infants find attractive change over the first several months of life for reasons that are probably independent of experience. The infant's increasing preference for complexity and contour in visual stimulation has important implications for social interaction, and most writers connect these developmental changes to changes in the infant's preferences for looking at faces. Increasing preference for familiar stimuli has also been demonstrated, and this has been thought relevant to the preference for familiar faces that is usually evident by 4 or 5 months and that coincides with the discriminative social responding emerging at that time. It is important to note that these changes, while localized in the child, precipitate changes in the behavior of *both* child and caregiver in their interaction with one another. Mothers respond with pleasure to signs that the infant recognizes or prefers her to other people as represented, for example, in discriminative smiling. Thus, changes in the child modify not only its behavior vis à vis the significant other but change the actions of the significant other as well.

As the infant grows older, its response to separation from the caregiver undergoes considerable change: Crying and distress in response to separation from the mother are relatively uncommon prior to 5 or 6 months-of-age, increase thereafter, and reach a peak in the first part of the second year; after this, they decline. Rearing conditions and cultural setting seem not to affect the timing of these developmental changes in a major way (Kagan, Kearsley, & Zelazo, 1978). "We can only conclude that the disruptive effects of separation seem to be governed by a cognitive-developmental timetable that is similar in widely different life situations. This timetable seems to determine whether children are old enough to organize voluntary protest behavior and to perceive the uncertainties of a situation and whether they are young enough to feel helpless in the face of these uncertainties" (Maccoby, 1980, p. 58). The profound implications of these changes for the manner in which mother and child manage their relationship are obvious.

Still later, children increase the distance between themselves and their mothers that they can tolerate in exploring the environment. The relationship can be said to facilitate this exploration but one must consider that changes in the child also underlie the increasing distance that children can put between themselves and their mothers. The children have learned that distance signals will work in place of proximal signals for maintaining contact; they have learned to be reassured by the fact that contact *can* be established rather than its actual occurrence. For example, by 30 months-of-age, children play more comfortably in a strange environment if they can see the mother rather than if she is behind a screen, even though they do *not* look toward her more frequently when she is in view (Carr, Dabbs, & Carr, 1975). At this same time, the presence of a peer encourages exploration away from the mother, and the integration of the peer into the exploratory activity becomes increasingly evident (Gunnar, Senior, & Hartup, 1984). The developmental changes occurring toward the end of the second year thus affect the patterning of the child's interactions with the mother, the utilization of other children as "bridges" in exploring the environment away from the mother, and the patterning of the child's interactions with them. While the relationship with the mother and the relationship with the other child may each contribute to changes in the target child, it is clear that changes in the child touch off changes in the patterning of these relationships.

We know relatively little about the developmental changes in the child that generate transformations in the mother-child relationship during the preschool and middle childhood years. Some writers (Maccoby, 1980; Marvin, 1977) suggest that relevant changes consist of the child's growing appreciation of the mother as a separate self—someone who evidences her own thoughts and intentions—as well as the child's increasing capacity to inhibit seeking immediate contact with her. These changes enable the child to participate in relationships based on the sharing of ideas, goals, and plans—as these occur between separate persons—permitting the relationship to be maintained through separations with more assurance than earlier. The preschool and middle childhood years also bring changes in the child's understanding of the motives and intentions of others (Shantz, 1983) and in the ability to inhibit ongoing behavior. It is difficult to believe that these changes are not reflected in the nature of the child's attachment to the mother and, simultaneously, that these changes would not elicit changes in the mother's actions toward the child. Consider, for example, the strategies used in regulating the child's social activities. Social regulation in the preschool years is achieved largely through the use of external guidance. Parents supervise their children closely and intervene when they behave inappropriately; concomitantly, children acknowledge their parents' authority mainly on the basis that "might makes right" (Damon, 1977). In middle childhood, however, mother-child relations are "co-regulated," based on the understanding by both mothers and children that, in certain situations, the child's actions can safely be self-regulated as long as each party knows the whereabouts of the other (Maccoby, 1984). These changes may be precursors of the more extensive decline in external guidance and the concomitant increase in self-regulation that occurs in adolescence. Some writers regard the major changes occuring in parent-child relations in adolescence as changes in strategies for social regulation rather that detachment (Hill, in press). In any case, these transformations seem to be adaptations to the cognitive and emotional development of the child.

Developmental changes are also reflected in peer interaction. These interactions change, over the first 2 years, from simple "interacts" to more complex and coordinated interactions, from loosely coordinated exchanges to coordinated interaction, and from primitive awareness of the needs of others to more complex reciprocities. Some investigators (e.g., Brownell, 1982) consider the second birthday to be a turning point, before which early skills for coordinating one's actions with those of another immature individual are not fully formed and after which children seem ready to enter into give-and-take interaction with other children. Convergences in other domains suggest that changes in combinatorial skills (capabilities to hold two or more units in memory or manipulate them cognitively) may underlie the transitions in child-child relations.

Other cognitive changes contain implications for peer relationships among children. We know that children's conceptions of friendship change markedly in middle childhood; concrete reciprocities loose their centrality whereas intimacy issues become more important (Youniss, 1980). The implications of these changes for interaction among friends, however, are not clear. In fact, age differences in friendship interaction have not been closely scrutinized. Some data sets suggest that preschool-aged friends are not notably more "mutual" and "reciprocal" in their interaction than nonfriends (Hinde, Titmus, Easton, & Tamplin, in press) whereas school-aged friends are (Newcomb & Brady, 1982). Berndt (1981), too, found that fourth-grade friends assisted their partners and were more willing to share rewards with them than were first-graders. But in spite of a growing consensus that an increasing integration of ideas and plans is a general theme of development in middle childhood, very little thought has been given to these changes as a basis for change in friendship interaction during this time (Collins, 1984).

The manner in which the child's development generates changes in the patterning and functioning of relationships has thus received scattered attention. The relevant issues range from the extent to which children increasingly "drive" the relationships in which they are involved to the manner in which new understandings about the social world are reflected in the interactions occurring within a relationship. These issues are significant for the study of relationships involving the child and many different individuals including parents, peers, siblings, and teachers.

Changes in the Partner

Developmental change occurs among children's companions as well as among the children themselves. These changes, too, affect relationships. Especially important is the developmental status of the companion when the relationship begins.

Maternal development as a factor in the mother-child relationship is not well-studied. This oversight undoubtedly emanates from the assumption that the developmental trajectory is relatively "flat" during adulthood and that, during the child bearing years, there are few major reorganizations in cognitive and personality development. There is some question that this is a valid assumption, however, especially when one considers that the child bearing years extend from 12 or 13 years-of-age to 45.

What we know about the age of the mother and mother-child relationships is scattered and mostly tangential to the issue at hand. A small number of studies deal with child-rearing practices, as measured by self-reports among younger and older women. Recent interest in the adolescent mother has spawned a number of other investigations, now in progress, that are focused on the relationship between young mothers and their infants (Crockenberg, 1983), taking into account the life situations and social supports available to them. Indications are that, when adequate social support is available, adolescent mothers are sensitive and accessible to their babies and that attachment relations are not markedly different from those involving older women. Full-scale comparative investigations involving women in various age groups have not yet appeared in the literature. Many issues confront the investigator in conducting these studies, not the least of which is untangling the variations that can be attributed to the age of the mother from those variations that stem from the life situation. For example, teenage mothers, as compared to older mothers, are more likely to be poor and to be unmarried. It is necessary to consider the effects of stigmatization as well—an occurrence which is common in the situation of the adolescent mother and relatively uncommon in the situation of the "one-time" mother in her 20s or 30s.

Comparative studies are also needed that deal with relationships involving primiparous mothers in their late 30s and early 40s as contrasted with younger mothers. Population demographics indicate that an increasing number of women are bearing their first babies at these older ages in most industrialized countries. Studied by Daniels and Weingarten (1980), a "late-late" group of women who had their first children in their late 30s and early 40s reported themselves especially satisfied and ready to be parents but that, overall, there is no single "right time" to have children.

Other interesting and theoretically relevant issues involving maternal development and the mother-child relationship require longitudinal data. For example, the stresses commonly reported in the family relations of adolescents are almost always considered in terms of developmental pressures impinging on the adolescent (Hill, in press). And yet, children move through this period in close relationships with mothers who are themselves entering middle age. Transitional events, such as menopause, have never been examined in relation to these stresses, even though both cross-sectional and longitudinal methods could be used to study them. The relevant issues, of course, involve more than the demonstration that menopause is or is not a stress factor in mother-adolescent relationships. We need to know whether mid-life changes, in general, generate a reworking or restructuring of relationships between mothers and children that are mapped onto earlier transformations.

Some of the same considerations apply to the development of fathers and their relationships with their children. The literature in this area is sparse, although two investigative teams have studied differences in father-child relations as a function of the age of the father. Nydegger (1975, 1981; Mitteness & Nydegger, 1982) contrasted younger and older fathers, partialling out parental experience and other factors that are naturally confounded with paternal age. Older men seem to be better fathers than younger men in some respects—they are warmer, have better communications with their children, are more encouraging of intellectual achievement and individuality, and are less rejecting. On the other hand, older men, as compared with younger men, are less demanding for socialization and less firm in enforcing directives. Similar conclusions were reached by Daniels and Weingarten (1980) who found greater participation in child care by late-timing fathers than early-timing ones. Thus, a beginning has been made that provides information on the developmental status of the father at the outset of the relationship and the father's behavior toward the child. We do not know, however, what concomitant variations there may be in the quality of the relationships that older and younger men construct with their children. Longitudinal studies of the developmental transitions (e.g., mid-life growth and development) in the lives of men and their implications for their relationships with their adolescent and young adult children are also needed.

How does the developmental status of a sibling affect his or her relationships with the target child? Certain investigators have been interested in whether the quality of early sibling relations varies as a function of the age of the older sibling. For example, it has been reported that 6-year-old first borns provide more "teaching" to their younger siblings than 5-year olds do (Pepler, Abramovitch, & Corter, 1981) and that second borns accept directions more readily when the first-born child is 4 rather than 2 years older than the target child

(Cicirelli, 1973). These data are difficult to interpret, however, owing to the confounding of chronological age with the spacing interval between the children (Dunn, 1983). New analyses are needed in order to argue that these differences derive from the developmental status of one sibling or the other as opposed to the difference in age between them. This issue has considerable significance since sibling instruction is thought to be one element involved in birth order and family size effects on intellectual development (Zajonc & Markus, 1975). To elaborate this model fully requires information about sibling age as a determinant of interaction with the target child at the outset of the relationship as well as information about sibling development and changes in their interaction over time.

With regard to child-child relationships, the age of the child's companion relative to the target child makes a considerable difference in the nature of their interaction. The complexity of verbal messages, the amount of social activity, and teaching behaviors are different in interaction with younger associates from with same-age associates or older ones (Hartup, 1983; Holmberg, 1980). The content of the interaction also varies: for example, dependency is more common in interaction with older companions, aggression more common with same-age companions, and nurturance with younger ones.

Mixed-age and same-age *friendships* differ similarly. In one investigation, the interaction of 3-year olds with same-age preferred partners (children with whom the child socialized more than 10% of the time) was compared to interaction with preferred partners who were a year or more older (Attili, Hold, & Schleidt, in press). Same-age friendships were marked by greater reciprocity than occurred in cross-age preferred partnerships. Social play and playful aggression, specifically, were more common in same-age contacts with preferred partners than in contacts with older children. There is some suggestion, then, that mixed-age friendships and same-age friendships may differ in interactive content.

Friendship selection, of course, more frequently involves children of the same chronological age than assortments between children who differ in age (Kandel, 1978). Even so, mixed-age friendships are not unknown and some children form close relationships with children of more than one age (Attili et al., in press). The examination of these relationships thus offers a rich opportunity for assessing the variance in peer relationships generated by the developmental status of children's companions as well as the role of these relationships in socialization.

Concurrent Change in Both Partners

Thus far, changes in relationships have been considered as deriving separately from the child's development or the development of the partner. The extent to which these functions can be studied separately, however, is limited: both the child and the partner account for developmental variance simultaneously. At certain times, when the child's development is rapid and the partner's is slow, changes in the relationship may be attributed primarily to developmental pressures at work on the child. To illustrate: The older infant "drives" the interaction with its mother to a greater extent than does the younger infant as evidenced by differences in configurations of action and reaction in exchanges between them (Stern, 1977). Ordinarily, *development* is thought to underlie the child's contributions to these changes but not the mother's since 6 or 9 months is too short a period to capture anything very significant in maternal development. This is not to say that the mother contributes nothing to the time-related changes in the interaction between her and the child. Rather, we assume that observed changes in her behavior are made in reaction to the child's development (or in an effort to stimulate it) rather than being manifestations of developmental change in the mother herself.

Since maternal development is so slow in relation to the child's development, it is seldom possible to examine its consequences in the short term. For example, the implications of adolescent motherhood can only be identified by means of studies that also include new mothers who are in their late 20s and 30s. Since the children of adolescent mothers and older women may differ, however, it is not easy to untangle the effects of maternal status from child status in these situations.

This problem is even more complex when examining individual development and child-child relationships. One can contrast friendship formation among 4-year-old and 8-year-old children, but it is always necessary to remember that the 4-year old's companions are most commonly other 4-year olds while the companions of 8-year olds are other 8-year olds. The confounding between the child's age and the age of the child's companion is complete, of course, when relationships are studied over time. One child (e.g., a younger one) may develop more rapidly than its companion (e.g., an older one) but, in each case, both are changing.

The difficulties in untangling the developmental sources of changes in child-child interaction can be illustrated with data on siblings (Dunn & Kendrick, 1981). Second-born children were observed at 8 and 14 months in interaction with their siblings who were, on average, 25 months older than themselves. In same-sex pairs, there was a significant increase in the frequency of the infant's positive and negative behavior and an increase in the positive behavior of the older sibling. In different-sex pairs, there was an increase in negative behavior by both children but no change in the positive behavior of either. It would be difficult to argue that these changes do not reflect an increase, between 8 and 14 months, in the infant's competencies for engaging in both positive and negative play interactions. But the beginning of the third year (the time extending between these observations for the older siblings) is now known to be marked by relatively sharp increases in children's capacities for "integrating" their social activities with those of other children—both children of the child's own age and children who are slightly younger (Brownell, 1982). Thus, it is doubtful that the age changes in the behavior of *either* the younger or the older sibling observed by Dunn and Kendrick can be attributed only to the development of the younger ones. Concordantly, it is unlikely that the increasing salience of gender in these data can be attributed only to the emergence of gender norms among the older siblings. There is some possibility that, by 14 months-of-age, the younger siblings were themselves becoming conscious of their own gender and more interested in interaction with the older sibling on that basis (Dunn & Kendrick, 1981).

More differentiated analyses of the interaction between six sibling pairs from this study make it possible to disentangle developmental changes pertaining to the younger child from those pertaining to the older one (Dunn & Kendrick, in preparation). Between their first and second birthdays, the younger children showed increases in responsibility for initiating conflicts in sibling interaction, physical aggression and the appearance of teasing, and certain changes in the way they expressed anger (biting self, throwing things, etc.). Different changes marked their older siblings: for example, increases in verbal reference to social rules and rationales, prohibitions and moral references directed toward the younger child, and references to the older child's own needs and feelings. Thus, greater specificity in the assessment of social competencies across time in both members of the dyad assists in identifying the individual sources of change in these relationships. Considerable advances have been made in the assessment of self- and other-understanding, role emergence, communicative capacities, and play skills in infants and very young children (Shantz, 1983). Thus, we conclude that more carefully executed multivariate studies utilizing such measures could advance our efforts to isolate the individual developmental variance in relationships among children.

Exogenous Pressures (Age-Related)

Relationships are sensitive to situational variations. Ordinarily, the basic relationship does not change between mother and child as they travel from home to supermarket, to nursery school, to laboratory—even though their interactions may be different in these places (Maccoby & Martin, 1983). Setting conditions similarly affect child-child interaction: Children and their friends behave differently toward one another in cooperative and competitive situations (Hartup, 1983) even though these variations cannot be said to alter their relationships.

Relationships are not entirely buffered, however, from the effects of situational exigency. Profound changes in the life situation alter the quality of the mother-child relationship (Vaughn, Egeland, Waters, & Sroufe, 1979) and family disruptions can also change it. Following divorce, for example, mothers become more authoritarian and children, especially boys, less compliant and more aggressive. After a period of time, balance seems to be restored in divorced families, although this restoration occurs at varying rates in different families depending on a variety of factors (Hetherington, 1979). The weight of the evidence suggests that divorce itself stresses the mother-child relationship, i.e., the stress imposed by the conflict leading to the divorce does not account entirely for the changes in mother-child interaction (Hetherington, 1979; Wallerstein & Kelly, 1981). Economic instability, crises imposed by life-threatening illness, and bereavement are other examples of situational changes that may affect ongoing relationships.

In addition to crisis events, certain exogenous pressures on relationships occur normatively, that is, they occur for most individuals in a given culture and are correlated with the chronological age of one or the other member of the dyad. One example consists of the child's entrance into school, an event that is age-related and requires considerable restructuring of family routines. School entrance is a universal event in Western culture. Few good opportunities exist for examining schooling effects per se (e.g., by comparing children who go to school with similar children who do not) but schooling seems to entail changes in the parent-child relationship beyond those transformations that occur during the preschool years. New issues of co-regulation confront parents and children at this time, enabling them to function "together then apart" with some degree of certainty as to each other's whereabouts, normative compliance, and the child's achievement (see above). In addition, time spent in school subtracts from time spent with parents; time spent with peers increases, too, thereby reducing parent-child interaction still further.

Certain studies suggest that schooling effects on relationships may actually begin well before the first day of school. Some parents "lead" the child's development by sending the child to nursery school or arranging other preparatory activities. These tendencies are similar, in many ways, to the manner in which parents "lead" language development in the early years (Bloom, 1970). The content and patterning of parent-child relationships thus change as a function of school entrance in diverse and subtle ways.

It is probably as difficult to disentangle the effects of exogeneous events on relationships from organismic effects as to unconfound the effects of developmental change occurring in the two partners. Cross-cultural research would obviously be useful (see Weisner, this volume). At this time, however, we know relatively little about the salience of life events such as school entrance in terms of interpersonal expectations, partner attitudes, and time-use within relationships. And more is needed than an assessment of parent attitudes toward these events and children's attitudes toward the same. Rather, it is the manner in which schooling is woven into the content and patterning of relationships that constitutes one relevant issue, and the manner in which these transformations are assimilated into previous relationships that constitutes another.

Exogenous events such as school entrance have implications for child-child relationships as well. Peer interaction becomes salient for children beginning in the preschool years, but more extensive "coming to terms" with the peer context is a major challenge in middle childhood. Child-child relations, in some ways, are the "social frontiers" of the classroom (Minuchin & Shapiro, 1983), with the nexus defined by the peer culture and the school taking on new coloration at this time. Schooling effects on child-child relations are difficult to establish as are these effects on parent-child relations. Many interesting issues, however, can be identified in existing studies. Hallinan (1976), for example, found relatively rigid sociometric hierarchies in traditional classrooms, as compared with open classrooms, along with more clear-cut consensus concerning the identities of popular and isolated children. More diffuse social organizations were observed in open classrooms, with unreciprocated choices occurring less commonly and persisting over a shorter time than in traditional ones. Open settings thus seem to encourage the continuing reorganization of close relationships to a greater extent than traditional settings do—another illustration of exogenous pressures and their impact on relationships.

RELATIONSHIPS AND THEIR IMPACT ON THE INDIVIDUAL

Relationships may account for significant variance in the behavior of individual children, variation that is manifest in interaction with the partner, in other behavioral contexts, and across in time. Since relationships are enduring rather than momentary entities, this means that it is actually the relationship *history* that accounts for individual variation in personality and social development.

These "conclusions" are among the oldest and most controversial notions in developmental psychology. A consensus about them is not evident, even today. To what extent are the various dimensions of relationships (e.g., quality, patterning, commitment) stable over time? To what extent are the child's modes of action and reaction specific to partner and to place? To what extent do developmental transformations "erase" earlier adaptations? Does the individual carry forward templates or schemata of relationships or does the individual carry forward "bits and pieces" of relationships into later social experience? Clear-cut answers to none of these questions can be drawn from the literature even though the size of this literature is great.

With respect to the early child-caregiver attachment and its bearing on the personality development of the child, three situations have been examined: (a) the failure to form a specific attachment (mostly animal models), (b) instances in which primary attachments are disrupted, and (c) instances of "insecure" or malfunctioning attachments. The experimental evidence concerning these conditions and their effects derives entirely from animal studies (for obvious reasons); correlational strategies are used with children.

Overall, we read this evidence as supporting the conclusion that relationships bear a causal relation to individual differences in personality development. The substance of what we have learned through recent empirical studies forms a large part of the present book and so will not be repeated here. Suffice to summarize this material: First, the failure to become attached has devastating consequences for individual development. The classic animal studies (Harlow and others) have not been contravened in demonstrating both short- and long-term consequences. Turning to instances of attachment "failures," these have been difficult to determine in case studies with children but, where presumptive evidence exists, the consequences appear to be debilitating (Kagan, 1976). Both the animal studies and case studies with children further indicate that rehabilitiation is difficult (Suomi & Harlow, 1972).

Second, disruptions in early attachments produce strong and persisting reactions (monkey studies) although reasonably adequate adaptations may eventuate if familiar animals are present to adopt them. Among children, institutional rearing extending over the first several years creates initial problems in the development of relationships with adoptive parents, although these gradually work themselves out (Tizard, 1977). Shifts from one caregiver to another through adoption have similar consequences (Yarrow & Goodwin, 1973). There is some indication in these studies, however, that social relations with other individuals (adults other than the child's parents or other children) may show long-term effects.

Third, infants who are securely attached to their caregivers show more appropriate adaptations, both within and outside the relationship, as time goes on, than infants who are not securely attached. Their engagements in play and problem solving, as well as their reactions to strangers, differ as 2-year olds; their interactions with other children differ as 4-year olds (see Sroufe & Fleeson, this volume).

Significant issues remain in the interpretation of these findings, the most important ones concerning the nature of the mechanisms that link variations in early relationships and subsequent individual differences. Does the early experience leave residuals in the child that are carried forward more or less directly, thus constraining future adaptations? This possibility remains although many investigators question this hypothesis. Do certain qualities in the relationship persist over time, serving to involve the child in a "chain" of transactions that cumulates toward the individual differences we observe later? It is known that certain qualitative features in early attachments may persist for upwards of two years (Waters, 1978), thus suggesting that continuities exist in the nature of the child's experiences with the mother. These continuities have not been traced more extensively, however, so we must speculate about whether early transactions have qualities that persist over long periods. Nevertheless, this idea remains attractive—namely, that the quality of early relationships predicts to their quality subsequently which, in turn, accounts for individual differences among the children.

The success of recent research on the impact of early attachment on individual development rests heavily on certain methodological and strategic conventions. First, investigators abandoned the counting of discrete actions and reactions within mother-child interaction as a means of assessing the quality of early relationships. In turn, global or summary assessments were employed in order to measure general dimensions in mother-child interaction at critical times, e.g., reunion following separation. It is still the case that *presence* or *absence* of specific behavioral indices provides the examiner with a basis for classifying the overall configuration. Consequently, the shift from use of *frequencies* to the use of *qualities* in the assessment of attachment relationships is not quite as dramatic as sometimes claimed.

Second, recent advances are attributable, in considerable degree, to the use of child measures that center on developmentally relevant issues. Thus, the individual characteristics among 2-year olds that have been most successfully predicted from the attachment history consist of resourcefulness in problemsolving (including use of the mother as a resource) and exploration away from the mother, rather than individual differences in reunion behavior. Similarly, the outcomes predicted most successfully among 4-year olds include the initiation and maintenance of social relations with other children (a special challenge of that period) as well as effective, nondependent interactions with preschool teachers (another special challenge of the period). Again, proximity maintenance vis à vis the mother seems not to be an especially relevant outcome.

Third, the most convincing evidence that early attachment relations bear on long-term personality development involves assessments made outside mother-child interaction. Otherwise, one cannot argue that the relationship accounts for variations in the children as *individuals*. Much remains to be accomplished in this area, but the indications—as mentioned earlier—are encouraging.

The quality of the mother-child relationship and its impact on the *mother* has not been studied extensively, although the existence of these effects is frequently mentioned, especially in the literatures on psychopathology and family therapy. An accumulation of recent studies suggests an impact on the mother's affective state. For example, mothers who become involved in relationships with "difficult" infants were more at risk for symptoms of depression during the child's second year (Wolkind & De Salis, 1982). Most of this evidence derives from assessment of the child's temperament rather than the assessment of the early relationship between mother and child but these measures make extensive reference to the infant's interaction with the mother and are frequently based on the mother's perceptions of the infant. In any case, arguments about whether infant "difficult" scores derive from the infant or from the mother's reactions should not obscure the fact that the scales are correlated with the presence of difficult transactions between mother and child. Moreover, the evidence suggests that these early transactions are not connected to maternal depression at the time but, through maternal variables such as physical fatigue and lowered self-esteem, to later breakdown. The connection to psychiatric disorder thus occurs between early difficulty with the relationship and maternal state a year or more later. The model best fitting these data seems to be one that highlights difficulties in dyadic interaction that cycle through time, that include the mother's relationships with individuals other than the child, and that later eventuate in generalized psychiatric symptoms.

There are many other reasons for being interested in the impact on mothers of their relationships with their children. The "self system" of women in many cultures seems to develop closely in relation to children, and these relationships are also important in women's relationships with their husbands and their friends. Beyond the prediction of psychiatric disorder, the nature of these relationships may be relevant to the prediction of marital satisfaction and/or breakdown as well as participation in the workforce. It has been known for some time that working women who report that they are satisfied with their children are also more satisfied with their jobs (Maccoby & Gibbs, 1954). But a clearer understanding of the causalities underlying these correlations needs to be obtained.

Child–child relationships appear to have long-term consequences, too. Poor peer relations in childhood are characteristic of children "at risk" for emotional and behavioral disturbances in adolescence and adulthood. Early childhood assessments may not be strong predictors, but individual differences during middle childhood are correlated with subsequent adjustment. Negative reputations and social rejection among third- and fourth-graders predict poor mental health and psychosexual difficulties; beginning in early adolescence, irritability, aggressiveness, and negativistic behaviors are characteristic of preschizophrenic individuals. Similar comments can be made about poor peer relations and crime (Hartup, 1983).

Consistent as these results are, it is difficult to interpret them. Childhood indicators of later maladjustment include somatic disturbances, family difficulties, and school failures as well as trouble with other children. It is hard to believe that difficulties with contemporaries do not contribute directly to negative self-attitudes, alienation, and reductions in social effectiveness. Even so, what children learn and how much they learn in the peer context is difficult to specify. Peer socialization and its relevance to sexual socialization, the regulation of aggression, and a prosocial orientation have been posited; little is known, however, about the cycles of social interaction that mediate these correlations.

We are only beginning to document the contributions that friendships themselves make to child development although much has been written about their role in the socialization of intimacy (Sullivan, 1953). We do not know whether children who have friends differ from those who do not; only one investigation suggests that adolescents who have chums are more altruistic generally than those who do not participate in such relationships (Mannarino, 1976). Otherwise, we need to know more about the socializing consequences of friendships, e.g., their role in increasing similarities between children, the status implications of having a "best friend," and the value of friendships as "protective" factors in times of stress. It is not a given that children turn to their friends for support when, for example, stress within the family disturbs relationships at home. One investigation indicates that friends and other associates assist in the amelioration of the anxiety associated with divorce, in the resolution of loyalty conflicts, and in coping with the economic and practical exigencies deriving from divorce— among boys, but not among girls (Wallerstein & Kelly, 1981). The extent to which children use their friends *instead of* or *in addition to* their families for emotional and social support is an interesting question, but one to which an answer is not currently available.

Peer relationships are known to differ along dimensions of "intensity" and "exclusivity." Some children have close, intimate friendships; others do not. Some have many friends, others a few, still others none at all. Earlier attempts at constructing a typology of child-child relationships were based on the use of sociometric techniques, thus emphasizing dimensions of popularity and social power in the classification of individual differences (e.g., Peery, 1979). One recent attempt to go beyond a sociometric typology was based on interviews and observations of 6, 10, and 12-year old children in three classes in an elementary school (Krappman & Oswald, 1983). Extensive assessments of these children resulted in the identification of five types of peer "integration":

1. *Intimate friends*—children who have intimate friends with whom they pursue negotiation actions and shared interests, either to the exclusion of others (subtype 1) or supplemented by other, nonintimate relationships (subtype 2);

2. *Partners*—children who move back and forth from social networks to alliances with one or two other children and who expect involvement with one another but not on an intimate basis;

3. *Mates*—children who are members of a manifold social network and who either have high (subtype 1) or low social power (subtype 2);

4. *Ramblers*—children who oscillate between solitary activities and social participation without establishing enduring relationships and who are either accepted (subtype 1) or rejected (subtype 2);

5. *Isolates*—children who have very few interactive partners.

It is not presumed that this typology is universally applicable, but the investigators believe that these classifications will predict certain features of the child's socioemotional development. Longitudinal measures are being obtained to test this assumption. Meanwhile, this investigation exemplifies a strategy that is badly needed: namely, a classification of peer relationships—not according to popularity or the amount of contact that the children have with one another but, rather, on the basis of sociability, exclusivity, acceptance-rejection, and social influence *taken together*. Differentiation among mother-child relationships in terms of manifold qualities was the key to significant advance in the study of those relationships and their impact on the individual child; the same could be true for peer relations and their influence on the individual.

A similar state of affairs marks the literature on sibling relationships. Earlier studies indicate that having a sibling has certain implications for individual development according to the sex of the child and the sex of the sibling. Relationships with same-sex siblings, for example, seem to extend the sex-typing of behavior in normative directions whereas relationships with opposite-sex siblings, especially older ones, attenuates these extensions (Sutton-Smith & Rosenberg, 1970). Current studies are focused primarily on the interactive processes involved in early sibling interaction rather than on sibling relationships as antecedents of individual differences. No one has yet attempted a typology of sibling relationships so that variations in the nature of these relationships have not been explored in terms of their sequelae in individual development.

The importance of doing this, however, can be illustrated with the results of one investigation focused on the joint pretend play of twenty 2-year olds and their 4- to 5-year-old siblings. Based on maternal interviews, these sibling relationships were classified as "very friendly," "quite friendly," or "unfriendly." Home observations revealed that pretend play was five times more frequent in the interaction of very friendly siblings than between quite friendly ones, and more than ten times as frequent than between unfriendly siblings. The significance of these findings is considerable since it is known that pretend play emerges in mother-child and sibling interaction before being evident in the child's interaction with peers or in laboratory assessments (Dunn & Dale, 1984). Social cognitive development, in some aspects, thus may be supported not so much by having a sibling as by the affectional quality of the sibling relationship.

RELATIONSHIPS AND RELATIONSHIPS

Across Time

Changes occurring within relationships set the stage and/or determine subsequent changes in these same relationships. Among infants and their mothers, for example, the emergence of secure attachments marked by effective proximity-seeking in one another's presence and comforting during reunion is followed by more extensive exploration away from the mother (Rheingold & Eckerman, 1970) and mutual cooperation in confronting problem situations (Sroufe & Fleeson, this volume). In the third year, these mothers and their children substitute distal modes of contact for the proximal ones used earlier (Maccoby & Feldman, 1972). The progression is different for other mothers and their children: From "avoidant" interactions during reunion and mutual interference during caretaking, these infants and their mothers move toward a lack of connectedness in confronting problems in the second year that has been likened to "ships that pass in the night (Sroufe & Fleeson, this volume)." With variation from dyad to dyad, then, certain relationships move through predictable sequences or progressions.

As Maccoby and Martin (1983) point out . . . "At each stage, the quality of prior relationships must have an impact on the quality of the relationships that can grow out of the child's developing capacities for interaction. But the nature of the cross-age linkages is something that is only beginning to be explored" (p. 72). And the issue is more than establishing the normative changes or continuities existing across the various dimensions with which relationships can be measured; the issue consists of identifying those transformations in the nature of the relationship that underlie whatever continuities exist.

The evidence suggests that the qualities in relationships may be linked across time through multiple processes—through dispositions and expectations generated in the individuals vis à vis, and through the bases that the relationship provides for change and growth. Thus, the exploration away from the mother that is a consequence of secure early attachments contains certain elements that, in itself, stimulate change and reorganization of the relationship as time passes. One must remember, too, that the attachment between mother and child only *permits* the child's exploration; it is a necessary but not sufficient condition for the exploration. Among other things, the presence of interesting items in the environment is also necessary in order to bring this activity about. Only when these forces operate together does the developmental trajectory move forward.

Various writers have suggested that relationships "set the stage" for their own development by establishing "bounds" or "set goals" within which the two partners function. When one individual is propelled beyond these bounds, disequilibrium ensues until activity is either brought back within bounds or a new accomodation within the relationship is worked out. Thus, it seems to be slowly emerging stages of coregulation that mark relationships (Maccoby & Martin, 1983); both constraint and change are evident. Partly for this reason, relationships have developmental trajectories that are wobbly rather than smooth, and that can sometimes be disrupted altogether.

The research agenda is formidable with respect to discovery of both patterns of normative change in childhood relationships and their various stabilities— especially extending into middle childhood and adolescence. They have not been addressed, except in one or two instances, in the earliest years of sibling relationships (Dunn, 1983), and are virtually unstudied with respect to children's friendships. Again, the issue is more than description; we need to know the complex manner in which relationships are linked to themselves across time.

Across Relationships

The notion that early relationships constrain other ones has persisted in theories of child development for a long time (Erikson, 1950; Freud, 1933). The hypothesis has almost always been stated with reference to the child's relationship with the primary caregiver and its sequelae, although occasional mention is made of the constraining effects of early sibling relationships on future relationships. Father-child relationships have rarely been thought to carry forward into subsequent relationships although their importance in middle childhood and adolescence has been suggested (Hetherington & Parke, 1979). The importance of the mother-child relationship, however, has been emphasized again and again in relation to the child's subsequent friendship-choices, and to second-generation family relationships.

Research on these issues seems now to be emerging from a long period of uncertainty and doubt. Earlier theories were probably misleading in terms of the processes thought to underlie these continuities. Nevertheless, the mother-child relationship in early childhood appears to be linked to certain others: (1) Secure attachments in the first two years are antecedents of sociability, empathy, and effectiveness in child-child relations in the third and fourth years, as well as popularity (Waters, Wippman, & Sroufe, 1979). (b) Anxious attachments tend to predict either negative interactions with other children, ignoring, or withdrawal (Pastor, 1981). These studies, however, center on the connection between the early relationship and later characteristics of the individual child; their implications for the formation and functioning of later relationships are less clear. One would expect, on the basis of the evidence, that children with histories of secure attachment, as compared with insecurely attached children, would: (a) be more frequently involved in mutual friendships; (b) have friendships that function more smoothly, and (c) have friendships that are more stable. To date, none of these notions has been tested empirically, but the interest of investigators is evident. Similarly, new work is beginning to clarify the manner in which mother-child relationships predict teacher-child relationships after earlier efforts largely failed (see Sears, Whiting, Nowlis, & Sears, 1953).

Data are also beginning to emerge that link relationships across generations. Frommer and O'Shea (1973) found that mothers reporting major difficulties with their year-old infants were more likely to have had poor relationships with their own mothers and fathers than were mothers not reporting difficulties with their infants. Uddenberg (1974) interviewed 95 new mothers 4 months after the baby was born, their mothers with respect to parent-child relations some 20 years earlier, and their children after they had reached the age of 4½ years. First, the nature of the mother's relationship with her own mother predicted psychiatric difficulties in the postpartum period, feelings of inadequacy as a parent, and ambivalent or negative reactions to the infant. Second, the mother's relationships with her parents were correlated with her children's perceptions of her 4 years after delivery. These associations were sex-linked: Good relations between the mother and her father were associated with positive descriptions of the mother by sons; poor relationships with the father were associated with negative descriptions by sons. On the other hand, the early relationship between the mother and the grandmother expressed itself in the descriptions of the mother by their daughters and not by their sons.

These results foreshadow recent evidence linking relationship disturbance in the mother's family of origin and quality of her relationship with her offspring. First, Ricks (1983) found that mothers of year-old infants seen as secure in relation to themselves had more positive recollections of childhood relationships with their mothers, fathers, and peers than did mothers of infants seen as insecure. Second, Main, Kaplan, and Cassidy (in press) administered an "attachment interview" to the mothers and fathers of infants whose own attachments were classified in Ainsworth's "strange situation." The child's avoidance of the parent following separation was related to parental reports of rejection in their own childhoods; resistance in the mother-infant relationship was related to continuing anger and conflict regarding the mother's own parents; and parents rated as secure in their earlier relationships were seen as having secure attachments with their own offspring. (It is also interesting that parents of securely attached babies were coherent and consistent in these recollections of their childhoods while those with insecurely attached infants were often confused and "frequently insisted that they could not remember anything.") In addition to these results is the growing evidence connecting relationship disturbance across generations in instances of sexual abuse (see Sroufe & Fleeson, this volume).

The processes mediating these outcomes are undoubtedly complex but the results indicate that the nature of early relationships exert important influences on the construction of future ones. Obviously, the circumstances under which these continuities do not hold are important, as are the processes underlying continuities when they exist. Expansion of this data base has significance for intervention (Guerin, this volume) as well as theoretical advancement.

CULTURAL VARIATIONS AND HISTORICAL CHANGE

Considered as either independent or dependent variables, relationships and their developmental implications may vary according to social and historical context. These issues are beyond the scope of this chapter and, indeed, beyond the scope of this book. Questions can be raised, however, concerning the extent to which those qualities in relationships that are found in middle-class America to be associated with individual differences in social competence are the same as those observed in other cultures. Although the onset of specific attachments in the second half-year of life seems to be a universal phenomenon, small variations in the timing of this event seem to be traceable to cultural variations; qualitative differences have also been reported (Grossman & Grossman, 1982). And, in this volume, Weisner traces variations in relationships to the ecological cultural niche. It is likely to be a long time, however, before developmental dialectics and the full range of the child's relationships are placed in cross-cultural perspective.

The same can be said of relationships and individual development in historical perspective. The data base on which this essay is based derives mainly from relationships as studied in the United States and Great Britain since 1970. This has been a period of considerable change in the lives of both men and women in industrialized societies, in the structure and stability of families, and in the ecology of both family and peer relations. It is quite possible, of course, that contemporary social changes have not altered the most basic aspects of relationships and their impact on the development of individuals. As maternal employment outside the home has become normative, for example, there seem not to have been major changes in the qualities of early mother-child relationships (Hoffman, 1984). Nevertheless, the manner in which these relationships connect to individual differences and the manner in which relationships are carried forward in time may be modified by historical change. Thus, the most important outcomes of recent research may be the demonstration that a dialectic exists between relationships and development rather than the specific connections demonstrated.

CONCLUSION

We have attempted to construct a framework into which most of the other chapters included in this book will fit. It is not a summary of the other chapters nor a compendium of cross-cutting themes and issues. Rather, we have been concerned with what it means to take a developmental perspective in the study of relationships. Key issues include, on the one hand, the impact of individual development on relationships and, on the other, the impact of relationships on individual development.

The relevant studies vary greatly in the extent to which individuals and their actions were measured as opposed to the measurement of ''interaction'' or ''relationships.'' We have sometimes made inferences about relationships on the basis of measures that were actually taken on individuals. At other times, we have made inferences about individuals from transactional measurements. In each case, we think there are acceptable reasons for doing this. Nevertheless, we acknowledge that the available data do not always ''fit'' the questions we have raised.

The evidence makes clear that cognitive and emotional development are reflected in various dimensions of children's relationships. As individuals mature, they do different things with their partners, organize their interactions differently with respect to control and compliance issues, manifest different expectations, and communicate differently with one another. Developmental trajectories affecting both individuals in a relationship are relevant. The weight of the evidence also indicates that experience in well-functioning relationships is associated with good functioning in individuals and that important continuities in relationships exist across time and generation.

The issues involved in the dialectic between relationships and development are complex. The conceptual scheme that we have laid over these issues is relatively simple. We nevertheless assume that the developmental dynamics involved in relationships are knowable, and that they can be inferred through the use of experimental and nonexperimental observations applied both cross-sectionally and longitudinally.

ACKNOWLEDGMENT

Preparation of this manuscript was supported by Grant No. 5 PO1 HD 05027 from the National Institute of Child Health and Human Development. It was written while the author was in residence at the MRC Unit on the Development and Integration of Behavior, Cambridge University. The contributions of Judy Dunn, Robert Hinde, Joan Stevenson-Hinde, and Zick Rubin are gratefully acknowledged.

REFERENCES

Ainsworth, M., & Bell, S. (1974). Mother-infant interaction and the development of competence. In K. Connolly & J. Bruner (Eds.), *The Growth of competence*. New York: Academic Press.

Attili, G., Hold, B., & Schleidt, M. (in press). Relationships among peers in kindergarten: A cross-cultural study. In M. Taub & F. A. King (Eds.), *Proceedings of the IXth Congress of the International Primatological Society*, New York: Van Nostrand Reinhold.

Berndt, T. J. (1981). Effects of friendship on prosocial intentions and behavior. *Child Development, 52*, 636–643.

Bloom, L. (1970). *Language development: Form and function in emerging grammars*. Cambridge, MA:MIT Press.

Bowlby, J. (1969). *Attachment*. New York: Basic Books.

Brownell, C. A. (1982). *Peer interaction among toddler aged children: Effects of age and social context on interactional competence and behavioral roles*. Unpublished doctoral dissertation, University of Minnesota.

Carr, S. J., Dabbs, J. M., & Carr, T. S. (1975). Mother-infant attachment: The importance of the mother's visual field. *Child Development, 46*, 331–338.

Cicirelli, V. G. (1973). Effects of sibling structure and interaction in children's cateorization style. *Developmental Psychology, 9*, 132–139.

Collins, W. A. (Ed.). (1984). *Development during middle childhood*. Washington: National Academy Press.

Crockenberg, S. (1983, April). *Social support and the maternal behavior of adolescent mothers*. Paper presented at the meetings of the Society for Research in Child Development, Detroit, MI.

Damon, W. (1977). *The social world of the child*. San Francisco: Jossey-Bass.

Daniels, P., & Weingarten, K. (1980). *Sooner or later: The timing of parenthood in adult lives*. New York: W. W. Norton & Co.

Dunn, J. (1983). Sibling relationships in early childhood. *Child Development, 54*, 787–811.

Dunn, J., & Dale, N. (1984). I a daddy: Two-year olds' collaboration in joint pretend with sibling and with mother. In I. Bretherton (Ed.), *Symbolic play: The representation of social understanding*. New York: Academic Press.

Dunn, J., & Kendrick, C. (1981). Social behavior in young siblings in the family context: Differences between same-sex and different-sex dyads. *Child Development, 52*, 1265–1273.

Dunn, J., & Kendrick, C. (in prep.). *Siblings and development*. Cambridge University.

Erikson, E. (1950). *Childhood and society*. New York: Norton.

Freud, S. (1933). *New introductory lectures in psychoanalysis*. New York: Norton.

Frommer, E., & O'Shea, G. (1973). Antenatal identification of women liable to have problems in managing their infants. *British Journal of Psychiatry, 123*, 149–156.

Grossman, K., & Grossman, K. (1982, March). *Maternal sensitivity to infants' signals during the first year as related to the year old's behavior in Ainsworth's Strange Situation in a sample of northern German families*. Paper presented at International Conference on Infant Studies, Austin, Texas.

Gunnar, M. R., Senior, K., & Hartup, W. W. (1984). Peer presence and the exploratory behavior of 18- and 30-month-old children. *Child Development, 55*, 1101–1109.

Hallinan, M. T. (1976). Friendship patterns in open and traditional classrooms. *Sociology of Education, 49*, 254–265.

Hartup, W. W. (1983). Peer relations. In E. M. Hetherington (Ed.), P. H. Mussen (Series Ed.), *Handbook of child psychology*, Vol. 4, *Socialization, personality and social development*. New York: Wiley.

Hetherington, E. M. (1979). Divorce: A child's perspective. *American Psychologist, 34*, 851–858.

Hetherington, E. M., & Parke, R. D. (1979). *Child psychology: A contemporary viewpoint*. New York: McGraw-Hill.

Hill, J. P. (in press). Early adolescence: A research agenda. *Journal of Early Adolescence*.

Hinde, R. A. (1979). *Towards understanding relationships*. New York: Academic Press.

Hinde, R. A., Titmus, G., Easton, D., & Tamplin, A. (1985). Incidence of "friendship" and behavior with strong associates versus non-associates in preschoolers. *Child Development, 56*,234–245.

Hoffman, L. (1984). Maternal employment and the young child. In M. Perlmutter (Ed.), *Minnesota symposia on child psychology* (Vol. 17). Hillsdale, NJ: Lawrence Erlbaum Associates.

Holmberg, M. (1980). The development of social interchange patterns from 12 to 42 months. *Child Development, 51*, 448–456.

Kagan, J. (1976). Resilience and continuity in psychological development. In A. M. Clarke & A. D. B. Clarke (Eds.), *Early experience: Myth and evidence*. New York: The Free Press.

Kagan, J., Kearsley, R. B., & Zelazo, P. R. (1978). *Infancy: Its place in human development*. Cambridge, MA: Harvard University Press.

Kandel, D. B. (1978). Similarity in real-life adolescent friendship pairs. *Journal of Personality and Social Psychology, 36*, 306–312.

Kelley, H. H., & Thibaut, J. W. (1978). *Interpersonal relations: A theory of interdependence*. New York: Wiley.

Krappmann, L., & Oswald, H. (1983, April). *Types of children's integration into peer society*. Paper presented at the biennial meetings of the Society for Research in Child Development, Detroit.

Maccoby, E. E. (1980). *Social development*. New York: Harcourt Brace Jovanovitch.

Maccoby, E. E. (1984). Middle childhood in the context of the family. In W. A. Collins (Ed.), *Development during middle childhood*. Washington: National Academy Press.

Maccoby, E. E., & Feldman, S. S. (1972). Mother-attachment and stranger-reactions in the third year of life. *Monographs of the Society for Research in Child Development, 37* (Whole No. 146).

Maccoby, E. E., & Gibbs, P. K. (1954). Methods of child rearing in two social classes. In W. E. Martin & C. B. Stendler (Eds.), *Readings in child development*. New York: Harcourt & Brace.

Maccoby, E. E., & Martin, J. A. (1983). Socialization in the context of the family: Parent-child interaction. In E. M. Hetherington (Ed.), P. H. Mussen (Series Ed.), *Handbook of child psychology*, Vol. 4, *Socialization, personality and social development.* New York: Wiley.

Mahler, M. S., Pine, F., & Bergman, A. (1975). *The psychological birth of the infant.* New York: Basic Books.

Main, M., Kaplan, N., & Cassidy, J. (in press). Security in infancy, childhood and adulthood: A move to the level of representation. *Monographs of the Society for Research in Child Development.*

Mannarino, A. P. (1976). Friendship patterns and altruistic behavior in preadolescent males. *Developmental Psychology, 12,* 555–556.

Marvin, R. S. (1977). An ethological-cognitive model for the attentuation of mother-child attachment behavior. In T. Alloway, P. Pliner, & L. Krames (Eds.), *Attachment behavior.* New York: Plenum.

Minuchin, P. P., & Shapiro, E. K. (1983). The school as a context for social development. In E. M. Hetherington (Ed.), *Handbook of child psychology*, Vol. 4, P. H. Mussen (Series Ed.), *Socialization, personality and social development.* New York: Wiley.

Mitteness, L. S., & Nydegger, C. N. (1982, November). Dimensions of parent child relations in adulthood. Paper presented at meetings of the Gerontological Society of America, Boston.

Newcomb, A. F., & Brady, J. E. (1982). Mutuality in boy's friendship relations. *Child Development, 53,* 392–395.

Nydegger, C. N. (1975, October). *Age and parental behavior.* Paper presented at meetings of the Gerontological Society of America, Louisville, KY.

Nydegger, C. N. (1981, November). *The ripple effect of parental timing.* Paper presented at meetings of the Gerontological Society of America, Toronto.

Pastor, D. L. (1981). The quality of mother-infant attachment and its relationship to toddlers' initial sociability with peers. *Developmental Psychology, 17,* 326–335.

Peery, J. C. (1979). Popular, amiable, isolated, rejected: A reconceptualization of sociometric status in preschool children. *Child Development, 50,* 1231–1234.

Pepler, D. J., Abramovitch, R., & Corter, C. (1981). Sibling interaction in the home: A longitudinal study. *Child Development, 52,* 1344–1347.

Rheingold, H. L., & Eckerman, C. O. (1970). The infant separates himself from his mother. *Science, 168,* 78–83.

Ricks, M. (1983). *The origins of individual differences in competence: Attachment history and environmental support.* Unpublished Ph.D. dissertation, University of Massachusetts.

Sears, R. R. (1951). A theoretical framework for personality and social behavior. *American Psychologist, 6,* 476–483.

Sears, R. R., Whiting, J. W. M., Nowlis, V., & Sears, P. S. (1953). Some child-rearing antecedents of aggression and dependency in young children. *Genetic Psychology Monographs, 47,* 135–234.

Shantz, C. U. (1983). Social cognition. In J. H. Flavell & E. Markman (Eds.), P. H. Mussen (Series Ed.), *Handbook of child psychology,* Vol. 3, *Cognitive development.* New York: Wiley.

Sroufe, L. A. (1983). Infant-caregiver attachment and patterns of adaptation in preschool: The roots of maladoption. In M. Perlmutter (Ed.), *Minnesota symposia on child psychology* (Vol. 16). Hillsdale, NJ: Lawrence Erlbaum Associates.

Stern, D. (1977). *The first relationship: Infant and mother.* London: Fontana/Open Books.

Sullivan, H. S. (1953). *The interpersonal theory of psychiatry.* New York: Norton.

Suomi, S. J., & Harlow, H. F. (1972). Social rehabilitation of isolate-reared monkeys. *Developmental Psychology, 6,* 487–496.

Sutton-Smith, B., & Rosenberg, B. (1970). *The sibling.* New York: Holt, Rinehart, & Winston.

Tizard, B. (1977). *Adoption: A second chance.* London: Open Books.

Uddenberg, N. (1974). Reproductive adaptation in mother and daughter. *Acta Psychiatrica Scandanavia, 254* (Suppl).

Vaughn, B., Egeland, B., Waters, E., & Sroufe, L. A. (1979). Individual differences in infant-mother attachment at 12 and 18 months: Stability and change in families under stress. *Child Development, 50,* 971–975.

Wallerstein, J. S., & Kelly, J. B. (1981). *Surviving the breakup: How children and parents cope with divorce.* New York: Basic Books.

Waters, E. (1978). The stability of individual differences in infant-mother attachment. *Child Development, 49,* 483–494.

Waters, E., Wippman, J., & Sroufe, L. A. (1979). Attachment, positive affects, and competence in the peer group: Two studies in construct validation. *Child Development, 50,* 821–829.

Wolkind, S. N., & De Salis, W. (1982). Infant temperament, maternal mental state and child behavioral problems. In *Temperamental differences in infants and young children* (Ciba Foundation Symposium 89). London: Pitman.

Yarrow, L. J., & Goodwin, M. S. (1973). The immediate impact of separation reactions of infants to a change in mother figures. In L. J. Stone, H. T. Smith, & L. B. Murphy (Eds.), *The competent infant.* New York: Basic Books.

Youniss, J. (1980). *Parents and peers in social development: A Sullivan-Piaget perspective.* Chicago: University of Chicago Press.

Zajonc, R., & Markus, H. (1975). Birth order and intellectual development. *Psychological Review, 82,* 74–88.

2 Relating Childhood Relationships to Individual Characteristics

Robert A. Hinde
Joan Stevenson-Hinde
*M.R.C. Unit on the Development and
Integration of Behaviour,
Madingley, Cambridge*

In this chapter we present first an overview of some issues which we believe are crucial for the understanding of relationships in general and of relationships in childhood in particular. These include the provision of an adequate descriptive base and an understanding of the dialectics between individual characteristics and relationships, on the one hand, and between relationships and the social situation, on the other. We then briefly sketch some findings from two studies in which we have attempted to study the effects of individual characteristics on relationships and vice versa.

PRINCIPLES OF DYNAMICS AND THE NEED FOR DESCRIPTION

The great bulk of research on interpersonal relationships has involved attempts to establish or refine principles providing an understanding of their dynamics. These include principles of learning; of attribution; of balance and dissonance; of exchange, equity and interdependence; and of positive and negative feedback. None of these principles is ubiquitously applicable: each has had its successes and its failures.

The classic learning theories, for example, throw considerable light on the dynamics of childhood relationships. Lott and Lott (e.g., 1974) used a classical conditioning paradigm to explain how children were more likely to choose members of a three-child group as future companions if they had been rewarded in their presence than if they had not. Gewirtz (1961, p. 237) explained the development of an infant's attachment to its mother by operant principles, arguing that an infant will form an attachment with the person "who mediates most of the important environmental consequences of his behavior." And, in both human (Zajonc, 1968) and nonhuman species (e.g., Bateson, 1964) simple exposure learning can form a basis for attraction in the young. Although such principles may be valuable for integrating data and generating hypotheses (Clore & Byrne, 1974), their explanatory value is limited. The classical conditioning paradigm neglects the cognitive intermediaries that are crucial in on-going relationships (cf. Bandura, 1977). The operant conditioning model requires prior knowledge of which are the "important environmental consequences" in which sort of relationship—they are certainly not similar across relationships. It neglects also the constraints and predispositions on what can be learned (Hinde & Stevenson-Hinde, 1973; Seligman & Hager, 1972) and the structure of behavior (Baerends, 1976) into which the learning experiences are assimilated. Some stimuli become attractive on exposure more readily than others: furthermore, internal constraints may determine that what is most attractive is always somewhat different from what is most familiar (Bateson, 1973). Many of these issues have been taken into account by the attachment theorists (e.g., Ainsworth, Blehar, Waters, & Wall, 1978; Bowlby, 1969), who emphasize the particular sequelae of action that are important in the development of the mother-infant relationship and the "behavioral systems" (Baerends, 1976) that each partner brings to the interactions. Of course, what the attachment theorists have found to be important in the mother-child relationship is not important in the development of all relationships (Parkes & Stevenson-Hinde, 1982).

In a comparable way balance theory is useful in some contexts, but not all (If Jack likes Jill and Joe likes Jill, Jack does not necessarily like Joe (Newcomb, 1971)). Exchange and interdependence theories must take cognizance of the differing properties of the resources exchanged (Foa & Foa, 1974) and of the fact that what is considered as *fair* differs between relationships of different types (Lerner, Miller, & Holmes, 1976) and, in children's relationships, with the age of child (Leventhal & Lane, 1970). Principles of negative and positive feedback are valueless unless we know which operates in which relationships in which circumstances.

Thus, rather than jousting for the honor of the particular principles they espouse, investigators would sometimes do better to attempt to specify the range of instances for which their principles are useful, and where they fail. For this, some framework for describing relationships is necessary. Although the way to achieve such a framework is by no means clear, it is possible to specify eight categories of dimensions that may be useful—that is, to classify into eight groups the sorts of things about relationships that are likely to be important for understanding their dynamics. These range from the properties of specific interactions to more global properties of the relationship, and from behavioral to more subjective aspects (Hinde, 1979). They are not all equally applicable to the relationships of childhood, but they can be useful both in ordering our knowledge and in locating lacunae within it. They are summarized briefly as follows.

The *Content* of the relationship refers to what the individuals do together. Whether we are concerned with differences between major categories of relationships (e.g., mother-child vs. teacher-child) or with differences within a category (e.g., between mothers who play with their children and mothers who do not), content dimensions provide an initial basis for differentiating among relationships. We know, for instance, that the content of the mother-child relationship may differ from that of the father-child relationship (Lamb, 1976; Lytton, 1980), and that preschool children do different things with friends and nonfriends (Hinde, Titmus, Easton, & Tamplin, 1985). What we do not know is whether it matters how interactions of different types are "parcelled up" into relationships. For instance, in two-parent families fathers are more often involved in physical play with the baby than mothers. If, in a one-parent family, the mother attempts to provide the same amount of physical play, would the fact that the rumbunctious play now came from the same individual who provided tender loving care make any difference (Hinde, 1971)?

The *Diversity* of the interactions refers to the number of different things the participants in the relationship do together. It depends in part on the level of analysis involved: thus a mother-child relationship could be described as uniplex, involving only maternal—filial responses, or multiplex, involving nursing, playing, protecting and so on. The greater the diversity of interactions, the more opportunities for interactions of one type to be influenced by those of another type. The diversity of interactions involved is surely one reason for the special nature of the mother-child relationship.

The *Quality* of the interactions within a relationship are one of its most crucial properties, and yet at the same time amongst the hardest to evaluate. What matters in the mother–child relationship is not just what they do together, but how they do it. If the mother responds sensitively to the child's needs (Ainsworth, Bell, & Slayton, 1974), or shows herself to enjoy physical contact (Main & Stadtman, 1981), the relationship may take a course quite different from that which it would take if the mother were insensitive or resistant to physical contact. Quality is equally important in peer relationships: how a child approaches a group may markedly influence its success in joining it (Putallaz & Gottman, 1981).

The qualities of a relationship, as opposed to those of its constituent interactions, may depend on the *Relative Frequency and Patterning* of those interactions. Several different issues may be involved here. First, if the properties of a number of different types of interaction covary, the participants (and outsiders) may be more prone to apply certain global labels to the relationship: thus a relationship is described as *warm* or *loving* on the basis of interactions in many social contexts, not one. This is likely to become important to children once they start to evaluate their relationships. Another issue, important from very early on, concerns the relative frequencies of interactions—what matters about a relationship may be not how often A comforts B, but how often A comforts B relative to how often B needs to be comforted. Yet another issue concerns properties of relationships that are consequent upon interactions of quite different sorts. For instance, a child who is always ready to play with another when invited might be seen as compliant, but one who sometimes refuses and at other times insists on playing might be seen as controlling.

Another important issue concerns the *Reciprocity vs. Complementarity* of the interactions comprising the relationship. Reciprocal interactions are those in which the participants each do the same thing (e.g., one chases the other and then the other chases the one), while in complementary interactions they do different but complementary things (the mother nurses and the baby sucks). Whereas mother-child or teacher-pupil relationships involve mainly complementary interactions, peer relationships involve more reciprocity. Most close personal relationships involve an interweaving of reciprocal and complementary interactions. As yet, we know virtually nothing about the patterning of reciprocity and complementarity in children's relationships, or about the extent to which children adjust their behavior in these terms within different relationships. On the one hand, it is said that indiscriminate behavior—behavior that is consistent across situations or relationships—tends to be characteristic of disturbed, less mature, or less intelligent persons (e.g., Schuster, Murrell, & Cook, 1980). On the other hand, the language used even by young children shows that they can and do adjust their behavior according to whom they are with (Gelman & Shatz, 1977; Garvey & Ben Debba, 1974; Shatz & Gelman, 1973; Snow, 1972). But at a subtler level, where an adult can boss another individual in one context and be bossed or nursed or led by him/her in another, does a young child have similar flexibility? To what extent do we acquire plasticity with social sophistication, or become more rigid as we grow older?

Intimacy, the extent to which the participants in a relationship reveal all aspects—experiential, emotional, and physical—of themselves to each other, is a crucial dimension of many relationships. Casual observation indicates that intimacy in the more limited sense of sharing secrets, is a matter of some significance to 6-year-olds, and perhaps to younger children. Although such secrets may not be very enduring, intimacy potential may be important before it is recognized in children's written reports (cf. Bigelow & La Gaipa, 1975). Intimacy in the sense of the extent to which the child is prepared to reveal him or herself to others could be said to appear much earlier. Clearly, there is work to be done in defining intimacy in childhood, as well as in tracing its developing importance in different contexts.

Interpersonal Perception involves a number of dimensions differing in their requirements for cognitive complexity—whether A sees B as B "really" is; whether A sees B as B sees B (i.e., Does A understand B?); whether B feels that A sees B as B sees B (i.e., Does B feel understood?), and so on. The issues here, of course, relate to those of empathy and role-taking, but nevertheless require study in their own right. To see B as B "really" is or as "B sees B" involves much more than sharing another's emotional state, for it is necessary to comprehend B even when B's thoughts and feelings are different from one's own (cf. Chandler & Greenspan, 1972; Smither, 1977). Studies of empathic and role-taking abilities may be of less help than at one time seemed likely, in part because anecdotal data permit the inference that children understand how to needle or comfort each other in the context of long-term relationships long before such abilities are revealed by laboratory assessments in less intimate situations (e.g., Dunn & Kendrick, 1982; Lewis, Young, Brooks, & Michalson, 1975; Mueller & Brenner, 1977; Yarrow, 1975). Chronologies involving verbal abilities may be especially suspect (see e.g., Rubin & Pepler's (1980) discussion of Selman (1976a, 1976b)). In any case, we know that adults who are capable of understanding another's point of view do not always do so, so we need to specify not just when children become capable of mutual understanding, but the extent to which it actually influences the course of their friendships. The study of interpersonal perception may be of crucial importance for understanding the development of the self-concept, of self-esteem, and thus of many aspects of personality. Many writers hold that reciprocal relationships, in which the child interacts with another individual who in some ways is like him or herself, have a special role here (Piaget, 1965; Sullivan, 1953; Youniss, 1980).

Finally, *Commitment* in adult relationships usually refers to the extent to which the partners accept their relationship as continuing indefinitely or direct their behavior towards ensuring its continuance or towards optimizing its properties. In the parent–child relationship commitment arises more or less inevitably as the relationship develops. Its role in peer relationships is less clear. Our knowledge of children's conceptions of friendship suggests that it is unlikely to be important before about 8–10 years-of-age (Bigelow & La Gaipa, 1975). However, this may well not be the whole story. Anecdotal evidence, involving such remarks as "Mary said she was my friend but she went and played with Jane," suggest that the related issue of fidelity begins to be important considerably earlier than this. We need a conceptual analysis of the nature of commitment before the issue can be taken much further (see, e.g., Lund, 1981).

Although there are certainly other ways of classifying the characteristics of interpersonal relationships, the earlier discussion provides a convenient starting point for description and analysis. We must now address other issues crucial to the understanding of relationships—the dialectics between the properties of relationships and the social situation, on the one hand, and the characteristics of the participants, on the other.

THE DIALECTICS BETWEEN INDIVIDUAL CHARACTERISTICS, RELATIONSHIPS, AND THE SOCIAL SITUATION

The Social Nexus and Relationships

Every relationship is embedded in a nexus of other relationships which influence its course (see Fig. 2.1). Within the family, this is clear enough. The relationship between mother and child may both affect and be affected by the marital relationship of the parents (Fletcher, 1966; Glenn, 1975; Humphrey, 1975; Slater & Woodside, 1951). The relationship between first and second-born siblings varies with, and presumably both influences and is influenced by, the relationship between the mother and the firstborn (Cicirelli, 1975; Dunn & Kendrick, 1982). A sick child can have an impact on the whole family (Burton, 1975; Gath, 1978). Similar issues arise in peer relationships: "Mary says she is Ann's best friend, so she can't be mine" is a remark heard from very early on in the playground— though we do not know exactly when it starts to be important. In each case the effects are reciprocal: we must thus attempt to understand an ongoing dialectic between properties of the relationship and those of the social situation.

The processes involved in these dialectics are certainly complex and diverse. For example, the advent of a secondborn will have an immediate effect on the mother-firstborn relationship merely because the baby occupies the mother's time and attention, and affects her physical and mental state. But much may also depend on how the mother handles the situation. She may succeed in establishing the firstborn as a partner in coping with the baby, so that the child comes to view itself as "on the mother's side." This could lead to a profound change in the first child's self-image, enhancing self-perceptions as the big one, the elder and not the baby, the girl and not the boy, and so on. Alternatively, the firstborn may use the newcomer as a rival and become alienated, or may use the baby as a model and regress (Dunn & Kendrick, 1982). The extent to which either happens no

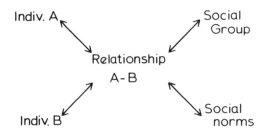

FIG. 2.1.   Dialectics between Relationships, Personality, and Social Structure.

doubt depends indirectly on the mother's relationships with her husband, her own mother, and the new baby, as well as on her relationship with the firstborn.

A related issue concerns the social norms which affect the goals and expectations of the participants in a relationship. Mothers try to build a mother-child relationship which they judge as "good" by criteria acquired from the social group(s) in which they have lived and, in addition, each family engenders its own systems of rules and expectations (Wertheim, 1975a, 1975b, 1975c). Similarly, children come to have expectations about friends (Bigelow & La Gaipa, 1975). However, the precise role of social norms in children's relationships has been little studied. One interesting starting point might lie in the nicknames that codify the roles that children are to play in relationships (Harré, 1975). Whilst these social norms influence the goals and expectations of the participants in relationships, they are themselves transmitted and transmuted in part through the agency of dyadic relationships. In the modern world, of course, other agencies, such as the media and advertisements, also play a role (Goffman, 1978).

In practice the dialectics illustrated in Fig. 2.1. represent only a portion of a more complex system. We must also envisage the social means and social norms as embedded in the 'socio-cultural structure'—the system of beliefs, and myths, the institutions and the relations between them shared by the members of the society. Furthermore there are reciprocal relationships between societies, and every social group affects and is affected by its physical environment. However, further discussion of these issues is not possible here (Hinde, 1985).

Individual Characteristics and Relationships

In a similar way, the properties of a relationship depend on the characteristics of the participants: individuals behave differently according to whom they are with. This is well illustrated in the work of the symbolic interactionists (e.g., McCall, 1970) who emphasize how, on entering a relationship, we select from all the possible ways in which we might behave in accordance with our hopes for and expectations about the relationship and our assessment of the other participant. The future of every relationship depends in part on the "role support" that each partner gives to the "roles" the other selects to play.

Although this issue may seem to be an obvious one, two consequences of crucial importance for studies of children's friendships must be mentioned. One is that measures derived from interactions within an ongoing relationship must be seen as measures of that relationship, and not as measures of the characteristics of one or the other participant (Hinde, 1969, 1974). This is clearly shown by the manner in which one caregiver can behave differently to individual twins or infants of similar ages (e.g., J. W. B. Douglas, personal communication; Hinde, 1969; Spencer-Booth, 1968; Yarrow, 1963; Yarrow, Waxler, & Scott, 1971). Assessments of sensitive mothering may depend on the infant, and assessments of "security of attachment" in infants may depend on the accompanying caregiver (Main & Weston, 1981). The same principle applies to all interpersonal relationships.

A second implication is that the effects of the home or school environment on the development of a child's behavior or personality must not be studied with assessments deriving from just one context. Too often, a child's propensity to behave aggressively is assessed by the total frequency of all aggressive acts made toward all others encountered in school; prosocial behavior may be assessed by a test in an irrelevant social context. The danger of these conventions is considerable: to give but one example, the degree of interpersonal perception shown by young siblings towards each other far outstrips what children of similar ages would be thought capable of, as measured in laboratory tests (Dunn & Kendrick, 1982).

Not only do the properties of a relationship depend on the characteristics of the individual participants, but the characteristics of individuals depend in large measure on the relationships in which they are and have been involved. In the short term, as noted earlier, individuals select from their repertoire according to their assessment of the relationship. In the longer term, the nature and extent of that repertoire depends on the relationships experienced. Thus, we must come to terms not only with a dialectic between the properties of relationships and those of the social situations in which they are embedded, but also between the properties of relationships past and present and the personalities of the individuals involved.

This is, perhaps, the fundamental issue in the study of child development. What are the processes whereby children influence and are influenced by the relationships they experience? In a study of the relations between the home relationships of preschool children and their behavior in school (some aspects of which are discussed next) we found few simple isomorphisms between the ways in which the children behave in home and school. On the other hand, many meaningful regularities were obtained across these situations. For example, children who experienced much warm intercourse with their mothers tended not to interact frequently with peers or to initiate interactions with the adults in the preschool. Their interactions with peers, however, were unlikely to be negative in character, and they were likely to *receive* initiations from adults (Hinde & Tamplin, 1983). We now consider a possible strategy for coming to terms with this dialectic.

STUDIES OF THE DIALECTICS BETWEEN INDIVIDUAL CHARACTERISTICS, RELATIONSHIPS, AND THE SOCIAL SITUATION

Gradual realization of these issues has influenced the research projects we have been carrying out at Madingley. They have been based on the premise that, for full understanding, the study of interindividual relationships cannot be wholly divorced from that of personality, or vice-versa. This is, of course, recognized by students of childhood relationships in so far as they have studied how relationships change as children develop cognitive and emotional sophistication, but we feel it is necessary to extend this to individual differences within specific age periods. We have therefore attempted for particular relationships to combine studies of the two dialectics (between the relationship and the personalities of the participants on the one hand, and between the relationship and the social situation on the other), with studies of the behavior of one or other participant in another social context. The (idealized) design of each study is shown in Fig. 2.2, which may be compared with Fig. 2.1. The dialectic between mother and child is studied by comparing assessments of their behavior in interaction, with characteristics of each assessed (so far as possible) independently of the other. Although influences between mother and child are mediated primarily through their relationship, we also make direct comparisons between them. The dialectic between the mother-child relationship and the social situation is similarly assessed. Finally, the child's behavior is assessed also in one or more additional social situations or relationships.

It is apparent that the design shown in Fig. 2.2 is applicable also to other relationships—e.g., child/sibling and child/peer. The two studies discussed in the following paragraphs are primarily correlational, but additional sources of evidence have been used to impute causality.

Mother and Infant Rhesus Monkeys

The first example concerns the relations between individual characteristics of rhesus monkey females and their infants. The animals lived in small captive groups, each consisting of a male, two-to-four adult females, and their offspring. Individual characteristics were assessed by a behavior rating questionnaire completed every November by observers thoroughly familiar with the animals. It consisted of 25 behaviorally defined adjectives, each of which was rated on a 7-point scale. Definitions of the items, reliability and validity, and principal component analyses are given by Stevenson-Hinde, Stillwell-Barnes, and Zunz

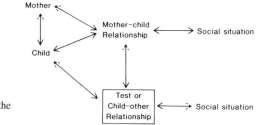

FIG. 2.2.   Schematic Design for the 2 studies discussed here.

(1980a). Principal component analyses yielded three dimensions, termed Confident–Fearful, Excitable–Slow and Sociable–Solitary. Items loading highly on each dimension were summed, to give a Confident, Excitable, and Sociable score for each animal.

Consistency of Mothers' Scores.   Once the monkeys had reached adulthood, their scores tended to be consistent from year to year. For example, for 11 adult females who had been rated over 4 successive years, the consistency was .90*** ($p<.001$) for Confident scores, .80*** for Excitable scores and .59** ($p<.01$) for Sociable scores (Kendall coefficients). For the 25 mother/infant pairs that we shall be considering here, correlations between mothers' scores from the November of the year of the infant's birth to the next November were: .81*** ($p<.001$, two-tailed) for Confident scores, .84*** for Excitable scores and .74*** for Sociable scores (Spearman coefficients). In addition, there were no significant increases or decreases over time. A similar picture held when the group was broken into 11 mother/daughter pairs and 14 mother/son pairs, except that mothers with daughters had especially high consistency in their Confident scores, with a coefficient of .92*** compared with .71** ($p<.01$) for mothers with sons.

Mothers' and Infants' Individual Characteristics.   Taking the Confident, Excitable, and Sociable scores, there were no sex differences among the youngest age group (i.e., 58–85 week-olds), nor did scores of mothers with young sons differ from scores of mothers with daughters. However, mothers' scores were correlated with the scores of their infants, and in ways different for sons and for daughters. That is, daughters tended to be ranked in a way that was very similar to their mothers, so that Confident mothers had Confident daughters (r_s = .79**), Excitable mothers had Excitable daughters (.66*, $p<.05$), and Sociable mothers had Sociable daughters (.68*). On the other hand, for mothers and sons, there was essentially no correlation between either their Confident scores (.07) or their Excitable scores ($-.29$). Sociable mothers tended to have Sociable sons (.56*), but Excitable mothers produced sons with relatively low Confident scores ($-.76**$).

Given these correlations and the stability of the mothers' scores over time, one may infer causal effects from mother to infant. If so, this could operate through sex-linked genetic factors and/or the mother/infant relationship. The latter possibility was investigated by asking how mothers' characteristics correlated with measures of mother/infant interactions.

The Dialectic Between Mothers' and Infants' Characteristics and the Nature of Their Interactions.   Since mothers' Confident and Sociable scores were significantly correlated (r_s = .59**), further discussion is confined to the Confident and Excitable scores, which were not ($-.25$). Table 2.1 (top half) indicates what

Confident mothers tended to do with their sons or daughters over each infant's first year of life. The more Confident the mother, the less she left or rejected her daughter at the age of weaning (16 weeks). By 52 weeks, Confident mothers still left daughters relatively infrequently, but daughters left them and played a low role in maintaining proximity with mothers (% approach—% leave). By the end of the year, their daughters themselves tended to be Confident (.79**).

TABLE 2.1
Mother/infant Interaction Measures (at 8, 16, and 52 weeks)
which Correlate with Individual Scores of Either Mothers or Infants
(at 58–85 weeks)

	Age of Infants		
	8 weeks	16 weeks	52 weeks
CONFIDENT SCORES			
Mothers	———	−M leave*	−M leave*
↑		−M reject*	I leave
.79**			−%app − %leave*
↓			
Daughters	———	−M reject*	−M reject
Mothers	M reject*		−M reject*
↑	%M reject*	———	−time contact*
.07			
↓			
Sons	———	———	−I approach*
			−I leave*
EXCITABLE SCORES			
Mothers	M restrict	M restrict*	
↑	M approach*	M approach*	M approach*
.66*		M leave*	M leave
↓		I approach*	
Daughters	———	———	M leave**
			I approach
Mothers	−time contact	M restrict*	I approach**
↑	M leave*	M approach*	%app − %leave
−.29	%app − %leave*	M leave*	
↓			
Sons	M restrict**	———	———
	M approach*		
	I approach*		
	I leave		

n = 11 mother/daughter pairs; 14 mother/son pairs.
no star, $p<.10$; *$p<.05$; **$p<01$; two-tailed, Spearman rank-order correlations.

Daughters' Confident scores were correlated with few maternal rejections at both 16 and 52 weeks.

On the other hand, Confident mothers did reject their sons early on (at 8 weeks). By 52 weeks, the frequency of rejections was low, but so also was total time in contact. They did not tend to have Confident sons (.07). Instead, sons with high Confident scores tended to have mothers who were not Excitable (−.76**). These mothers (Table 2.1, bottom half, please reverse signs of correlations), who were *not* Excitable but relaxed and slow, spent time in contact with sons and left them infrequently early on. Nonexcitable mothers did not restrict, approach, or leave much at 16 weeks, while their sons played a relatively low role in maintaining proximity with mothers.

To the extent that both types of mothers left their infants relatively infrequently and had infants who played a low role in maintaining proximity with mothers, one sees parallels with "sensitively responsive" mothers providing a "secure base" from which the infant may explore the environment (Ainsworth et al., 1978; see also Sroufe and Fleeson, this volume).

The correspondence between Excitability in mothers and daughters between 58–85 weeks (.66*) may also be traced to antecedent interactions (Table 2.1, bottom half). Excitable mothers tended to restrict and approach as well as to leave their daughters. In turn, their daughters tended to approach them. The sons' Excitable scores were not highly correlated with mothers' scores on the Confident, Excitable, or Sociable dimensions, nor were they correlated with contemporaneous mother/infant interaction (i.e., with interactions at 52 weeks). However, the more Excitable the son at 58–85 weeks, the more their mothers had restricted and approached, and the more the son both approached and left, during observations conducted at 8 weeks.

Thus, in the case of both sons and daughters who were Excitable, mothers seemed to be *overprotective* early on, restricting and approaching their offspring. With daughters, these interactions were coupled with being left by mothers. In addition, sons who were later to be rated Excitable both approached and left their mothers, and daughters who would become Excitable approached frequently. The patterns are strikingly similar to what has been called "insecure" attachment. Unlike "avoidant" (Group A) infants, however, the Excitable monkeys approached their mothers, and their mothers could not be described as rejecting. The parallel here is closer with "ambivalent" (Group C) infants, who act to maintain contact and whose mothers behave noncontingently (Ainsworth et al., 1978).

Mother and Offspring Characteristics: Cross-Situational Predictability. The colony observations at 52 weeks were followed by removal of the infant and its mother to a situation away from the colony, for a series of behavioral tests. Although the sons of Confident mothers were not necessarily Confident in the colony (r_s = .07), they did behave confidently when in the test situation. There, sons (n = 10) with Confident mothers spent less time in contact with their mothers ($-.79^{**}$), showed less nervous pacing ($-.60$) and spent more time looking in a mirror ($.72^*$) than sons of non-Confident mothers. On the other hand, sons of Excitable mothers showed lack of confidence in the test cage. They distress-called more ($.82^{**}$), snatched food more quickly ($.74^*$), and were slower to approach a novel object ($.84^{**}$) than the sons of non-Excitable mothers.

In summary, the sons' behavior in the test situation was related to the ratings their mothers obtained in the colony (Stevenson-Hinde & Simpson, 1981), as well as to their own (Stevenson-Hinde, Stillwell-Barnes, & Zunz, 1980b). This was not the case for daughters, whose behavior in the test situation was not related to either their mothers' or their own colony scores. Perhaps daughters' characteristics are more situation dependent than sons': daughters remain in their natural troops throughout their lives whereas males usually transfer to another troop in early adulthood.

Social Situation and the Mother-Infant Relationship.   The mother-infant relationship influences, and is influenced by, the social nexus in which it is embedded. When a baby is born, other animals are more attracted to the mother, and she becomes more avoidant of other animals, than before the birth (Hinde & Powell Proctor, 1977). This is in part a consequence of attempts to interfere with the infant and/or aggression from other animals in the group. Not surprisingly, mothers are more restrictive of their infants when in a group than when alone (Hinde & Spencer-Booth, 1967). Subordinate mothers reject their infants less than do dominant mothers, presumably because they need to maintain proximity with them more. The situation is in some ways exacerbated by the presence of an elder female sibling, for such animals direct more aggression to their mothers and/or younger siblings than do male elder siblings. In addition, since female infants attract more aggression from other females than do males, the sex of the infant affects the protectiveness of the mother: primiparous (but not multiparous) mothers restrain daughters more than they restrain sons, and dominant mothers reject sons more than they reject daughters (Simpson, personal communications). The complexity of the issues involved is exemplified by the facts that dominant mothers are more likely to bear daughters than sons, and that mothers with sons on average conceive again more quickly than mothers with daughters (Simpson, 1983; Simpson, Simpson, Hooley, & Zunz, 1981).

Studies of the relatively simple case of rhesus monkey mother–infant relationships thus demonstrate relations between the characteristics of the mother and those of her offspring mediated by characteristics of the mother-infant relationship, which itself may be affected in diverse ways by the social nexus in which it is embedded. The relation between mother and offspring characteristics, however, differs according to the sex of the latter, and the relations between male infants' characteristics and their behavior in a strange situation differs from those for females. Comparable complexities arise even more clearly in the human case, as discussed below.

DIFFICULT CHILDREN: HOME RELATIONSHIPS AND
BEHAVIOR IN PRESCHOOL

We have attempted to assess children's temperament and relationships at home, and to compare these assessments with the children's interactions in preschool. The children, who all attended the same preschool, were assessed when 42 months old (n = 26 boys and 21 girls) and again at 50 months (n = 24 and 17). Each child had one, but only one sibling, younger by 14–26 months or older by 16–52 months. The data sources were as follows:

1. The Garside, Birch et al., (1975) *Tempermental Characteristics Interview,* to assess the child's style of behavior (see also Thomas & Chess, 1977). This was behaviorally based, with mothers describing recent interactions in different settings (e.g., waking, dressing, mealtime). From a tape recording of the interview, the interviewer rated each item on a 5-point scale. A Difficult score was produced by summing the six Mood items (inequable, irritable, or sulky), the four Intense items (extreme in the expression of feelings), and the two Unmalleable items (refusing to come when asked). Thus, like Thomas & Chess's Difficult score, ours includes an assessment of Mood and Intensity. However, it does not include Irregularity, Approach-Withdrawal, or Adaptability, and it provides a continuous score rather than a categorization.

2. A *Relationships Interview,* to obtain background information and either frequencies of occurrence or ratings of interactions with the mother, father, and sibling. Again, the mothers described recent interactions, and the ratings were made by the interviewer from a tape recording.

3. The *Bené-Anthony Family Relations Test,* administered to the child, to assess feelings (Positive, Negative, and Dependency) toward each family member.

4. The *Irritability, Depression and Anxiety Scale* (Snaith, Constantopoulos, Jardine, & McGuffin, 1978). This is a questionnaire, with mothers rating themselves, designed to give scores for outward and inward Irritability, Depression, and Anxiety.

5. Two observational sessions of about 60 minutes in the home.

6. Two (42 months) or four (50 months) observation sessions of 40–60 minutes in the preschool classroom, and three sessions (both ages) of 30 minutes in the playground.

7. A teacher questionnaire concerned with social behavior.

For present purposes we have selected for discussion the relations between the children's Difficult scores (or its constituent characteristics) and various interaction measures at home and at school.[1]

---

[1]Further details of this study, including data on the measures and their reliability, can be found in Stevenson-Hinde & Simpson, 1982; Hinde, Easton, Meller, & Tamplin, 1983; Stevenson-Hinde, Hinde, & Simpson, in press; Hinde & Stevenson-Hinde, in press; Hinde & Tamplin, 1983; Simpson & Stevenson-Hinde, 1985 and Hinde, Stevenson-Hinde, & Tamplin, 1985.

Home Data

The Child. Children with relatively high Difficult scores were reported by mothers in a different interview as having a relatively high incidence of the sum of tantrums, difficult-to-manage behavior, and refusals (r_s = .36*, .41**, at each age, $p<.05$ and .01, 2- tailed).

In the Bené-Anthony test, the more Difficult the child, the more negative messages the child gave him/herself (.35*, $p<.05$) and the more positive messages to "nobody" (.33*) at 42 months, indicating that the children themselves may have some awareness of their own characteristics (for further detail, see Stevenson-Hinde & Simpson, 1982).

The Mother. None of the interview items on the mother's background was significantly correlated with Difficult temperament. However, at 50 months (when the mother's mood was assessed), Difficult children tended to have mothers who were anxious (.41**), inwardly irritable (.50***) and outwardly irritable (.46**). When the three characteristics comprising the Difficult score were separately correlated with the maternal mood scores, Unmalleable produced no significant correlations, while Moody and Intense were each significantly correlated with maternal Anxiety, Inward Irritability, and Outward Irritability. Thus, it was the two "mood" characteristics of the child that were correlated with the mother's mood.

The Mother-Child Relationship. Mothers reports indicated that, although Difficult children were (surprisingly) more prone to comply with their mothers after a tantrum at 42 months (.34*) than non-Difficult children, they were less so at 50 months (−.45**). At both ages, having refused to do something, they tended to fail to comply when asked again (−.42** and −.36*) and, by 50 months, their mothers tended to be harsh when this occurred (.35*). At both ages, the more Difficult the child, the less accepting were mothers of the child's offers of help (−.40**, −.50***).

When the observational data on mother-child interactions were related to the temperament assessment, associations with the constituent characteristics Intense and Moody were found to be more revealing than those with the Difficult score. At 42 months, children scoring highly on Intense tended to have frequent friendly (.36*) and hostile (Ch. active hostile, .34*; M. reactive hostile, .32*; Ch. Controls .39**) interactions with their mothers; the Moody score was also associated with maternal reactive hostility (.37*). The conversations of Intense children tended to involve abstract topics (.52***) and, at this age, both the Intense and Moody measures were significantly correlated with the frequency of questions to the mother (.31* and .33*).

At 50 months, both these temperamental characteristics were negatively associated with maternal friendliness (−.32*, −.43**), although physical friendliness was common (.33*, .33*).[2] There were also negative correlations between the Moody score and other positive or neutral items (e.g., M. neutral speech, −.42**; M. conversational questions −.46**), as well as positive correlations between this score and maternal hostility (M. reactive hostility, .33*; M. active hostility .32*).

Surprisingly, few significant correlations between the home observational items and the Unmalleable score appeared. Negative correlations linking this score and maternal inhibitions suggest that mothers may have adjusted their behavior to their perceptions of their children and/or to the observer's presence.

These data from the maternal interviews and home observations indicated some tenseness in the mother-child relationships of Difficult children. Moreover, the Bené-Anthony tests suggested that the children had some awareness of this. At 42 months, the more Difficult the child, the fewer Dependency (−.58***) and Positive (−.36*) messages went to the mother. At 50 months, however, for reasons which are not apparent, these correlations disappeared even though the problem behavior and negative interactions continued.

Father-Child Interactions.   The maternal interview yielded only limited data on father-child interactions. Fathers high in the Registrar-General's classification of occupations tended to have more Difficult children (−.30*). The maternal interview data showed no significant correlations between father-child interactions and Difficult ratings at 42 months. At 50 months, the more Difficult the child, the more likely were fathers to be reported as being harsher than mothers (.31*), even though, as we have seen, the mothers were themselves relatively harsh. In addition, the more Difficult the child, the less did the mother feel that the father was aware of her daily life (−.43**), the less the father did with the child (−.33*), and the more often the child annoyed the father (.35*). The difference between the associations at 42 and 50 months suggests a change in parental expectations—a hope that the Difficult child would improve in preschool, which was not fulfilled.

Sibling-Child Interactions.   The maternal interview indicated that Difficult Children tended to have a less enjoyable relationship with siblings (−.33*) and to have a high rate of squabbling (.35*). Since firstborns tended to be more Difficult than secondborns (Mann-Whitney *U,* p<.02, two-tailed), one of the effects of a secondborn on a firstborn may be to make at least some firstborns more Difficult (see also Dunn & Kendrick, 1982).

---

[2]Physical friendliness was a rather ambiguous item, giving near zero correlations with maternal verbal friendliness, expressions of pleasure or solicitude, but in girls significant positive correlations with the four dimensions of mother's mood (depression, anxiety, inward and outward irritability).

Preschool Data

It is first necessary to stress that the children's behavior with adults in preschool bore no simple relation to their behavior with peers. Children who interacted frequently with peers showed no tendency to interact frequently with adults, and showed only limited tendencies to show the same type of behavior to adults and to peers. Not surprisingly, the behavior shown to peers tended to resemble the behavior received from peers, whereas interactions with adults tended to be complementary. For these reasons, child-adult behavior and child-child behavior have been considered separately in terms of their relation to the temperament scores (Hinde, Easton, Meller, & Tamplin, 1983).

Child-Teacher and Child-Child Interactions.   Again, it proved to be more profitable to examine relations with the constituent items of the Difficult score separately. At 42 months, children rated as Intense on the basis of maternal descriptions of behavior at home frequently played excitedly (.43**) and made play noises (.30*), and seldom scanned the environment (−.36**), or were fearful (−.34*). They were often with peers(.47**), their interactions including high proportions of control (.36*), dependency (.47**), and active and reactive hostility (.37* and .33*). Their behavior with adults differed little from that of non-Intense children. At 50 months, these correlations largely disappeared but, when the sexes were examined separately, girls continued to show a pattern similar to that evidenced at 42 months.

Moody children interacted with adults more frequently than non-Moody at 42 months (.36*), making frequent control statements (.32*), and showing reactive hostility to them (.30*) as well as to their peers (.30*). They also tended to cry (.30*). At 50 months, Moody children showed more involvement with peers than children not so rated (.43**) with their interactions including both control (.50**) and active hostility (.50**). Their interactions with adults differed little from those of non-Moody children, but they tended not to comply with them (.41**) and to receive reactive hostility from them (.45**).

Unmalleable children tended not to interact with adults, and at 50 months many of the interactions with adults tended to have a negative character. They tended to play boisterously with their peers at both ages. At 42 months, they were often excited and, at 50 months, they showed high frequencies of a number of neutral items, but no tendency to show the hostility seen in Intense and Moody children.

The Mother-Child Relationship and Hostility.   It is important to stress that the home situation associated with a particular pattern of behavior in school cannot be described in terms of one or even a few variables, but is liable to involve a complex pattern of factors (e.g., Baumrind, 1967, 1971). To exemplify this, we consider here the relations between the observational data on the mother-child relationship and a type of behavior in school that is perceived by teachers as "difficult," namely, hostility to peers. For present purposes active hostility (which included verbal hostility, criticism, threats, and physical interference or hitting) was differentiated from reactive hostility (nonverbal resistance and verbal refusals or protests accompanied by a hostile manner). To summarize the data in general terms, children who showed frequent hostility to peers in school tended to have infrequent positive (−.34*) and neutral (−.40**) interactions with their mothers at home. Active hostility to peers was also associated with frequent strong control of the mother by the child at 42 months (.37*), and with its absence at 50 months (child inhibits −.35*). At the latter age, Active hostility to peers was associated with maternal reactive (.40*) and active (.35*) hostility and inhibitory control (.32*) with which the child did not comply (.35*), but often disconfirmed the mother (.48**). Reactive hostility to peers was associated also with maternal hostility (.33*) at 42 months, and with dependent behavior (.42**) and mutual absence of control (−.33*, −.41*) at 50 months.

It is worth noting that, at 50 months, lack of involvement with the mother coupled with maternal permissiveness (i.e., mother compliant and/or low on control) was associated with high frequencies of *both* friendly behavior *and* hostility at school, but in the latter case there were also significant correlations with maternal or mutual hostility at home. And these are only some of the variables associated with friendly and hostile behavior in school: for instance, the maternal interview data indicated that relationships between the child and other family members were also related to behavior in school (Stevenson-Hinde, Hinde, & Simpson, in press).

General.   What we are dealing with here is, of course, a complex web of cause–effect relationships which a correlational approach can describe but not unravel. Nevertheless it will be apparent that there were meaningful patterns of relations between difficult behavior and the child's various intrafamilial relationships and between the child's intrafamilial relationships and behavior in school. These do not involve so much direct parallels between the one and the other—for instance agressiveness to peers in preschool was not closely linked to aggressiveness at home. Rather the relations were between patterns of variables—aggressiveness in preschool to a mother/child relationship lacking in warmth and characterized also by either permissiveness or by control and hostility (according to age).

CONCLUSION

Understanding social development demands a multipronged attack, and this chapter is, in essence, a plea that four of those prongs should not lose touch with each other. It is assumed that social development depends in large part on the relationships experienced. First, to understand how relationships form, are maintained or change, we need principles concerned with their dynamics. Second, to specify the limits of applicability of those principles, we need a means for describing relationships. The description of relationships can also help us to pinpoint gaps in our knowledge. But the nature and dynamics of relationships will be affected by the characteristics of the individuals involved—characteristics themselves that are partly consequent upon relationships. Thus, third, the study of relationships must be integrated with the study of personality. Finally, since relationships also affect and are affected by the social situation, relationships must also be studied in relation to their social context. In this chapter we have briefly summarized two studies designed with these issues in mind.

Although we believe that this strategy has considerable potential, five points about the tactics need to be emphasized. First, one must choose whether to go straight for global variables with which to describe individual characteristics, behavior, and relationships, such as the "secure" vs. "insecure" attachment (see Ainsworth et al., 1978), or whether to use more particulate items. We chose the latter, primarily because the use of global variables permits much individual variation to slip through. In addition, we found that attempts to produce summary scores by principal component analysis produced components insufficiently replicable across sexes, ages, and situations for the comparisons we wished to make. Second, we suggest that, in studies of the effects of one set of interpersonal relationships on another, it is useful to assess a considerable number of variables in each case. In the present instance, insofar as the effects are from home to school, one must expect each aspect of school behavior to depend on numerous aspects of the home environment, with the influences interacting in complex ways. Furthermore, the child's behavior is constantly influenced by the current situation. If one looked only at aggression to peers in school, for instance, one might be led to conclusions about home environments conducive to aggression which would be incorrect for aggression to adults. Furthermore, a home environment conducive to little hostility in school is not necessarily propitious for much friendliness: a broader perspective is necessary. Of course the result of considering numerous variables is a formidable problem of data reduction and the possible criticism that the empirical effort lacks focus—but these are problems that the complexity of life requires one to live with.

Third, as presented here, ours are correlational studies. Correlational studies are notoriously difficult to replicate, and attempts to repeat them are essential (and currently in hand). In addition, the yield of correlational studies in terms of causal understanding is limited. For the purposes of this chapter we have glossed over some of the complexities (for instance the problem of ubiquitous sex and birth order differences—see the papers cited and especially Hinde & Stevenson-Hinde, in press). Partly because of these very complexities, we have not used a multivariate approach: principle components analyses showed the structure of the behavior to differ between boys and girls, between classroom and playground, between 42 and 50 months. It seemed more important to try to understand the factors related to each of the variables considered.

Ultimately, of course, the goal must be an understanding of process. If we are to come to terms with the dialectic between personality and relationships, an attack on process is essential. Some aspects of the present study will contribute to that end. The use of diverse instruments has in some cases provided us with insights about the directions of effects. The longitudinal element, not discussed in this chapter, also provides insights into process—though we must remember that the factors responsible for changes with age are not necessarily the same as those responsible for individual differences at one age (Hinde, 1969). Study of the data on individual children, selected as being extreme by one or more criteria, will also, we hope, bring further understanding of process. Beyond that, studies of process require identification of child characteristics that affect behavior in home and school in addition to the characteristics of temperament used here. Comparisons of behavior between home and school can contribute towards the finding of such characteristics, but is itself only a step along the road.

Finally, we must emphasize the ubiquitous problem of meaning. Any attempt to classify instances of behavior into categories involves pooling events that are diverse in at least some characteristics. The necessity for data reduction exacerbates the issues. Our data suggest that some of our categories may have included events subtly different for boys and for girls. But, too often, this difficulty is used as a counsel for despair. If we recognize it as a problem intrinsic to *all* studies of behavior, and are constantly aware of it, it loses its potency.

ACKNOWLEDGMENT

This work was supported by the Medical Research Council and the Royal Society. We are grateful to W. W. Hartup for his editorial comments.

REFERENCES

Ainsworth, M. D. S., Bell, S. M. & Slayton, D. J. (1974). Infant-mother attachment and social development: "Socialisation" as a product of reciprocal responsiveness to signals. In M. P. M. Richards (Ed.), *The integration of a child into a social world.* Cambridge: Cambridge University Press.

Ainsworth, M. D. S., Blehar, M. C., Waters, E., & Wall, S. (1978). *Patterns of attachment: A psychological study of the strange situation.* Hillsdale, NJ: Lawrence Erlbaum Associates.

Baerends, G. P. (1976). The functional organization of behaviour. *Animal Behaviour 24,* 726–738.

Bandura, A. (1977). *Social learning theory.* Englewood Cliffs, NJ: Prentice Hall.

Bateson, P. P. G. (1964). Effect of similarity betwen rearing and testing conditions on chicks' following and avoidance responses. *Journal of Comparative Physiological Psychology 57,* 100–103.

Bateson, P. P. G. (1973). Preference for familiarity and novelty: A model for the simultaneous development of both. *Journal of Theoretical Biology 41*, 249–259.

Baumrind, D. (1967). Child care practices anteceding 3 patterns of preschool behaviour. *Genetic Psychology Monographs, 75*, 43–88.

Baumrind, D. (1971). Current patterns of parental authority. *Developmental Psychology Monographs, 4*, No. 1, Pt. 2, 1–103.

Bigelow, B. J., & La Gaipa, J. J. (1975). Children's written descriptions of friendship: A multidimensional analysis. *Developmental Psychology, 11*, 857–858.

Bowlby, J. (1969). *Attachment and loss. Vol. 1. Attachment.* London: Hogarth Press.

Burton, L. (1975). *The family life of sick children.* London: Routledge & Kegan Paul.

Chandler, M. J., & Greenspan, S. (1972). Ersatz egocentrism: A reply to H. Borke. *Developmental Psychology, 7*, 104–106.

Cicirelli, V. G. (1975). Effects of mother and older siblings on the problem solving behavior of the older child. *Developmental Psychology. II*, 749–756.

Clore, G. L., & Byrne, D. (1974). A reinforcement-affect model of attraction. In T. L. Huston, (Ed.), *Foundations of interpersonal attraction.* New York: Academic Press.

Dunn, J., & Kendrick, C. (1982). *Siblings: Love, envy and understanding.* Cambridge, MA: Harvard University Press.

Fletcher, R. (1966). *The family and marriage in Britain.* Harmonsworth, UK: Penguin.

Foa, U. G., & Foa, E.B. (1974). *Societal structures of the mind.* Springfield, IL: CC Thomas.

Garside, R. F., Birch, H., Scott, D.Mcl., Chambers, S., Kolvin, I., Tweddle, E. G., & Barber, L. M. (1975). Dimensions of temperament in infant school children. *Journal of Child Psychology and Psychiatry, 16*, 219–231.

Garvey, C., & Ben Debba, M. (1974). Effects of age, sex and partner on children's dyadic speech. *Child Development, 45*, 1159–1161.

Gath, A. (1978). *Down's Syndrome and the family—Early years.* London: Academic Press.

Gelman, R., & Shatz, M. (1977). Speech adjustments in talk to 2-year olds. In M. Lewis & L. A. Rosenblum (Eds.), *Interaction, conversation and the development of language.* New York: Academic Press.

Gewirtz, J. L. (1961). A learning analysis of the effects of normal stimulation, privation and deprivation on the acquisition of social motivation and attachment. In B. M. Foss (Ed.), *Determinants of infant behaviour. Vol. 1.* London Methuen.

Glenn, N. D. (1975). Psychological well-being in the post-parental stage: Some evidence from national surveys. *Journal of Marriage and the Family, 37*, 105–112.

Goffman, E. (1978). *Gender advertisements.* London: McMillan.

Harré, R. (1975). The origins of social competence in a pluralist society. *Oxford Review of Education, 1*, 151–158.

Hinde, R. A. (1969). Analysing the roles of the partners in a behavioural interaction—mother-infant relations in rhesus macaques. *Annals of the New York Academy of Science, 159*, 651–667.

Hinde, R. A. (1971). Some problems in the study of the development of social behaviour. In E. Tobach, L. R. Aronson, & E. Shaw (Eds.), *The biopsychology of development.* New York: Academic Press.

Hinde, R. A. (1974). *Biological bases of human social behaviour.* New York: McGraw-Hill.

Hinde, R. A. (1979). *Towards understanding relationships.* London: Academic Press.

Hinde, R. A. (1984). Why do the sexes behave differently in close relationships? *Journal of Social and Personal Relationships. 1*, 471–501.

Hinde, R. A., Easton, D. F., Meller, R. E., & Tamplin, A. (1983). Nature and determinants of preschoolers' differential behaviour to adults and peers. *British Journal of Developmental Psychology, 1*, 3–19.

Hinde, R. A., & Powell Proctor, L. (1977). Changes in the relationships of captive rhesus monkeys on giving birth. *Behaviour, 61*, 304–321.

Hinde, R. A., & Spencer-Booth, Y. (1967). The effect of social companions on mother-infant relations in rhesus monkeys. In D. Morris (Ed.), *Primate ethology*. London: Weidenfeld and Nicolson.

Hinde, R. A., & Stevenson-Hinde, J. (Eds.). (1973). *Constraints on learning: Limitations and predispositions*. London: Academic Press.

Hinde, R. A., & Stevenson-Hinde, J. (in press). Relationships, personality and the social situation. In R. Gilmour & S. Duck (Eds.), *The emerging field of personal relationships*. Hillsdale, NJ: Lawrence Erlbaum Associates.

Hinde, R. A., Stevenson-Hinde, J., & Tamplin, A. (1985). Characteristics of 3- to 4-year-olds assessed at home and their interactions in preschool. *Developmental Psychology, 21,* 130–140.

Hinde, R. A., & Tamplin, A. (1983). The relations between mother-child interactions of 3-4 year olds and their behaviour in preschool. *British Journal of Developmental Psychology, 1,* 231–257.

Hinde, R. A., Titmus, G., Easton, D. and Tamplin, A. Incidence of "Friendship" and behavior towards associates vs nonassociates in preschoolers. *Child Development, 56,* 234–245.

Humphrey, M. (1975). The effect of children upon the marriage relationship. *British Journal of Medical Psychology, 48,* 273–279.

Lamb, M. E. (Ed.). (1976). *The role of the father in child development*. New York: Wiley.

Lerner, M. J., Miller, D. T., & Holmes, J. G. (1976). Deserving and the emergence of forms of justice. In L. Berkowitz & E. Walster (Eds.), *Advances in experimental social psychology. Vol. 9,* 133–162.

Leventhal, G. S., & Lane, D. (1970). Sex, age and equity behavior. *Journal of Personality and Social Psychology, 151,* 312–316.

Lewis, M., Young, G., Brooks, J., & Michalson, L. (1975). The beginning of friendship. In M. Lewis & L. A. Rosenblum (Eds.), *The origins of behavior: Friendship and peer relations*. New York: Wiley.

Lott, A. J., & Lott, B. E. (1974). The role of reward in the formation of positive interpersonal attitudes. In T. L. Huston (Ed.), *Foundations of interpersonal attraction*. New York: Academic Press.

Lund, M. (1981). *The development of commitment to a close relationship*. Ph.D. thesis. University of California, Los Angeles.

Lytton, H. (1980). *Parent-child interaction*. New York: Plenum Press.

Main, M., & Stadtman, J. (1981). Infant response to rejection of physical contact by the mother. Aggression, avoidance and conflict. *Journal of the American Academy of Child Psychiatry, 20,* 292–307.

Main, M., & Weston, D. R. (1981). The quality of the toddler's relationship to mother and to father: Related conflict behaviour and the readiness to establish new relationships. *Child Development, 52,* 932–940.

McCall, G. J. (1970). The social organization of relationships. In G. J. McCall, M. McCall, N. K. Denzin, G. D. Suttles, & S. B. Kurth (Eds.), *Social relationships*. Chicago: Aldine.

Mueller, E., & Brenner, J. (1977). The origins of social skills and interaction among playgroup toddlers. *Child Development, 48,* 854–861.

Newcomb, T. M. (1971). Dyadic balance as a source of clues about interpersonal attraction. In B. I. Murstein (Ed.), *Theories of attraction and love*. New York: Springer.

Parkes, C. M., & Stevenson-Hinde, J. (Eds.). (1982). *The place of attachment in human behavior*. New York: Basic Books.

Piaget, J. (1965). *The moral judgment of the child*. New York: The Free Press. (Original publication in English in 1932 by Routledge and Kegan Paul, London.)

Putallaz, M., & Gottman, J. M. (1981). Social skills and group acceptance. In S. R. Asher & J. M. Gottman (Eds.), *The development of children's friendships*. Cambridge: Cambridge University Press.

Rubin, K. H., & Pepler, D. J. (1980). The relationship of child's play to social-cognitive growth and development. In H. C. Foot, A. J. Chapman, & J. R. Smith (Eds.) *Friendship and social relations in children.* New York: Wiley.

Schuster, S. O'D., Murrell, S. A., & Cook, W. A. (1980). Person, setting, and interaction contributions to nursery school social behaviour patterns. *Journal of Personality, 48,* 24–37.

Seligman, M. E. P., & Hager, J. L. (1972). *Biological boundaries of learning.* New York: Appleton-Century-Crofts.

Selman, R. L. (1976a). Social-cognitive understanding: a guide to educational and clinical practice. In T. Lickona (Ed.), *Moral development and behavior.* New York: Holt, Rinehart and Winston.

Selman, R. L. (1976b). Towards a structural analysis of developing interpersonal relations concepts: research with normal and disturbed preadolescent boys. In A. D. Pick (Ed.), *Minnesota Symposia on Child Psychology,* Minneapolis: Minnesota University Press.

Shatz, M., & Gelman, R. (1973). The development of communication skills: Modification in the speech of young children as a function of the listener. *Monographs of the Society for research in Child Development. 38,* No. 5.

Simpson, A. E., & Stevenson-Hinde, J. (1985). Temperamental characteristics of three- to four-year-old boys and girls and child-family interactions. *Journal of Child Psychology and Psychiatry, 26,* 43–53.

Simpson, M. J. A. (1983). Effect of the sex of an infant on the mother-infant relationship and the mother's subsequent reproduction. In R. A. Hinde (Ed.), *Primate social relationships.* Oxford: Blackwells.

Simpson, M. J. A., Simpson, A. E., Hooley, J., & Zunz, M. (1981). Infant-related influences on birth intervals in rhesus monkeys. *Nature, 290,* No. 5801, 49–51.

Slater, E., & Woodside, M. (1951). *Patterns of marriage.* London: Cassell.

Smither, S. (1977). A reconsideration of the developmental study of empathy. *Human development, 20,* 253–276.

Snaith, R. P., Constantopoulos, A. A., Jardine, M. Y. & McGuffin, P. (1978). A clinical scale for the self-assessment of irritability. *British Journal of Psychiatry, 132,* 164–171.

Snow, C. (1972). Mother's speech to children learning language. *Child Development, 43,* 549–564.

Spencer-Booth, Y. (1968). The behaviour of twin rhesus monkeys and comparisons with the behaviour of single infants. *Primates, 9,* 75–84.

Stevenson-Hinde, J., Hinde, R. A., & Simpson, A. E. (in press). Interactions at home and friendly or hostile behavior in preschool. In J. Block, D. Olweus, & M. R. Yarrow (Eds.). *Development of antisocial and prosocial behavior.* New York: Academic Press.

Stevenson-Hinde, J., & Simpson, M. J. A. (1981). Mothers' characteristics, interactions, and infants' characteristics. *Child Development, 52* 1246–1254.

Stevenson-Hinde, J., & Simpson, A. E. (1982). Temperament and relationships. In Temperamental differences in Infants and Young Children. *Ciba Foundation symposium 89.* London: Pitman Books.

Stevenson-Hinde, J., Stillwell-Barnes, R., & Zunz, M. (1980a). Subjective assessment of rhesus monkeys over four successive years. *Primates, 21(1),* 66–82.

Stevenson-Hinde, J., Stillwell-Barnes, R., & Zunz, M. (1980b). Individual differences in young rhesus monkeys: consistency and change. *Primates, 21(4),* 498–509.

Sullivan, H. S. (1953). *The interpersonal theory of psychiatry.* New York: Norton.

Thomas, A., & Chess, S. (1977). *Temperament and development.* New York: Brunner/Mazel.

Wertheim, E. S. (1975a). Person-environment interaction: The epigenesis of autonomy and competence. II Review of developmental literature (normal development). *British Journal of medical Psychology, 48,* 95–111.

Wertheim, E. S. (1975b). Person-environment interaction: the epigenesis of autonomy and competence. III Autonomy and para-/pre-linguistic and linguistic action systems: review of developmental literature (normal development). *British Journal of medical Psychology, 48,* 237–256.

Wertheim, E. S. (1975c). The science and typology of family systems II. Further theoretical and practical considerations. *Family Process, 14,* 285–309.

Yarrow, L. J. (1963). Research in dimensions of early maternal care. *Merrill-Palmer Quarterly, 9,* 101–114.

Yarrow, M. R. (1975). Some perspectives on research on peer relations. In M. Lewis & L. A. Rosenblum (Eds.), *The origins of behavior: Friendship and peer relations.* New York: Wiley.

Yarrow, M. R., Waxler, C. Z., & Scott, P. M. (1971). Child effects on adult behavior. *Developmental Psychology, 5,* 300–311.

Youniss, J. (1980). *Parents and peers in social development.* Chicago: University of Chicago Press.

Zajonc, R. (1968). Cognitive theories in social psychology. In G. Lindzey & E. Aronson (Eds.), *Handbook of social psychology.* Reading MA: Addison-Wesley.

3

Attachment and the Construction of Relationships

L. Alan Sroufe
June Fleeson
University of Minnesota

A perspective on the study of personality development recently has evolved, which is an integration of general developmental theory (Santostefano & Baker, 1972), ego theory (Loevinger, 1976; Sullivan, 1953) and adaptational theory (Bowlby, 1969; Breger, 1974; Sander, 1975, Sroufe, 1979). Within this organismic/adaptational perspective, personality development not only takes place in a social context but is, in fact, a direct outcome of social relations (Mead, 1934). At the same time, social relations are seen as the complex products of individual personalities (Hinde, 1979). *Studying the origins of personality and the origins of social relations becomes one and the same task.*

In modern terms personality is not a collection of static traits or even behavioral dispositions. It is not a thing, or even a collection of things, that persons *have* in certain degrees. Rather, it refers to the organization of attitudes, feelings, expectations, and behaviors of the individual across contexts (Block & Block, 1979; Loevinger, 1976; Sroufe, 1979).

As described by Ainsworth & Bell (1974), Sander (1975), and others, the first behavioral organization (the *anlage* of personality) is with reference to the caregiver. Organization exists from the outset, but the organization is a property of the dyadic relationship, rather than the individual infant. The newborn infant can exhibit a limited set of preadapted behaviors in certain behavioral contexts; for example, it cries when it is aroused (for whatever reason) and it looks at slowly moving objects having certain contrast features (Salapatek & Banks, 1967). But it is only when caregivers elicit and respond to these behaviors in a timely and appropriate fashion—that is, when they imbue them with meaning—that the infant becomes part of an organized dyadic system. Outside of this relationship the infant cannot be "competent"; that is, cannot be part of an organized whole.

Everything that the infant brings to this interaction in terms of behavioral capacities and dispositions becomes part of the dyadic organization. Such dispositions are profoundly transformed and transmuted within the relationship and have little significance outside of it. For example, studies with prematures (Cohen & Beckwith, 1979) and newborns having nonoptimal (but not life threatening) status (Crockenberg, 1981) converge to suggest that, in typical caretaking environments, such infant characteristics commonly will be countered and will have no lasting effects (see also Sameroff & Chandler, 1975).

With time, a new organization emerges which is not an organization around the caregiver, but an organization around an emergent self. What was dyadic regulation becomes self-regulation as the child learns he/she can perturb and reinstate the dyadic system (Sander, 1975). This transition from dyadic organization to self-organization is of fundamental importance for it profoundly shapes the direction of future relationships. The young child seeks and explores new relationships within the framework of expectations for self and other that emerges from the primary relationship.

Although, ultimately, the personality organization is around the self, and thus transcends particular relationships, this organization is always with reference to others. In less than ideal circumstances, the organization of some young children may continue to be "around" another (as in the overly dependent child) and, in pathological circumstances, some children are virtually devoid of social relations. The emotional withdrawal and flat affect of such nonrelating children, might be described as the "absence" of personality.

This view of personality as organization makes it clear why developmentalists would want to study social relations and, in particular, the child's primary attachment relationships. But it also has implications for the study of individuals as they participate in social relations. Once the infant has been involved in the attachment relationship, its inherent dispositions are both subsumed and transformed by the relationship. These dispositions cannot be reclaimed as the infant moves forward to new relationships. Congenital temperament, could it be assessed, in large part ceases to exist as a separate entity. An earlier view of the developmental process was that, as the infant moved out from the attachment relationship to the larger social world, he or she took forward congenital temperamental dispositions plus aspects of the relationship history, like suitcases in each hand. But what the child brings to new relationships (with peers, teachers and others) is not an additive combination of dispositions plus relationship history. The child brings forward *only* an organization of feelings, needs, attitudes, expectations, cognitions, and behavior; that is, only the relationship history as processed and integrated by the developing individual (i.e., everything is in the same suitcase). One implication of this argument, to be developed below, is that relationships with peers and others formed in early childhood (and later in more complex ways) would be strongly predictable from the quality of the early primary relationships.

A major question addressed in this chapter is how early relationships and their histories influence the form and quality of subsequent relationships. It is assumed that relationships are not constructed afresh, nor are new relationships based on the simple transfer of particular responses from old relationships. Instead, it is assumed that previous relationships exert their influence through the attitudes, expectations, and understanding of roles that they leave with the individual. Each relationship may be unique, but relationships are also lawfully determined by the relational histories of the individuals. Individuals are complex and, of course, when two complex individuals enter into a dyadic system the potential complexity is enormously increased. Still, as is argued in this paper, the complexity is limited, and predictability enhanced, by the fact that individuals select and shape each other in terms of the dispositions, inclinations, and expectancies brought from prior relationships. Individuals tend not to combine these dispositions in random fashion, but to recreate aspects of relationship systems previously experienced.

INFANT-CAREGIVER ATTACHMENT AS A RELATIONSHIP

Large numbers of new studies have been focused on infant attachment. Strong links between individual differences in infant attachment and later socioemotional functioning have been established at a time when continuity of individual behavior was being challenged (Sroufe, 1979). Developed here is the thesis that these links emerged largely because the early assessments are valid measures of the infant-caregiver *relationship,* not just the individual infant.

Examined closely, Ainsworth's strange situation (e.g., Ainsworth, Blehar, Waters, & Wall, 1978) is actually a method for assessing the quality of the infant-caregiver attachment relationship rather than infant attachment behaviors per se. In this laboratory procedure, which has been shown to relate to exploration and crying in the home, the infant is observed across a series of episodes involving increasing stress. The way the infant adjusts his or her behavior across the episodes and, especially, the changing balance between exploration and proximity, contact, and interaction with the caregiver is assessed. Infants are classified according to the flexibility of behavioral organization with *respect to the caregiver.* Infants who use the caregiver as a base for exploration and for coping with novelty, and who, following the stress of separation, are active and direct in seeking contact or interaction (which also promotes exploration) are said to have secure attachment relationships, and by inference, to have been part of a responsive caregiver-infant system. Infants who are unable to use the caregiver as a base for exploration and are not readily comforted by contact (usually mixing contact seeking with anger) are said to have anxious/resistant attachment relationships. Infants who withhold contact and avoid the caregiver following these brief laboratory separations (with more avoidance the greater the stress) are said to have anxious avoidant attachments. Like the resistant infants, this inability to derive comforting from renewed contact (physical or psychological) interferes with exploration and mastery of the environment. (See Table 3.1 for a summary of the Ainsworth classification scheme.)

Using the Ainsworth assessment procedure, the interest is in capturing the infant-caregiver relationship even though only infant behavior is examined. One cannot know how the procedure (including the presence of a camera, which generally is focused on the infant) influences caregiver behavior, and there is

TABLE 3.1
Patterns of Attachment[a]

Pattern A: Anxious/Avoidant Attachment
   A. Exploration Independent of Caregiver
      1. readily separate to explore during preseparation
      2. little affective sharing
      3. affiliative to stranger, even when caregiver absent (little preference)
   B. Active avoidance upon reunion
      1. turning away, looking away, moving away, ignoring
      2. may mix avoidance with proximity
      3. avoidance more extreme on second reunion
      4. no avoidance of stranger
Pattern B: Infants Secure in Their Attachment
   A. Caregiver as Secure Base for Exploration
      1. readily separate to explore toys
      2. affective sharing of play
      3. affiliative to stranger in mother's presence
      4. readily comforted when distressed (promoting a return to play)
   B. Active in Seeking Contact or Interaction Upon Reunion
      1. If distressed
         (a) immediately seek and maintain contact
         (b) contact is effective in terminating distress
      2. If not distressed
         (a) active greeting behavior (happy to see caregiver)
         (b) strong initiation of interaction
Pattern C: Anxious/Resistant Attachment
   A. Poverty of Exploration
      1. difficulty separating to explore; may need contact even prior to separation
      2. wary of novel situations and people
   B. Difficulty Settling Upon Reunion
      1. may mix contact seeking with contact resistance (hitting, kicking, squirming, rejecting toys)
      2. may simply continue to cry and fuss
      3. may show striking passivity

[a]Adapted from Ainsworth, Blehar, Waters, & Wall, 1978. Reprinted by permission of Lawrence Erlbaum Associates.

reason to question whether the separation–reunion procedure in this context has the same salience for the caregiver as for the infant. But the infant, one can argue, will behave according to established dyadic patterns and, in so doing, will reveal qualities of the relationship history. Relationship patterns can be seen even in examining individual behavior when both partners are present. For example, it is the infant's *expectations* concerning caregiver responsiveness that promote exploration in the novel setting. Infants who have visual access to caregivers explore more actively than infants whose caregivers are behind a screen (Carr, Dabbs, & Carr, 1975), as do infants whose mothers are watching them compared to mothers who are instructed to read a magazine (Sorce & Emde, 1981). Individual differences when all caregivers are literally available reflect a history of availability and responsiveness (as is shown below). Should the infant become distressed or threatened, he or she relies on the knowledge that the caregiver is available and will respond promptly and effectively. Infants secure in their attachments settle quickly following the distress of separation, because these pairs have evolved an efficient distress-terminating routine and because the infants are confident that stress will be terminated by the opportunity for contact. When distressed, secure infants go *immediately* to the caregiver for contact upon reunion, and they end this approach either by clambering up or with a clear gesture for pick-up. Such purposeful behavior necessarily reflects a history not only of infant behavior but of caregiver behavior (e.g., routine responses made to these signals by the infant).

In sum, we believe that the Ainsworth attachment assessments are actually measures of the relationship between the infant and the caregivers. Moreover, we believe that infant-caregiver attachment has all of the basic definitional features of relationships as described by Hinde (1979). It is characterized by its enduring qualities and patterning. It transcends the momentary interaction, being a product of the interactional history. It is unique to the particular partnership. And it is not reducible to the characteristics of one individual. These features of the attachment relationship are illustrated by recent research.

Attachment as Characterized by Qualitative Aspects

Like other relationships, variations in infant-caregiver attachment are marked by differences in the quality and patterning of behavior (Hinde, 1979). Infant behaviors exhibited within the attachment relationship may be shown toward others, but their organization within the attachment relationship is unique. For example, infants approach other persons, but approaches when distressed or approaches ending in pick-up gestures are shown almost exclusively to attachment figures (Tracy, Lamb, & Ainsworth, 1976). Infants smile at strangers, but "affective sharing" (turning automatically to smile, vocalize, and show a newly discovered toy) is uniquely characteristic of attachment relationships (Waters, Wippman, & Sroufe, 1979).

Perhaps more compelling, frequencies of particular behaviors serving the attachment system are not stable over time; yet the quality of the relationship shows both coherence across contexts and impressive temporal stability. When, following the method and procedure of Ainsworth, attachment is defined in terms of the efficiency and effectiveness of the dyadic system in modulating affective arousal and promoting commerce with the environment, variations in attachment relationships show strong stability from 12–18 months (Waters, 1978), despite dramatic changes in infant development (Sroufe & Waters, 1977). Secure infants may need less physical contact when they are 18 months old but the quality of the relationship is still apparent through greeting behaviors, affective sharing of play, and exploration promoted by the caregiver's presense. The attachment relationship, like other relationships, shows stability in the *patterning* of behaviors over time. It "endures over time and space" (Bowlby, 1969), despite changes in its form.

Infant-Caregiver Attachment as a Product of Caregiver Responsiveness

It now has been shown in at least five separate studies, based on five diverse samples, that the quality of infant-caregiver attachment is related to earlier assessments of caregiver responsiveness (Ainsworth et al., 1978; Bates, Maslin, & Frankel, in press; Grossman & Grossman, 1982, Egeland & Farber, 1984, Smith & Pederson, 1983). It is not related to assessments of infant temperament (Farber & Egeland, 1980). Infant behavior (crying, activity, and so forth) in the early weeks fails to show temporal stability and does not predict later attachment, but maternal responsiveness to the infant's signals during this same period strongly predicts it (Blehar, Lieberman, & Ainsworth, 1977). Thus, the quality of the attachment relationship appears to be a product of the relationship history.

It is the case that nonoptimal newborn status (as assessed by the Brazelton exam) adds stress to the interaction, as evidenced among dyads from an urban poor sample, and the frequency of anxious/resistant attachment increases (Ainsworth type C; Waters, Vaughn, & Egeland, 1980). Even these results are best interpreted in terms of the infant-caregiver relationship rather than infant characteristics per se, because similar assessments of newborns in middle-class samples do not predict attachment outcome. In one study, Crockenberg (1981), too, found that some babies were irritable and difficult to console. But, in contrast to the Waters et al. (1980) study, there was no relation between such newborn status and later attachment, presumably because in this low-stress sample the quality of care overrode these early difficulties. This is supported by within-group analyses. When there was newborn irritability in the absence of adequate social support for the mother, anxious attachments were found. But, when there was adequate social support, as was common in this middle-class sample, secure attachments resulted—presumably because care was responsive within such a context.

Attachment as Unique to the Particular Partnership

There is other evidence that attachment, as assessed by the Ainsworth procedure, is an assessment of relationships and not individuals. First, the quality of the attachment may not be the same with different partners. Ainsworth attachment classifications of infant-mother and infant-father attachment may differ; the infant may show a secure attachment relationship with one parent and an anxious attachment with the other (Main & Weston, 1981).[1] Such nonconcordance in strange situation assessments for mother and father cannot derive simply from lack of reliability, since each of these relationships shows stability over time (6 months). Thus, each relationship has its own enduring qualities. Second, the quality of attachment within dyads is subject to change. In one recent study of an urban lower-class sample, substantial changes in life stress were accompanied by major changes in the quality of attachment. Mothers of infants who changed from anxious to secure patterns of attachment reported significantly greater reductions in life stress than mothers of infants changing in the other direction (Vaughn, Egeland, Waters, & Sroufe, 1979). Such changes in maternal life stress presumably alter the nature of the interaction and, over time, the quality of the infant-mother attachment. In support of this, other factors which would be expected to influence caregiver responsiveness have been shown to be related to Ainsworth attachment assessments, including amount of available social support for the mother (discussed earlier) and her own early care (to be discussed below). The fact that only the infant's behavior is examined in Ainsworth's assessment procedure makes these findings especially compelling with regard to the relationship construct. Even though one focuses upon the infant's behavior, factors in the caregiver's life predict the assessment outcome. Clearly, the quality of attachment cannot be reduced to characteristics of the infant.

Attachment Assessments as Predictors of Caregiver Behavior as well as Infant Behavior

If, in assessing infant behavior in the strange situation, one is capturing certain qualities of the relationship between the baby and its caregiver, the assessment should be predictive of later caregiver behavior as well as infant behavior. In fact, this is the case. Ainsworth assessments not only predict later infant behavior in a variety of contexts (see below), they also strongly predict later maternal

---

[1] It is interesting to note that the quality of infant-mother attachment more strongly predicts behavior in a novel setting than does infant-father attachment. However, secure attachment with both mother and father predicts the most positive outcome.

behavior (e.g., Matas, Arend, & Sroufe, 1978). Caregivers of infants with secure attachments are observed later (at 2 years and 3½ years) to be emotionally supportive and appropriate in the timing, pacing, responsiveness, and flexibility of their guidance. From a relationships perspective, these caregivers must have had these capacities earlier (and the freedom and support to exhibit them) or the infant would not have shown the secure pattern of behavior in the first place. Ultimately, infant behavior in contexts in which the caregiver is not present, including social situations with peers, can also be predicted from 12- 18-month-attachment assessments (Sroufe, 1979, 1983). This is not because attachment assessments merely tap temperamental variations among the infants (which clearly they do not), but because, ultimately, the relationship becomes "internalized." In this way, the organization of behavior with respect to the caregiver becomes an initial personality structure.

PROPOSITIONS CONCERNING RELATIONSHIPS

Having reviewed these definitional features of salient relationships, as illustrated by attachment research, we now advance certain propositions about relationships and how they function. We believe these propositions have general applicability:

1. Relationships are wholes, i.e., they are more than simple combinations of individual characteristics.
2. There is a continuity and coherence to close relationships over time.
3. The whole relationship "resides" in each individual.
4. Previous relationship patterns are carried forward to later close relationships.

These propositions are illustrated with further examples derived from the study of early development and from clinically oriented research and clinical practice.

Relationships as Wholes

We suggested earlier that relationships are not properly viewed as additive combinations of partner characteristics. If infant characteristics simply added a constant to relationships, one would expect some correlation between infant–mother and infant-father attachment. If one thinks of infant crankiness as a constant factor, for example, that combines with parent characteristics (some anti-crankiness factor) to produce an anxious/resistant attachment then one would expect some concordance between anxious–resistant attachment with the mother and anxious–resistant attachment with the father. But, as indicated by the Main and Weston data, this apparently is not the case. The infant may be easily settled with one parent and difficult to settle with the other, a qualitative difference.

A study by Pastor (1981) also illustrates the nonadditive nature of relationships. Initial peer encounters were observed between toddlers who were earlier rated as either secure or anxious in their attachments: (a) Securely attached children were sociable and positively oriented toward *both* peer and mother (both mothers were present). Their mothers were supportive and promoted success in peer interaction. (b) The anxious/avoidant children showed a more negative orientation toward peers even though they were active in the play sessions. (c) The anxious/resistant children were very incompetent in the situation, becoming upset, ignoring peer overtures, and being negative toward their mothers.

A somewhat different picture emerges from this investigation when dyadic interaction rather than individual behavior was measured. When both toddlers had histories of secure attachment, their interaction was characterized by reciprocity and smoothness. When secure toddlers were paired with anxious resistant toddlers, there also was little strife. In fact, the secure children tended to be more sociable and to more often redirect activities after object struggles with these toddlers than with securely attached partners (i.e., they were tolerant). When secure toddlers were paired with avoidant toddlers, however, there was a substantial increase in aggressive interaction—to which *both* partners contributed (and more intervention on the part of the secure toddler's mother). The amount of aggression was not uniform with the two types of anxious partners: Secure children were *not* aggressive with anxious resistant children, but with anxious avoidant children the dyad was often characterized by aggression. We believe that it is not simply that children behave differently depending on the relationship histories of their partners, but that relationships with different partners themselves vary in quality.

A study by Olweus (1980) with older children is relevant here. He found that some boys were characteristically aggressive (over a period of years) and that being the target of such aggression was also a stable characteristic. *Both* "bullies" and "whipping boys" had distinctive family histories. The parenting of the bullies was marked by discord and rejection of the child, power assertion, and permissiveness for aggression, and that of the whipping boys by "eschewing of aggression" and anxious overinvolvement by the mother. Thus, bullying seems to be a *relational* pattern and, moreover, a product of two *relational* histories. In support of this, it should be noted that "well-adjusted" boys (nominated by teachers as were the others) were not aggressed against by the bullies, nor were they involved in aggression against the whipping boys. Their parents also eschewed violence, but other aspects of the parenting relationship (e.g., responsive involvement) seem to have supported the emergence of self-assertion as an adaptive pattern.

Continuity and Coherence in Relationships

Changes in the child's behavioral repertoire are both extensive and rapid in the early years, making the coherence of the parent-child relationship over time even more dramatic. Children who were secure in their early attachments, for example, are smoothly cooperative with their mothers in a tool-problem situation at age 2 years. They inform their mothers when the problem is beyond their own resources, they attend to her verbal and postural cues, and they comply with her requests—ultimately solving problems beyond their own capacity. None of these behaviors was in their repertoires when attachment was assessed nor was reciprocal maternal responsiveness examined at that time (Matas, Arend, & Sroufe, 1978). Indications that the quality of the relationship remains coherently manifest among securely attached infants have now been documented in two other samples (Gove, 1983; Londerville & Main, 1981).

Anxious/resistant infants had shown poverty of exploration, low threshold for threat, great difficulty settling and, frequently, contact seeking mixed with explicit anger in the attachment assessment, presumably all based in a history of inconsistent care. At age two, these infants were easily frustrated in the problem situation, and they were whiney and negativistic—even when faced with relatively simple problems (Gove, 1983; Matas et al., 1978). Their mothers reciprocated with inconsistent support, unclear cues, and a *pot pourri* of coercive tactics (threats, bribes, anger, commands). These pairs were seemingly embroiled in a struggle of wills that took precedence over the problem solving, and the interaction deteriorated as task difficulty was increased. The ambivalence of both partners was clear-cut in these observations.

As infants, members of the anxious/avoidant group were characterized by avoidance of the caregiver during reunion, following brief separations. Earlier in the first year, the mothers of these infants were less responsive to the infants' signals and more interfering in their care (as was the case with the mothers of anxious/resistant infants). Although they did not differ in *amount* of holding or interacting with the infant, they were likely to rebuff the infant when he/she sought physical contact (Ainsworth et al., 1978). Presumably, this underlies the infants' later refusal to seek contact following the separation experience in the laboratory. Seemingly, these infants come to expect that, in times of stress, the caregiver will not be emotionally available. And, by age two, these infants sought little assistance from their mothers, even with the most difficult problem. They show little affective investment in the problem solving and little involvement with their mothers (with much ignoring and indirect expression of anger). Their mothers, predictably, showed little emotional involvement with their children and offered minimal assistance and emotional support, even when problem difficulty was increased. These dyads were reminiscent of ''ships passing in the night.''

Relationships Reside Within Individuals

Earlier we argued that even in looking at one partner one can, with appropriate assessment, capture aspects of the relationship. This is because each partner's behavior reflects expectations and feelings built up over time in the course of the relationship. Thus, the mother's support and the quality of her instruction in the tool-problem situation when the child is 2-years-of-age is as strongly predicted by the infant's behavior in the earlier dyadic assessments as is the child's behavior itself at age two (Matas et al., 1978). Similarly, secure attachment, reflecting a history of sensitive, responsive care is predictive of the child's empathy later in the nursery school, based on teacher Q-sort descriptions (Sroufe, 1983). Avoidant attachment tends to be associated with later hostility; resistant attachment with ineptness with peers and chronic emotional dependency upon teachers. *An ambivalent child thus seems to have internalized an ambivalent relationship; an empathic child to have internalized a responsive relationship.*

We believe this two-way transaction between individuals and relationships has more general implications. In this way, for example, abused children learn not only the role of the exploited but the role of the exploiter, in accord with the finding that abusing parents frequently were themselves abused (Egeland & Jacobvitz, 1984; Kempe & Kempe, 1978).[2] Each partner "knows" all "parts" of the relationship and each is motivated to recreate the whole in other circumstances, however different the required roles and behavior might be.

Beginning documentation for this proposition is being obtained in an ongoing study of preschool play pairs, whose development has been studied since the first year of life. In general, these partners form relationships that are consistent with their histories; for example, children with histories of anxious/resistant attachment are socially motivated and oriented, but immature and inept in social interaction; anxious/avoidant pairs are hostile or distant. Most important, five pairs have been identified in which one child victimizes or systematically exploits the other (e.g., by hitting the partner when the partner indicates an area of soreness; by continued sarcasm, derogation, and hostility; by lying on top of the same-sex partner and not letting up). In each case, the "victimizing" child was previously identified as having experienced one or another form of parental abuse and had been classed as anxious/avoidant (Egeland & Sroufe, 1981). Moreover, the "victim" in each case had been anxiously attached. It thus seems that mistreated children carry forward both the capacities for being mistreated and for mistreating others.

Relationship History is Carried Forward

As implied in the preceding section, relationships are not only internalized by the individual, but are carried forward to new relationships. This applies in general and in quite specific terms. In general terms, children who have histories of

---

[2]Being abused, of course, does not automatically lead to being an abusing parent. There are many ways that the relationship history may be expressed, and persons may explicitly develop patterns in reaction to their relationship history.

secure attachment are more socially competent in the preschool, as assessed through sociometrics, direct observation, or teacher reports (LaFreniere & Sroufe, 1984; Sroufe, 1983; Waters, Wippman, & Sroufe, 1979). They have more friends, are more capable of reciprocity, are more socially oriented, more empathic, more frequently imitated, and more popular. They approach and respond to others with more positive affect and less negative affect (Sroufe, Schork, Motti, Lawroski, & LaFreniere, in press).

The nature of subsequent relations is also influenced in more specific ways. *Both* children who were avoidant and those who were resistant as infants turn out to be highly dependent on their preschool teachers, but the manifestation of the dependency—the particular quality of the child–teacher relationship—differs between the two groups (Sroufe, Fox, & Pancake, 1983). The avoidant group, having strong needs for nurturance but having developed doubts about the availability of others and their own worthiness, show their dependency through desperate contact seeking in restricted (safe) circumstances. They are somewhat slower than other children to show their dependency once the school term begins, and often approach teachers in indirect ways. Frequently, they do *not* seek teachers when injured, disappointed, or otherwise stressed. Nevertheless, owing to the intensity of the behavior when it is expressed, they are judged by teachers to be just as dependent as the anxious/resistant children. The resistant children, however, show frequent chronic, low-level dependency, being constantly near or oriented to the teachers; they routinely wait at the edge of the group for the teacher to invite them in. Compared to the securely attached children, children with histories of both kinds of anxious attachment receive more discipline, guidance, and support from teachers, though in different ways.

Just how relationship histories are carried forward is a central question. We would take a lead from modern self-theorists who talk about motivation for maintaining coherence or consistency within the self (Breger, 1974; Cottrell, 1969; Epstein, 1973, 1980; Sullivan, 1953). An important part of this coherence would be continuing or reestablishing relationships that are congruent with one's past relationship experience. In our preschool classroom (Sroufe, 1983), when we observed a teacher get so angry at a child that she wanted to "stuff him across the hall," this was inevitably a child that had experienced chronic maternal rejection. When the teacher was strongly drawn to cuddle, caress, and otherwise be in physical contact with the child, the child had inevitably experienced a history of seductive maternal behavior. We believe that the "rejected" child misbehaves until a punitive reaction occurs in order to reproduce a familiar relationship pattern (what is known and understood). The "seductively treated" child, on the other hand, has been treated as cute, charming, and appealing; he or she knows how to be appealing to other adults—at times at the expense of peer relations. Once our teachers learned not to confirm the child's expectations, these behavior patterns soon changed. This occurrence makes clear that the individual child, himself, cannot recreate the earlier relationship pattern. We return to these issues in our discussions of clinically oriented studies.

CONVERGENT EXAMPLES FROM CLINICAL WORK

The relationship propositions we have outlined are well-illustrated in clinical practice and clinically oriented research. In fact, an assumption underlying most clinical work is that relationship histories are brought forward into future relationships, including the therapy situation itself (called transference by psychoanalysts, triangulation by family systems theorists). Further, most disorders are viewed as springing from disordered relationships, including delinquency and psychopathy, which decades of research suggest are marked by an absence of adequate relationships between children and their parents (Bandura & Walters, 1959; Rutter, 1979).

A clinical case study presented by Cottrell (1969) provides a useful starting point for elaborating our propositions concerning relationships. Cottrell's case, Otto B., was referred by his parents for "incorrigibility" at age 15 (including truancy, theft, and "unmanageability"). Otto's father was a harsh disciplinarian and, partly in response to moving to an unsupportive community, the two had entered into a very negative interactive spiral. The father became increasingly abusive (broomstick beatings, pepper in Otto's eyes), and Otto became increasingly noncompliant. This pattern continued, escalating for a substantial period. Ultimately, Otto was placed with an uncle who treated him with "friendly kidding," and his behavior changed dramatically. In time he finished trade school and seemed oriented toward a stable occupation, though before working for his uncle he had been fired repeatedly for becoming angry with his bosses. Some years later Mrs. Otto B. came to the same clinic with her 2½-year-old-son, complaining in particular about her husband's (Otto's) harsh treatment of the boy (including bruises left from his hitting). This harshness occurred in spite of the fact that Otto treated his wife with fondness (reminiscent of the close relationships that Otto had with his mother and with a younger sister) and his two apprentices at work with "good natured kidding."

Cottrell (1969) extracts certain propositions from this material, quite similar to those we have presented:

First, established relationships, as between Otto and his father, are quite difficult to modify (our continuity principle).

Second, relational patterns (both being defiant son and harsh father) are learned and "reproduced in appropriate context" in the absence of obvious "rewards." That is, relational patterns are learned merely by being in relationships.

Third, a relationship learned in one situation will be evoked in similar situations, and in that new situation, either "action position" may be occupied. Otto defied his bosses and was harsh with his son (our propositions that relationships are carried forward and that the *whole* relationship is learned).

Fourth, self-other patterns are perpetuated because: (a) persons select relationships in which the pattern is readily enacted, and (b) ambiguous situations are "structured to permit the pattern to be expressed."

Fifth, patterns carried forward will evoke responses in others "called for by the pattern" which "support and validate it."

Given that Cottrell's propositions were drawn from clinical case material and ours were drawn independently from research on early social development this is a remarkable congruence. The basic addition that we make is to suggest that it is relational features that are learned rather than two "action positions." This elaboration will become clear in considering systematic research on intergenerational transmission of maladaptation and clinical work with incest families.

Intergenerational Transmission of Relationship Patterns

Similarities in patterns of relationships across generations are of direct relevance to the propositions under discussion (Cohler & Grunebaum, 1981; Hill, 1970). Of particular importance are three retrospective studies of childrearing history and subsequent infant-caregiver attachment (Main, Kaplan, & Cassidy, in press; Morris, 1980; Ricks, in press). Each of these investigators found that mothers' reports of *their* early nurturance (or lack thereof) were strongly associated with secure or anxious patterns of attachment. Main's data are especially clear in demonstrating a relation between early rejection and lack of nurturance, on the one hand, and anxious-avoidant patterns of attachment in the next generation, on the other. The Morris study is described here, however, because it was coordinated with independent assessments of later parenting and child development, including a pattern of seductive maternal behavior directed toward male toddlers. As such, it serves as a bridge to our discussion of the occurrence of incest within families, and also as a means for describing how particular relational qualities may be carried forward.

Like Main and Ricks, Morris found that maternal histories (interviews coded by blind judges) were associated with independent assessments of infant-caregiver attachment. In particular, lack of a stable family relationship structure and the subject's perception of her own mother as not nurturant and not competent in the maternal role predicted anxious patterns of attachment in the offspring. In addition, within the 36 subjects included in this study, 12 were identified as evidencing pronounced "spousification" (either presence of incest or notable emotional exploitation of the daughter by her father). The second generation child outcomes of these cases are of special interest and are discussed below.

Concurrently, a sizable group (N = 18) of "seductive" mother-toddler dyads was identified within the larger sample from which Morris' subjects were drawn. These cases were characterized by the mother's use of sensuality, fondling, affectional bribes, or sensual teasing, both as control techniques and for seeking affection from the child during a toy clean-up task.

> Examples of seductive behavior actually observed included the following: (1) a mother asking her child for a kiss, then grabbing his buttock after he said no and was twisting away, and, finally, calling him to her and kissing him on the lips; (2) a mother whispering sensually, "What did you do?" and rubbing the child's buttock when he was being noncompliant; (3) a mother losing control of her child, then calling to him plaintively and kissing him twice on the lips when he finally came over to her; (4) a mother putting her hand on her child's genital area in the course of physical contact. Not considered seductive was physical contact as a source or comforting, a restraining arm around the shoulder ("physical guidance"), hugging or other affection in response to the child completing the task (unless, of course, it was forced on the child), or other examples of physical contact or affection (e.g., reassuring pats) viewed as responsive to the needs of the child. (Sroufe & Ward, 1980, p. 1224)

Such behavior was addressed almost exclusively to boys, was associated with physical punishment or threats of physical punishment, and the use of many, alternating control techniques (i.e., ambivalence). Seductive maternal behavior had distinctly different correlates from affectionate behavior and, in general, was associated with a *lack* of emotional support in this and other settings (Sroufe & Ward, 1980). The origins and consequences of such maternal behavior are thus of great interest.

Nine of the mothers involved in these seductive relationship patterns were included in the Morris study. Of these nine, eight were in the "spousification" subset, having had family histories in which the mother had been emotionally exploited earlier by her father. Given that only 12 of 36 were "spousification" cases, this is a highly significant result. (It is of interest to note that the one "miss" physically abused her child and that, in the other 3 "spousification" cases, the child was a female.)

The most important implication from this study concerns the nature of the relationship learning involved, which seems to go beyond simple modeling. Not only is it suggested that there is continuity in relationships and that the whole of the relationship is learned but, in addition, it seems to be the relational components per se that are carried forward. These mothers did *not* exhibit the same behaviors their fathers showed to them. They were emotionally exploited by their fathers; they, in turn, emotionally exploited their sons, not in ways identical to the paternal behavior they experienced, but in ways consistent with cultural definitions of the adult female sex-role. These mothers did not necessarily do what their fathers did to them but, rather, recreated the basic relational pattern, however different the expressed behavior might be. It is meanings, not behaviors, that are carried forward from relationships.

As this intergenerational pattern is carried forward, the boys from these relationships still later showed distinctive patterns of behavior in the preschool (Sroufe, 1983). They were coy, passive, and dependent, and/or hyperactive and impulsive, and elicited contact from their female teachers through being "cute" and "cuddly" or through acting out. All were emotionally immature. One can speculate that, later, they may be vulnerable to exploitation in other ways, but they may also exploit those around them, especially the weak and vulnerable. Like their mothers, they have learned that adults may (must?) meet their emotional needs with children, being ill prepared to meet their needs in mutual, symmetrical relationships.

We have now examined how these mothers treat their daughters. We found them often to be rejecting and demeaning (shaming) of their daughters, congruent with the way we suspect they feel about themselves (Sroufe, Jacobvitz, Mangelsdorf, DeAngelo, & Ward, 1985). A case in point is one mother who constantly criticized her daughter, desexualized her appearance, and was heard to reproach her as a toddler, "Don't you be so sexy!" This mother subsequently gave birth to a son, with whom she is explicitly seductive. Still another way in which these mothers are vulnerable is in the selection of partners who would be sexually exploitative of the daughters. We emphasize this latter idea because it illustrates the complex ways in which relationships may be internalized and carried forward.

Lessons From Therapeutic Work With Incest Families

All of the propositions outlined by Cottrell (1969) and by us can be seen quite clearly in clinical work with families in which there is father-daughter incest. Most notably, work with such families suggests strong homeostatic tendencies (continuity) even in the face of active intervention efforts, and illustrates the way in which individuals carry forward internalized relationships.

In treating such families, terminating the incest is more easily accomplished than altering basic relationship patterns. For example: One characteristic of such families is secretiveness, including, of course, the incest secret shared between father and daughter to the exclusion of the others. Girls have great difficulty in talking about the incest in treatment, a testimony to the power of this aspect of the relationship, since disclosure represents betrayal, even in cases where the father is hated. Following "successful" treatment (i.e., the incest is terminated and the family has changed in many ways) the exclusive relationship between daughter and father is often maintained in new ways. In one case from a 3-year follow-up study, the daughter is now pregnant with her fiance's baby. She had shared this fact only with her father who promised to keep the information from mother, although this clearly would be against treatment recommendations.

Clinical experience suggests that, not only were fathers in incest families frequently exploited as children, mothers were as well. Not only have the mothers selected partners congruent with their family histories, they tend to have "special" relationships with a son, serving to balance the father-daughter incest. Further, in treating these families, ongoing issues with sexually abused girls are their fears of men and their deep beliefs that men only want sexual contact from them. Often accompanying this, however, is seductive behavior directed at the men they are in contact with, including the men they most fear—i.e., those who remind them of their fathers. A common clinical observation, meriting systematic research, is that former incest victims become rape victims with very high frequency. They also are highly represented among teenage prostitutes. All of these observations suggest that relationship histories are carried forward to new situations.

CONCLUSION

It is now clear that relationships can be described in qualitative terms and that when so described they have coherence and stability, even in the face of change. Patterns of relationships, once established, seem especially difficult to change, undoubtedly owing to the systemic nature of relationships. Changes in one partner elicit "corrective" reactions in the other which, in turn, press that partner back toward the familiar pattern. One member may change and yet, if the partner changes in a complementary manner, the relationship may remain the same even though the behavior of each has changed. As complexly integrated systems, relationships would seem more difficult to change than individuals, even given the intractability of certain habitual behaviors.

Relationships seem to exert powerful influences over the individuals participating in them, and also to shape future relationships. We suggest four ways in which such an impact occurs: First, early relationships have a profound impact upon personality formation. The infant-caregiver attachment relationship is the womb from which the incipient person emerges. The first organization is dyadic, and it is from that organization, and not from inborn characteristics of the infant, that personality emerges. Whatever raw material the newborn brings to the interaction cannot be sorted out like particles of colored sand; rather, the material is transformed and encompassed within the relationship, like sand in glass. Having experienced the relationship, it is not even clear that the infant retains its original temperament, even apart from the caregiver. A person has been created within a relationship (or primary relationship network). It is this person, with characteristic ways of coping with arousal, preferred modes of dealing with impulses and feelings, and a particular organization of needs, attitudes, and beliefs about self and environment, who constructs future relationships with others.

Second, early relationships forge one's expectations concerning relationships. Expectations are the carriers of relationships. Carrying forward all of the specific behaviors and response chains from previous interactions would be an overwhelming task, but a limited set of expectations can generate countless behavioral reactions, flexibly employed in a variety of situations. One's orientation concerning others, one's expectations concerning their availability and likely responses, and what, in general terms, one can do (or cannot do) to increase the likelihood of familiar responses are strongly shaped by early relationships. Cottrell (1969) has argued that earlier patterns are especially persistent because they lead to "selectivity and structuring of interactional situations" such that early patterns are confirmed. Early patterns are therefore "likely to appear more general in the sense of being operative in a wider range of situations than are later ones which are more likely to be situation specific" (p. 565). It is because persons select and create later social environments that early relationships are viewed as having special importance (Sroufe, 1979).

Third, and related to one and two, early relationships shape what one knows how to do, what one understands. That is, one learns how to be in relationships by being in relationships. This would apply on the behavioral level as well as the more global attitudinal level. If the child has known (and therefore expects) hostile, punitive relationships with adults, positive reactions to his behavior are less likely to be perceived (or perceived as valid). Rather, they may be perceived as ambiguous and calling for clarification. The circuit remains open. When, on the other hand, acting out behavior is met with punitiveness the relationships pattern is validated. The circuit is closed; familiarity is achieved once again. It feels "right," however painful. With development and with different persons, such acting out or other behavior could take countless forms. Important research questions concern the process whereby attitudes and expectations are translated into particular behaviors; that is, what governs the forms and ways in which relational learning is manifest with different people.

Research on the infant-caregiver attachment relationship has been drawn upon to illustrate each of these points. Attachment relationships, when assessed in terms of quality and patterning have been shown to be stable and coherent, even across periods of rapid development. Moreover, the quality of these relationships has been shown to be related to caregiver relationship history and current social support. Finally, individual variations in such relationships have been shown to forecast both individual differences in behavioral organization (personality) and qualities of later relationships. Children with histories including a responsive caretaking relationship later are more socially oriented, empathic, and socially competent, as well as being more self-confident and self-reliant. Children with histories of anxious attachment have distinct self-environment organizations, dependent relationships with teachers, and ineffective relationships with peers. To some extent, peer partnerships seem selective. Much research remains to be done on how children select peer partners and how two children with distinct relationship histories construct a relationship together. Of special interest are the circumstances and processes through which future relationships fundamentally alter previously established patterns.

ACKNOWLEDGMENT

This paper was supported in part by a program project grant from the National Institute of Child Health and Human Development (5 POI HD 05027).

REFERENCES

Ainsworth, M., & Bell, S. (1974). Mother-infant interaction and the development of competence. In K. Connolly & J. Bruner (Eds.), *The growth of competence.* New York: Academic Press.

Ainsworth, M., Blehar, M., Waters, E., & Wall, S. (1978). *Patterns of attachment.* Hillsdale, NJ: Lawrence Erlbaum Associates.

Bandura, A., & Walters, R. H. (1959). *Adolescent aggression.* New York: Ronald Press.

Bates, J., Maslin, C., & Frankel, K. (in press). Attachment security, mother-child interaction, and temperament as predictors of behavior problem ratings at age three years. In I. Bretherton & E. Waters (Eds.), *New Directions in attachment research. Monographs of the Society for Research in Child Development.*

Blehar, M. C., Lieberman, A. F., & Ainsworth, M. D. S. (1977). Early face-to-face interaction and its relation to later infant-mother attachment. *Child Development, 48,* 182–194.

Block, J. H., & Block, J. (1979). The role of ego-control and ego-resilience in the organization of behavior. In W. A. Collins (Ed.), *Minnesota Symposia on child psychology* (Vol. 13). Hillsdale, NJ: Lawrence Erlbaum Associates.

Bowlby, J. (1969). *Attachment and loss* (Vol. 1). *Attachment.* New York: Basic Books.

Breger, L. (1974). *From instinct to identity.* Englewood Cliffs, NJ: Prentice-Hall.

Carr, S., Dabbs, J., & Carr, T. (1975). Mother-infant attachment: The importance of the mother's visual field. *Child Development, 46,* 331–338.

Cohen, S. E., & Beckwith, L. (1979). Preterm infant interaction with the caregiver in the first year of life and competence at age two. *Child Development, 50,* 767–776.

Cohler, B., & Grunebaum, H. (1981). *Mothers, grandmothers, and daughters.* New York: Wiley.

Cottrell, L. (1969). Interpersonal interaction and the development of the self. In D. A. Goslin (Ed.), *Handbook of socialization theory and research.* Chicago: Rand McNally.

Crockenberg, S. (1981). Infant-irritability, mother responsiveness and social support influences on the security of infant-mother attachment. *Child Development, 52,* 857–865.

Egeland, B., & Farber, E. (1984). Infant-mother attachment: Factors related to its development and changes over time. *Child Development. 55,* 753–771.

Egeland, B., & Jacobvitz, D. (1984, May). *Intergenerational continuity of abuse: causes and consequences.* Paper presented at the Social Science Research Council Conference on Biosocial Perspectives in Abuse and Neglect.

Egeland, B., & Sroufe, L. A. (1981). Developmental sequelae of maltreatment in infancy. In R. Rizley & D. Cicchetti (Eds.), *Developmental perspectives in child maltreatment.* San Francisco: Josey-Bass.

Epstein, S. (1973). The self concept revisited. *American Psychologist, 28,* 404–416.

Epstein, S. (1980). Self concept: A review and the proposal of an integrated theory of personality. In E. Staub (Ed.), *Personality: Basic issues and current research*. Englewood Cliffs, NJ: Prentice Hall.

Farber, E., & Egeland, B. (1980). *Maternal, neonatal, and mother-infant antecedents of attachment in urban poor*. Paper presented at American Psychological Association, Montreal.

Gove, F. (1983). *Patterns and organizations of behavior and affective expression during the second year of life*. Unpublished doctoral dissertation, University of Minnesota.

Grossman, K., & Grossmann, K. E. (1982). *Maternal sensitivity to infants' signals during the first year as related to the year olds' behavior in Ainsworth's Strange Situation in a sample of Northern German Families*. Paper presented at the International Conference on Infant Studies, Austin, Texas.

Hill, R. (1970). *Family development in three generations*. Cambridge, MA: Schenkman Publishing Co.

Hinde, R. A. (1979). *Towards understanding relationships*. New York: Academic Press.

Kempe, R., & Kempe, C. H. (1978). *Child abuse*. Cambridge, MA: Harvard University Press.

LaFreniere, P., & Sroufe, L. A. (1984). Profiles of peer competence in the preschool: Interrelations between measures, influence of social ecology, and relation to attachment history. *Child Development, 21*, 56–68.

Loevinger, J. (1976). *Ego development*. New York: Josey Bass.

Londerville, S., & Main, M. (1981). Security of attachment, compliance, and maternal training methods in the second year of life. *Developmental Psychology, 17*, 289–299.

Main, M., Kaplan, N., & Cassidy, J. (in press). Security in infancy, childhood, and adulthood: A move to the level of representation. In I. Bretherton & E. Waters (Eds.), *New directions in attachment research. Monographs of the Society for Research in Child Development*.

Main, M., & Weston, D. (1981). The quality of the toddler's relationships to mother and to father: Related to conflict behavior and readiness to establish new relationships. *Child Development, 52*, 932–940.

Matas, L., Arend, R., & Sroufe, L. A. (1978). Continuity of adaptation in the second year: the relationship between quality of attachment and later competence. *Child Development, 49*, 547–556.

Mead, G. H. (1934). *Mind, self and society*. Chicago: University of Chicago Press.

Morris, D. (1980). *Infant attachment and problem solving in the toddler: relations to mother's family history*. Unpublished doctoral dissertation, University of Minnesota.

Olweus, D. (1980). Bullying among school boys. In R. Barnen (Ed.), *Children and violence*. Stockholm: Akademic Litteratur.

Pastor, D. (1981). The quality of mother-infant attachment and its relationship to toddlers' initial sociability with peers. *Developmental Psychology, 17*, 326–335.

Ricks, M. (in press). The social inheritance of parenting: Attachment across generations. In I. Bretherton & E. Waters (Eds.), *New directions in attachment research, monograph of the society for research in child development*.

Rutter, M. (1979). Maternal deprivation 1972–1978: New findings, new concepts, new approaches. *Child Development, 50*, 283–305.

Salapatek, P., & Banks, M. (1967). Infant sensory assessment: Vision. In F. Minifie & L. Lloyd (Eds.), *Communicative and cognitive abilities—Early behavioral assessment*. Baltimore: University Park Press.

Sameroff, A., & Chandler, M. (1975). Reproductive risk and the continuum of caretaking casualty. In F. D. Horowitz (Ed.), *Review of child development research* (Vol. 4). Chicago: University of Chicago Press.

Sander, L. (1975). Infant and caretaking environment. In E. J. Anthony (Ed.), *Explorations in child psychiatry*. New York: Plenum.

Santostefano, S., & Baker, A. (1972). The contribution of developmental psychology. In B. Wolman (Ed.), *Manual of child psychopathology*. New York: McGraw Hill.

Smith, P., & Pederson, D. (1983). *Maternal sensitivity and patterns of infant-mother attachment*. Paper presented at the biennial meeting of the Society for Research in Child Development, Detroit.

Sorce, J., & Emde, R. (1981). Mother's presence is not enough: The effect of emotional availability on infant exploration and play. *Developmental Psychology, 17,* 737–745.

Sroufe, L. A. (1979). The coherence of individual development. *American Psychologist, 34,* 834–841.

Sroufe, L. A. (1983). Infant-caregiver attachment and patterns of adaptation in preschool: The roots of maladaptation and competence. In M. Perlmutter (Ed.), *Minnesota symposia on child psychology* (Vol. 16). Hillsdale, NJ: Lawrence Erlbaum Associates.

Sroufe, L. A., Fox, N., & Pancake, V. (1983). Attachment and dependency in developmental perspective. *Child Development. 54,* 1335–1354.

Sroufe, L. A., Jacobvitz, D., Mangelsdorf, S., DeAngelo, E., & Ward, M. (1985). Generational boundary dissolution between mothers and their preschool children: A relationship systems approach. *Child Development, 56,* 317–325.

Sroufe, L. A., Schork, E., Motti, F., Lawroski, N., & LaFreniere, P. (1984). The role of affect in social competence. In C. Izard, J. Kagan, & R. Zajonc. *Affect, cognition and behavior*. New York: Plenum.

Sroufe, L. A., & Waters, E. (1977). Attachment as an organizational construct. *Child Development, 48,* 1184–1199.

Sroufe, L. A., & Ward, M. (1980). Seductive behavior of mothers of toddlers: Occurrence, correlates and family origins. *Child Development, 51,* 1222–1229.

Sullivan, H. S. (1953). *The interpersonal theory of psychiatry*. New York: Norton.

Tracy, R. L., Lamb, M. E., & Ainsworth, M. D. (1976). Infant approach beahvior as related to attachment. *Child Development, 47,* 571–578.

Vaughn, B., Egeland, B., Waters, E., & Sroufe, L. A. (1979). Individual differences in infant-mother attachment at 12 and 18 months: Stability and change in families under stress. *Child Development, 50,* 971–975.

Waters, E. (1978). The stability of individual differences in infant-mother attachment. *Child Development, 49,* 483–494.

Waters, E., Vaughn, B., & Egeland, B. (1980). Individual differences in infant-mother attachment relationships at age one: Antecedents in neonatal behavior in an urban, economically disadvantaged sample. *Child Development, 51,* 203–216.

Waters, E., Wippman, J., & Sroufe, L. A. (1979). Attachment, positive affect, and competence in the peer group: Two studies in construct validation. *Child Development, 50,* 821–829.

4

Maternal Rejection: Determinant or Product for Deviant Child Behavior?

Gerald R. Patterson
Oregon Social Learning Center

It is the case that cold, rejecting parents have often been found along with the occurrence of delinquent behavior in their children (Eron, 1982; Fagan, Langner, Gersten, & Eisenberg, 1977; Glueck & Glueck, 1972; McCord, 1979). One of the hypotheses examined in this report is that parental rejection covaries with a wide spectrum of problem behaviors in children. As a general case, it is assumed that parent rejection covaries with deviant child behaviors of all kinds; the more extreme the deviancy, the greater the likelihood of the rejection. The primary hypothesis examined here is that parental rejection is a product, not a determinant, for deviant child behavior. In effect, it is assumed that parental rejection accompanies, or is produced by the deviant behavior or some aspects of the process that produced that deviant behavior, or both.

The relation between child deviancy and parental rejection is explored using correlational data from a sample of normal children and their families. Several aspects of the deviant behavior are examined to determine which variables account for the variance in maternal rejection (e.g., is it the daily discipline confrontations that accrue when living with the problem child, the daily rates of deviant behavior, or the information received from outside the family about failing school grades and teacher perceptions of deviancy that contribute to rejection?). It is not possible, of course, to use correlational evidence to explore causal relations, but the function of the present report is to make the argument that it is as reasonable to view maternal rejection as a product as it is to view it in its traditional role as a determinant of deviant child behavior.

It is assumed that relationships remain in flux. We can accept as perfectly reasonable the idea that the relation between two adults may change over time (e.g., it does not violate the conventional wisdom to say that adults often fall in

73

and out of love). In a similar vein, current attachment theories stress the impact of the mother's behavior on the alteration of the relationship between the child and the mother. The point of view taken here is that there are certain things children do that alter the esteem and affection in which they are held by their parents. A child who is obdurately abrasive in his or her exchanges with peers is very likely to be rejected by them, as shown in the studies reviewed by Hartup (1978, 1982). Similarly, we believe that the child who reacts abrasively to his or her parents will, over a period of time, also come to be rejected. It is hypothesized that both the abrasive daily exchanges and the pain that accrues from hearing negative reports about the child combine to determine the extent and duration of the rejection.

The second major hypothesis explored in this report is that it is disruptions in family management practices that serve as a primary determinant for deviant child behavior. As a general case, it is probably true that some interaction between parent skills and child temperament will account for most of the variance in measures of child deviant behavior. Measures of four parenting skills were used in this study to account for variance in several criterion measures of deviant child behavior. One implication of this hypothesis is that lack of parenting skill is indirectly responsible for some aspects of parental rejection.

As a methodological issue, it should be noted that the prior efforts to correlate parent and child behavior have seldom produced correlations above the .2 to .3 range, and many of these proved to be nonreplicable. However, most of the earlier attempts relied upon a single assessment procedure, such as an interview, a questionnaire, or a brief laboratory procedure. The recent emphasis within sociology (Bentler, 1980; Sullivan, 1974) on multiple indicators to define complex constructs should have a salutary effect when applied to measures of child rearing or deviant child behavior. The present report makes a consistent effort to employ multiple indicators for each of the main constructs, such as parent rejection, deviant child behavior, and parent skills. The expectation is that, in so doing, it should increase the likelihood of higher magnitude covariations, say in .4 to .5 range, and also increase the likelihood of the results being replicable.

FORMULATION

Speculations by Hartup (1982) and Youniss (1980) depict a mature adolescent as representing the outcome of two different relational experiences. On the one hand, the child learns constraint by interacting with his or her parents in hundreds of asymmetric exchanges, where the adult is in a dominant role and the child in a subordinate one. In exchange for learning constraint and social survival skills, the child receives approval from the adults. The adult teaches; the child learns. On the other hand, exchanges with peers tend to be more symmetric, and it is here that the child learns to cooperate. In these ways, both constraint and cooperation skills are acquired as the child matures. But what is the implication of the child's failure to develop an adequate relationship with the caretaker, and how does this breakdown come about? Is the breakdown in the child's ability to relate to the parents correlated with the breakdown in his ability to relate to peers? The analyses of families of antisocial children by Patterson (1982) suggested that the irritable parent-child exchanges probably generalize to the child's relations to peers. The failure of the parents to control coercive exchanges with the mother and the siblings leads to very high levels of coercive behavior in the home. The child introduces this same style of social interaction in the school setting, and is promptly rejected by peers because of the high rate of aversive behavior. The studies of peer rejection reviewed by Hartup (1982) are consistent with this idea. There is also some empirical support for the idea. The findings reported by Liberman (cited in Hartup 1978) showed that children observed in the home to have a good relationship with the mother were observed in the classroom to be more skilled in interacting with peers. In the present report, measures of peer rejection and parental rejection are used to test the hypothesis.

It is assumed that the antisocial child who fails in relationships with both peers and parents will be at serious risk for later adult adjustment problems. This is based on the follow-up studies by McCord (1978) and Robins (1966), which provided indirect support for the hypothesis. They found a significant correlation between early antisocial patterns and an increased risk of crime, marginal employment, unstable marriage, alcoholism, and mental illness as an adult. Although not specifically tested in those studies, the assumption would be that rejection by both parents and peers implies marked deficits for social survival skills. These deficits, in conjunction with high levels of antisocial behavior, are thought to place the child doubly at risk for adjustment problems as an adult.

Maternal affection and warmth is undoubtedly determined by a number of factors, but the present report is focused only on the reverse of this: What determines maternal nonacceptance or rejection of the child? There are, presumably, very different causal variables involved, depending on which question is being asked. The hypothesis to be examined here is that child deviant behavior is a prime determinant for maternal lack of acceptance. Mothers are the primary focus here because, due to the high prevalence of father-absent homes in the sample (28%), we have a higher incidence of mothers.

The second hypothesis is that the deviant child behavior may itself be due to a lack of parent skill in child-rearing or family-management practices. In effect, ineffective parental socialization of the child leads to his or her eventually being identified by family members, teachers, and peers as being a deviant child.

The general outline is summarized in Fig. 4.1. As shown there, the first step in the process is defined by a disruption in one or more of the family-management practices: monitoring, discipline, problem-solving, or parent positive reinforcement. The definitions for the family-management constructs are present in greater detail in Patterson, Dishion, & Bank (1984).

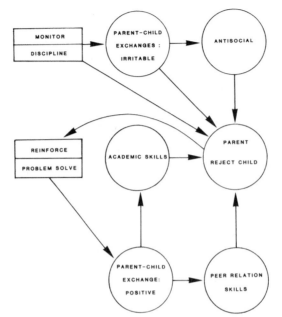

FIG. 4.1.   Family management, deviant behavior, and parental rejection.

There are two sets of parent skills thought to directly determine prosocial behaviors, and two sets of parent skills thought to directly determine antisocial behavior. In this context, the term *determine* implies that, if the parents were trained to increase their use of these skills, this would be accompanied by significant changes in relevant child behaviors. The hypothesis to be examined here is a weaker statement of this relation; the measures of parent reinforcement and parent problem solving skill should covary significantly with measures of child academic and peer relational skills. It is also assumed that disruptions in parental monitoring and in discipline would produce significant increases in a wide spectrum of antisocial child behaviors. Data are presented that examine the correlations among these measures.

It should be noted that there seem to be several reasons for a disruption in family-management practices (Patterson, 1982). Some parents are lacking in effective role models and simply do not know how to raise a child or manage a family; good child-rearing practices are not a given. Other parents may raise several children and demonstrate competence in these skills, but the partnership may then be disrupted by divorce (Hetherington, Cox, & Cox, 1978, 1979) or by prolonged marital discord (Rutter, 1976). Another major source of disruption for many families is thought to be the accumulation of familiar crises that impinge from outside (e.g., chronic illness, unemployment, difficulties at work). Stress variables have been shown to correlate with disrupted patterns of parent-child interaction (Patterson, 1982, 1983a; Wahler & Dumas, 1983).

The implicit assumption that underlies this formulation is that the disruptions in family process are thought to selectively involve the target child to a greater extent than other children in the family (Patterson, Dishion, & Bank, 1984). Home observation data showed that the target child interacts at a level significantly more coercive than siblings, and, while the siblings are highly coercive with the target child and all other siblings in the family, the problem child is highly coercive with the siblings and with the mother. The mother, in turn, is selectively more coercive with the identified problem child than with the other children. In fact, her coercive exchanges with the siblings are within the normal range. The fascinating question raised by these findings concerns the means by which two members of the family—the mother and the identified problem child—become the focus of this process. The current analyses, however, only indirectly address this important question.

As parents, most of us have the impression that the socialization of the child rests on the solid bedrock of a good relationship with that child. According to the present forumulation, however, a good relationship, as well as a bad one, is the outcome of a process centering on the interaction between familial crises and the quality of parenting skills practiced by the caretaker. Hence, prerequisites for a good parent-child relationship include having an adequate means for resolving crises, and effective parent skills for teaching the child both prosocial behaviors and the control of coercive ones. Given success in these endeavors, parents are likely to perceive their children as good or normal, and to judge the relationship between themselves and their children as a good one. The most interesting implication of the model presented in Fig. 4.1 is that each parent-child relationship is, in some sense, vulnerable. The remainder of the discussion delineates the nature of this vulnerability as viewed from an interactionalist perspective.

In the next section, the disruptions in family-management practices thought to produce antisocial behavior in children are briefly outlined. The subsequent section examines the relation between the measures of rejection of the one hand, and the variables thought to determine this reaction on the other.

DISRUPTIONS IN FAMILY MANAGEMENT AND CHILD BEHAVIOR

One hypothesis presented earlier was that the first step in the process leading to maternal rejection of the child may be found in a breakdown in child-rearing practices. This breakdown, in turn, was thought to produce a child who is antisocial or lacking in certain crucial social survival skills. These difficulties lead to a gradual perception of the child as being different, or deviant, and to a disruption in the mother-child relationship. To make a case for this formulation, it is necessary to first demonstrate some empirical links between family-management practices and child behavior.

As outlined in Patterson (1982), the antisocial problem child not only fights or steals, or both, but is also relatively lacking in social relations and academic skills. Both of these deviations from normal development presumably contribute to maternal rejection. The distinction between determinants for antisocial behavior and for social survival skills (peer relations and academic skills) is also emphasized in the selective disruption hypothesis. The development of social survival skills is thought to be determined by one set of parent skills, while the development of antisocial behaviors is determined by a disruption in another set. Specifically, the hypothesis to be tested here is that parent failures as measured by the problem solving and positive reinforcement constructs will correlate significantly with criterion measures of academic success and with measures of social competence. The second hypothesis is that parent failures to monitor and discipline will be correlated significantly with a wide range of measures of antisocial behaviors and other types of problem behaviors as well.

To test these hypotheses, multilevel assessment data were collected from families of 188 boys from the fourth, seventh, and tenth grades. Reports relating to child rearing, child behavior, and family background variables were obtained from parents and children. The family members each participated in interviews, responded to questionnaires, daily telephone interviews, and worked as a family in a laboratory analogue situation (Patterson, Dishion, & Bank, 1984). In addition to observations in the home, teachers and peers provided additional ratings, giving a broad base from which multiple indicators could be selected for each of the key constructs.

The family-management variables used in the study emerged as the result of a decade of clinical work and field studies of families of several hundred extremely antisocial children. The parent was the agent of change for altering the behavior of the problem child (Patterson & Forgatch, 1975; Patterson, Reid, Jones, & Conger, 1975). Clinical experience showed that families in each of the treated samples were characterized by disruptions in one or more of the parents' family-management skills. The treatment outcome data showed significant and long-term reductions in the problem child's antisocial behavior (Patterson & Fleischman, 1979). A series of comparison studies showed that the treatment effects were significantly greater than changes obtained for waiting-list control groups, placebo groups, or traditional treatment groups (Patterson, Chamberlain, & Reid, 1982; Walter & Gilmore, 1973; Wiltz & Patterson, 1974). However, it has not yet been established that these changes were brought about specifically by the parents' increased effectiveness in the use of family-management skills.

While the family-management variables are grounded in clinical experience, many of the variables have been noted in previous studies of antisocial children.

The inadequate presence of the monitoring variable was previously identified in longitudinal studies as characterizing families of delinquent youths. The parents of these children had limited awareness of where their children were, whom they were with, and what they were doing (Hirschi, 1969; McCord, 1979; West & Farrington, 1977; Wilson, 1980). The relationship between the discipline variable and antisocial child behavior has also been found in a number of studies (Glueck & Glueck, 1950; McCord, McCord, & Zola, 1959; Sears, Maccoby, & Levin, 1957; West & Farrington, 1973). The problem-solving variable does not have a long research history, although its importance is felt when treating these families. Disrupted problem-solving skills have been shown to significantly differentiate distressed and nondistressed married couples (Patterson, Hops, & Weiss, 1975). This literature is reviewed by Forgatch (1984). The fourth variable, positive reinforcement, emphasizes the contingent reinforcement by parents for prosocial behaviors of the child. While emphasized as a necessary component in the general social learning literature on socialization of the child (Bijou & Baer 1961), there are no studies that demonstrate a correlation between measures of parent reinforcement in the home and such measures of child competence as achievement test scores or school grades.

To test the first part of the selective parenting hypothesis, two criterion measures of antisocial behavior were constructed (see Table 4.1). The measure *fighting* is a composite score based on the sum of the standardized scores from ratings by the mother, teacher, and peers. The measure *stealing* is a composite based on the sum of the ratings by peers, the mother, and the child's self-report. The correlations were calculated separately for each of the three grades; the figures in parentheses described the size of the samples. In each case, the composite scores were keyed so that a high score indicated a disruption in the measure of parent skill.

The data showed that disrupted monitoring and discipline correlated significantly with the criterion measure of fighting at every grade level; the range of the correlations was from .28 to .51. It should be noted that the data indicated increases in stealing as a function of age of the child. The correlations of parent skills with the stealing criterion were in keeping with this trend. Monitor and discipline measures were significantly correlated with the criterion measure only for the adolescent samples, and here the range was from .30 to .62 Thus far, the findings are consistent with the selective parenting hypothesis. However, the hypothesis would also require that the positive reinforcement and problem-solving scores show only low positive or nonsignificant correlations with the antisocial criteria. The small sample size makes it impossible to carry out a proper multivariate comparison. However, a visual inspection of the findings for the positive reinforcement as compared to those for monitor and discipline suggest that the magnitude of the correlations are roughly comparable. The corresponding findings for the problem-solving variable are consistent with the differential status hypothesis.

TABLE 4.1
Correlation between Family Management
and Child Antisocial Variables

Family Management Variable	Fighting across settings				Multirespondent measure of stealing			
	grades				grades			
	4th	7th	10th	Total	4th	7th	10th	Total
Monitoring[b]	.28*	.44**	.51**	.37***	.08	.52***	.43**	.34***
N	(53)	(53)	(41)	(137)	(57)	(55)	(37)	(149)
Discipline[c]	.45**	.35**	.28[a]	.35***	.24	.62***	.30[a]	.38***
N	(25)	(27)	(21)	(73)	(24)	(28)	(26)	(78)
Pos. Reinforcement[d]	.39*	.45**	.32[a]	.40***	.19	.51**	.12	.29***
N	(21)	(26)	(21)	(68)	(21)	(27)	(26)	(74)
Problem Solving[e]	.38**	.27*	.06	.27***	.15	.09	−.04	.06
N	(54)	(65)	(36)	(155)	(58)	(67)	(44)	(169)

[a]$p < .10$, *$p < .05$, **$p < .01$, ***$p < .001$.

[b]A composite score based upon four variates: interviewer rating, mother rating, child rating, a difference score between mother and child daily telephone report from Patterson & Stouthamer-Loeber (1984).

[c]A composite score based upon three ratings by observers as to consistency and effectiveness of parent-child discipline confrontations in the home (Patterson & Stouthamer-Loeber, 1984).

[d]A composite score based upon the sum of three variates: (1) the sum of observation-based measures of mother distance, likelihood of approval for target child, mother positive affect in interaction with child, (2) child reports of positive reinforcement for prosocial behavior; and (3) observers' *global ratings* after each session on ''parents and child talk about fun things,'' ''parents teach child,'' ''talk together,'' ''talk to child about his day,'' ''parent promote child's interests.''

[e]A composite of five global ratings by the coders after viewing family problem-solving session (Forgatch, 1984): clarity of problem definition, staying on track, chaotic discussion, extent of resolution, quality of resolution.

Some additional weight is given to the selective disruption hypothesis by the analyses of police contacts for the adolescent sample (Patterson & Stouthamer-Loeber, 1984). The correlation with frequency of police contacts was .54 ($p < .001$) for monitor and .22 ($p < .05$) for discipline. In keeping with the hypothesis, the correlations for the remaining family-management variables were nonsignificant.

The second aspect of the selective disruption hypothesis would require that the positive reinforcement and problem-solving constructs correlate significantly with measures of the child's level of social survival skills. The reading score of the Wide Range Achievement Test (WRAT) was used as a preliminary test of academic skill and the mother's ratings on the social competence subscale of the Child Behavior Checklist (CBC) (Achenbach & Edelbrock, 1981) as a measure of social skill. As shown in Table 4.2, the data only moderately support the covariation of parent skills and social survival skills; most of the support is found in the older samples. It cannot be said that the contribution of positive reinforce-

TABLE 4.2
Correlations of Family Management with Academic and Social Skills

Family Management Variable	Reading achievement (WRAT)				Mother rating of social competence (CBC)			
	grades				grades			
	4th	7th	10th	Total	4th	7th	10th	Total
Monitoring	.04	−.06	−.11	−.04	.15	−.15	−.34**	−.12[a]
(N)	(57)	(58)	(45)	(160)	(56)	(57)	(43)	(156)
Discipline	.27	.35[a]	−.34[a]	−.16	.18	−.48*	−.65**	−.37**
(N)	(16)	(19)	(17)	(52)	(15)	(19)	(16)	(50)
Pos. Reinforce.	−.13	−.29[a]	−.33*	−.27**	−.13	−.54**	−.45**	−.15*
(N)	(21)	(28)	(31)	(80)	(20)	(27)	(30)	(77)
Problem Solving	.06	−.29**	−.47***	−.27***	−.08	−.10	−.28*	−.15*
(N)	(59)	(72)	(52)	(183)	(58)	(69)	(50)	(177)

[a]$p < .10$, *$p < .05$, **$p < .01$, ***$p < .001$.

ment and problem-solving variables is appreciably better than that provided by the monitor and discipline variables. The most reasonable conclusion is that the measurement of the positive reinforcement constructs and the problem-solving constructs leaves much to be desired.

It seems reasonable to conclude that a relationship exists between parent family-management skills and child antisocial behavior, and to a lesser extent, child prosocial behavior. Obviously, further work is required, including the construction of more powerful measures of these constructs, replication, larger samples, and a systematic multivariate analyses of these relations. While the appropriate studies are currently under way, the present findings are sufficient to make a case for parental child-rearing skills as a prime determinant for at least this one form of deviant child behavior.

SOME POSSIBLE DETERMINANTS FOR REJECTION

The first hypothesis examined in this section is that antisocial behavior may place the child at increasing risk for being rejected by the parents, particularly by the mother. To test this hypothesis, a measure of maternal acceptance/rejection is correlated with several different measures of antisocial child behavior. Then, to determine the degree to which the connection can be generalized, the rejection scores are correlated with a wide spectrum of child deviant behavior patterns.

What are the particular features of living with a problem child that might lead to maternal rejection? Is it the round of daily hassles that accrue from the mother's attempts to live with such a child or the clear signals from the community and family that she has failed in her responsibilities as a parent? The two possibilities are examined in separate multiple regression analyses. To examine the daily hassles hypothesis, measures were obtained of the frequency of the daily discipline confrontations with the target child plus the accompanying high rates of target child and sibling irritable exchanges. The three variables, discipline, likelihood of target child-sibling irritable exchange, and likelihood of target child-mother irritable exchange, are used in a stepwise multiple regression analysis to determine variance accounted for in a measure of maternal acceptance/rejection.

The alternative to the daily hassles hypothesis is that it is a parent's sense of failure as a parent that leads to rejection. Information from neighbors, friends, relatives and the school may lead to the reluctant conclusion that "my child is aggressive." By implication, the message received by the parent may be, "I am a failure." The parent may also learn that the child does not get along well with other children, and that he or she is failing in school. This kind of information is a clear indictment for some parents that they have failed in the crucial responsibilities assigned to them by the culture (Hartup, 1982; Youniss, 1980). It is expected, then, that measures of school failure and measures of perceptions of others that the child is aggressive will account for significant variance in a measure of parental rejection.

First, a composite score was developed that would assess maternal rejection. Based on separate interviews with parents and child, five variates were selected a priori as measures of maternal acceptance/rejection. Two involved ratings by the child, two by the interviewers, and one by the mother. The actual score was a composite based on the sum of the standardized scores from: (1) the child's report of father's/mother's positive/negative labeling of the characteristics of the child, (2) child's rating on how well he gets along with father/mother, (3) interviewer rating—father/mother seems to enjoy being a parent, (4) interviewer rating—father/mother seems to be accepting of target child, and (5) father/mother rating on how well s/he gets along with target child. The details of the scales and their intercorrelations are presented in Patterson, Dishion, & Bank (1984).

DEVIANT CHILD BEHAVIOR AND MATERNAL REJECTION

It is hypothesized that the maternal acceptance/rejection score will correlate significantly with both of the measures of antisocial behavior introduced earlier. The findings support the hypothesis. The correlation between the measures of child fighting and the rejection score was .46 ($p < .001$) for child steal .52 ($p < .001$). It will be recalled, however, that the two criterion measures of antisocial behavior were defined, in part, by reports from mothers as well as from teachers and peers. The overlap in assessment mode for the dependent and independent variables probably contributes somewhat to the magnitude of the correlation. For this reason, the child's self-reported delinquent behavior was examined as a third criterion measure. This measure, developed by Ageton and Elliott (1982), defines a delinquent lifestyle based on reports of persistence plus seriousness of self-reported offenses. The correlation of this score with the measure of maternal rejection was .29 ($p < .001$). The pattern of findings are consistent with the hypothesis that maternal rejection covaries with measures of antisocial child behavior.

It should be noted that the disposition to reject the child was shared by fathers and mothers alike. The correlation between mother and father rejection scores for the samples was .67 ($p < .001$) for fourth-grade boys, .73 ($p < .01$) for seventh-grade boys, and .55 ($p < .001$) for tenth-grade boys.

The possibility was raised earlier that the interpersonal style learned in the home might generalize to interactions with peers. This led to the hypothesis that rejection by parents would correlate significantly with rejection by peers. The correlation across all three samples was .22 ($p < .001$). There is, then, low-level support for the idea that rejection at home and at school covary significantly.

Does parental rejection covary with all forms of child deviancy (e.g., the greater the deviancy, no matter what its form, the more perceptible the rejection)? Is the covariation greater for some forms of child deviancy than others? The data base consisted of the Child Behavior Checklist (Achenbach & Edelbrock, 1981) completed by both mothers and fathers.

In Table 4.3 eight forms of child deviancy are ordered on an a priori basis, from left to right, from most to least antisocial. The ordering also corresponds to

TABLE 4.3
Correlation of Parental Rejection and Child Deviancy

	CBC Ratings by Parents Externalized and Mixed Problems				
	Delinquent	Aggressive	Hyperactive	Withdrawn Social[a]	Hostile[b]
Mother Reject	.48***	.43***	.44***	.48***	.55***
(N)	(188)	(188)	(188)	(188)	(123)
Father Reject	.32***	.27***	.37***	.29	.40***
(N)	(137)	(137)	(137)	(44)	(93)
	Internalizing Problems				
	Obsessive Compulsive	Immature[a]	Uncommuni-cative	Depressed[b]	Somatic Complaints	Schizoid
Mother Reject	.38***	.54***	.34***	.16	.26**	.19
(N)	(188)	(123)	(188)	(65)	(188)	(188)
Father Reject	.30***	.40***	.22**	.10	.22**	.13
(N)	(137)	(93)	(137)	(44)	(137)	(137)

[a]Scored only for older boys (12–16)
[b]Scored only for younger boys (6–11)
*$p < .05$, **$p < .01$, ***$p < .001$.

the bipolar dimension of externalizing to internalizing described by Achenbach & Edelbrock (1981). As shown there, the data provide strong support for the generalized form of the deviancy rejection hypothesis. It was also the case that the covariations held for both mothers and fathers.

With the exception of three problem behaviors, somatic complaints, schizoid, and depressed, the correlations were above .30 for one or both parents. With the exception of the more neurotic child, problems at the extreme of internalizing disorders, the relation between parental rejection and their perception of deviant child behavior seems highly generalized.

The bulk of the referrals to child guidance clinics consist of children characterized by one or more antisocial problems (Roach, 1958). If one included hyperactive, withdrawn, obsessive, immature, and noncommunicative problem behaviors, they would account for the vast majority of problem behaviors for which children receive treatment. The findings in Table 4.3 suggest that the deviancy-rejection hypothesis may be generalized to this wide spectrum.

The following two sections discuss some variables that may possibly serve as determinants for the relation between child deviancy and maternal rejection.

DAILY HASSLES AND MATERNAL REJECTION

The hypothesis to be examined here is that the round of daily hassles that accompany life with an antisocial child may determine the magnitude of maternal rejection. The more difficult and frequent the discipline confrontations, the more likely the parent is to be discouraged by these interchanges. The failure to discipline also means that antisocial child-sibling conflicts cannot be controlled; and they quickly escalate in frequency and intensity. Under these conditions, the target child increases his daily rates for temper tantrums, fighting, teasing, and so forth. Four variables were constructed that assessed the daily hassles associated with life with an antisocial child. The discipline score, described earlier, was based on global ratings made by observers following each session. Parent daily report is the sum of a series of brief telephone interviews, during which the parent is asked to list child problem behaviors occurring within the last 16 hours. The likelihood of maternal irritable exchanges with the target child is a summary score of three variables derived from the analysis of interaction sequences: the likelihood of the mother starting a conflict, the likelihood of her counterattacking given a coercive initiation by the child, and the likelihood that she will persist in being coercive regardless of his reaction to her. The details of this variable are discussed in Patterson (1982, 1983a, 1983b). The measure of target child irritability to siblings is a composite score summarizing the set of variables comparable to the mother-child exchange score.

The intercorrelation among the hassle measures, together with their correlations with maternal acceptance/rejection, is summarized in Table 4.4. It can be

TABLE 4.4
Intercorrelation Among Daily Hassle
and Maternal Rejection Variables

	Mother Reject	Discipline	Parent Daily Report	Mother-Child Irritable Exchanges
Maternal Reject				
Discipline	.52***			
(N)	(160)			
Parent Daily Report	.23**	.32**		
(N)	(160)	(54)		
Mother-Child Irritable	.16	.27*	.21*	
Exchanges (N)	(85)	(54)	(87)	
Child-Sib Irritable	.44***	.28*	.42***	.42**
Exchanges (N)	(66)	(44)	(69)	(67)

$*p < .05, **p < .01, ***p < .001.$

seen there that the discipline score is heavily correlated (.52) with maternal rejection; a finding consistent with the idea that disrupted discipline may initiate the sequence of events. It can also be seen that it is not the increase in mother–child irritable exchange (.16) that correlates with rejection, but rather, the increase in target child-sibling irritable exchange (.44). Furthermore, the mother's daily reports of frequency for antisocial behavior seems to add little (.23) to our understanding of the process.

The three variables—discipline, target child-sibling irritable exchanges, and parent daily report—were entered in that order in a stepwise multiple regression format with maternal acceptance/rejection as the criterion. The F values for the standard partial beta coefficients were 8.76 ($p < .001$), 5.94 ($p < .01$), and 3.17 ($p < .05$) respectively. The multiple R was .69, and the F value 12.45 ($p < .001$). In general, the findings are consistent with the hypothesis that the mother's disposition to reject covaries significantly with her daily round of abrasive experiences in discipline confrontations and her experiencing a myriad of target child sibling conflicts each day. As noted earlier, the correlational evidence attests to the fact that a connection exists; it is not evident from these data whether the hassles cause the rejection, rejection causes hassles, or both.

REJECTION AND FAILURE AS A MOTHER

It is our clinical impression that many mothers reject a child because they believe the child's behavior signals the mother is a failure. The child fails in school, then fails to fit into the peer group or is identified by teachers and friends as a problem child. Either or both of these would signify that, in some crucial respect, the mother has failed in her responsibility.

Three variables were selected to test the mother failure hypothesis. The first was the mother's perception of the child as being aggressive, measured by the Child Behavior Checklist.[1] It was assumed that this score measured not only her daily experiences with the child, but in addition, reflected information received from teachers, friends, relatives, and neighbors on the status of her child. Presumably, her description of the child as being aggressive would signify that she also perceived herself as having failed in this respect. The second variable, academic competence, was based on the sum of the standardized scores from child self-report, IQ tests, grades, and reading achievement score. The third variable was also a composite based on the standardized scores for child's report of his relations with parents, peers, and teachers, plus the score from the mother's ratings of his social competence. The latter is a subscale of the Child Behavior Checklist (Achenbach & Edelbrock, 1981).

It was assumed that the perception of the child as being aggressive would signify the greatest failure, academic incompetence the second, and a general lack of social skills as the third. The variables were entered in that order in a stepwise regression analyses with maternal acceptance/rejection as the criterion variable. As noted earlier, the mothers' perception of the child as being aggressive accounted for a significant amount of variance in the rejection scores. Adding the measure of academic competence increased the multiple R correlation to .494, with an F value of 25.84 ($p < .001$). Both of the standard partial beta values were highly significant. The measure of the child's social competence added little or nothing.

It seems then that the mothers' perception of the child as deviant and his poor status as a student were both associated with her rejection of him. Together, the two variables accounted for a modest 24% of the variance in the criterion score. In contrast, information about daily hassles accounted for 49% of the variance in the measure of rejection. Both sets of variables seem worthy of further exploration as possible determinants for parental rejection.

SOME SPECULATIONS ABOUT POSITIVE AND AVERSIVE CONTINGENCIES

We believe there is another set of mechanisms that play a key role in the deviancy-rejection process. While as yet we have only begun to construct a

---

[1]We have only recently began the construction of composite scores for academic and social skills. A preliminary test for the academic skill score based upon a composite of IQ plus reading acheivement, plus child self-report, plus school grades correlated significantly with all four measure of family management. The range of correlations was from .18 to .33.

technology for testing these speculations, it is our belief that later formulations about changes in mother-child relationships will make some provision for including a mechanism of this kind. The mechanism has to do with the relation between two different parent functions. First, there is their schema for categorizing devaint and prosocial child behavior. The second and related one is the parents' disposition to react in a positive or aversive fashion contingent on the behavior of the child. The larger issue has to do with the determinants for parent positive and aversive consequences for child behaviors. What determines parent rewards and punishment? What determines which child behaviors are reacted to in a contingent fashion? In that broader context, we believe that parent rejection, parental categorization of prosocial and deviant behaviors, and parental contingent reactions may all be significant factors in this crucial process.

Very early in our clinical contacts with families of antisocial children, we noted that the parents of boys who stole were extraordinarily reluctant to punish or even label thefts of any kind (Reid & Patterson, 1976). On the other hand, parents of socially aggressive boys seemed almost eager to scold and natter, but did not necessarily punish each incident of coercive behavior. As compared to parents of normal boys, parents of socially aggressive boys also seem to define a wider spectrum of child behaviors as deviant (Patterson, 1982). A good deal of parent training was focused on teaching the parent to ignore the more trivial instances of deviant child behavior, and to clearly define what was worthy of punishment and what was not.

The second feature that seemed to stand out in the field studies of these clinical samples was the fact that the parent seemed to use very low rates of approval or physical touching, hugging, etc. in their interactions with family members in general, and with the identified problem child in particular. Observation data collected in the homes of a normal and clinical sample showed many significant differences in interactions among members from distressed and non-distressed families (Patterson, 1979). In most comparisons, the family member from the normal family used about twice as much approval as did the comparable member from the families in the clinical sample. It was also the case that the conditional likelihood of parental approval, given interaction with the target child, was lower in distressed than in nondistressed families. A comparison of 37 families of social aggressors with 37 matched normal families showed an average likelihood of .004 for fathers and .007 for mothers from the clinical sample and .009 for both fathers and mothers of the normal sample.

The third, and perhaps most salient, characteristic of these clinical samples was the ubiquitous presence of aversive reactions. All dyads involving the target child showed significantly higher rates of coercive behaviors, and interactions among siblings were also significantly higher for the clinical as compared to normal samples (Patterson, 1976, 1982; Reid, Patterson, & Loeber, 1982). Most interesting of all of these findings was the fact that the mothers of problem children were significantly more likely than mothers of normal children to start conflicts when the problem child was behaving in a neutral or positive fashion. Why are mothers of problem children more likely to start conflicts even when the child is behaving? Our clinical experience in treating these families suggested that what they chose to classify as deviant was different from the classification schemes employed by normal mothers. They chose to view trivial instances of transgressions as worthy of a full scale scolding. In this formulation, scolding and threatening is not viewed as an exemplar of effective discipline because these parents almost invariably forgot to follow through on their threats to punish (Patterson, 1982). We suspected, but have never tested the idea, that rejecting mothers are more likely to have such highly inclusive categories for classifying deviant child behavior. We also suspected that the rejecting parents, with their overly inclusive categories for deviant behavior, have overly exclusive categories for prosocial behavior. The latter would be commensurate with reduced likelihoods for the use of positive reinforcement.

The first set of studies explored one of the variables we thought might determine the maternal use of overly inclusive categories for classifying what is deviant and what is normal child behavior. The hypothesis was that the abrasive daily interactions with the antisocial child might alter the manner in which the mother categorizes deviant child behavior. For example, it may be the case that such interactions broaden the definition to include more trivial behaviors as being symptomatic (and therefore worthy of negative attention). In the laboratory analogue study by Lorber, Reid and Simard (1979), male and female college students served as respondents. The task consisted of the respondents viewing videotapes of parent-child interaction, and pushing buttons when they perceived a prosocial or antisocial child behavior. Each of the respondents had previously viewed a set induction tape. One of the tapes consisted of 7½ min of coercive child behavior, and the other a tape of consistent prosocial behavior. In keeping with the hypothesis, viewing the coercive child behavior significantly reduced the tracking accuracy for that group of respondents and also lead to a more fine grained categorization. Both of these effects were significantly greater for the female than the male respondents. The findings were consistent with the idea that exposure to intense aversive interactions would be associated with more inclusive categorizing of deviant child behaviors.

The next study examined the hypothesis that parents of antisocial children might have a more inclusive definition of deviant child behavior than would be the case for mothers of normals (i.e., the category would include more examples of relatively trivial problem behaviors) (Lorber, 1981). Twenty-four parents of social aggressors and 24 parents of normal children viewed the videotape of parent-child interaction and again pushed buttons to identify events as prosocial or antisocial Lorber (1981). In keeping with the hypothesis, the parents of problem children were significantly more inclusive than were parents of normals. Their category of deviant included most of the events scored by our professional observers as deviant and, in addition, they included many events not classed as deviant by our staff. Lorder also showed that the scores from the laboratory task correlated significantly with field observation data describing the mother's interaction with the child in the home. Mothers who were overly inclusive were significantly more likely to react irritability to coercive child behavior. In the replication study by Holleran, Littman, Freund, Schmaling, & Heeren (1982), 17 parents of normal and 19 parents of oppositional children responded to a script containing 10 short vignettes. They were asked to underline events categorized as prosocial or antisocial child behaviors. Using a signal detection format, the investigators found that the parents from the clinical sample were significantly less sensitive than were parents of normals and also significantly overinclusive. Specifically, the parents of the problem children were more likely to classify many neutral behaviors as examples of deviant. The parents of the two samples were also asked to rate statements about deviant child behavior on their aversiveness. Parents in the clinical sample rated most forms of aggressive behavior as significantly more aversive than did parents of the normal children. A subset of 13 of the families were observed in the home. The sensitivity and inclusiveness scores for the comparison of neutral to deviant behaviors correlated significantly with the observed rates of prosocial and coercive behaviors observed in the home. Both studies were essentially in agreement that overly inclusive classification of deviant child behaviors is significantly correlated with higher rates of coercive behavior in the home.

The next replication study (Schmaling & Patterson, 1984) again employed videotapes in a laboratory task in addition to collecting observation data in the homes. The correlations between the laboratory task and observed mother-child behaviors in the home were highly significant and in keeping with the previous findings.

The findings from this brief series of studies, plus the programmatic studies by R. Lorber, currently under way, are very suggestive. It seems that mothers of antisocial and oppositional children are, indeed, likely to be overly inclusive in their willingness to classify some events most of us perceive to be neutral as deviant. The general thrust of these findings are consistent with the studies of attribution bias noted in the interactions of peers and aggressive children in the school settings (Dodge, 1980). In those studies, children who have experienced the interactions with the aggressive child are more likely to misattribute hostile intentions to neutral behavior (i.e., in a sense, they are overly inclusive). In the Dodge studies, the aggressive child is also more likely to misattribute hostile intentions to members of the peer group. At this point, the concepts of overly inclusive and misattribution seem equally useful. In fact, in the Schmaling and Patterson (1984) study, the correlation between the mothers' overinclusiveness score and the mean of the ratings made following each observation session was .44 ($p \leq .05$).

Is it that, as suggested in the Lorber (1981) study, interactions with a coercive child produce the overinclusiveness? We believe this is probably the case. Do these same parents also tend to be underinclusive in their classification of prosocial behaviors? Several of the studies note that the parents of distressed and normal children differ significantly in the manner in which they classify prosocial behaviors. If one is overly inclusive in classifying deviant behavior, does this also lead to underinclusiveness for prosocial behavior? Are the two classification schemata independent of each other?

It seems the case from two of the studies (Lorber 1981; Schmaling & Patterson, 1984) that parent overinclusiveness for deviant behaviors correlates with parent disposition to scold and nag when observed in the home. Is one a determinant for the other, or do both of these covary with some third variable? There is a suggestion in the same two studies that parental provision for positive consequences for prosocial child behavior may correlate with the manner in which they categorize prosocial behaviors. Again, is this a cause, an effect, or simply a correlational relation?

It is our impression that the point at which the parent labels the child as deviant is accompanied by an increase in aversive reactions and a commensurate decrease in supportive positions. It is perhaps this rapid shift in what one views as deviant and prosocial, plus a reduction in our positive reactions and increase in negative reactions, that define, in part, how we feel about another person. Do shifts in affect from warmth to rejection covary with shifts in inclusiveness? We think so. If we no longer accept the child this could function as a positive feedback loop. We may become increasingly critical of his or her behavior, tracking and nattering at little things that he or she does and overlooking more and more of the acceptable behaviors.

CONCLUSIONS

Correlational analyses provided support for the covariation between deviancy and rejection. The measure of parent rejection was available for each parent; the data showed a significant correlation for mothers and fathers suggesting a kind of parental trait of rejection that characterizes some families. In addition, it was shown that the relation between child deviancy and parent rejection held for both parents and across a wide spectrum of child problems. The findings showed that, for both parents, rejection covaried significantly with their reports on the CBC for the aggression, delinquency, and hyperactive scales, as well as with social and hostile withdrawal. Significant covariations also held for half of the scales (obsessive, immature, uncommunicative) on the internalizing dimension.

The next block of analyses explored the relation between child antisocial behavior and lack of parenting skills. The findings provided consistent support for significant correlations between failure to monitor and discipline and various measures of antisocial child behavior. Only marginal support was provided for the idea that parent positive reinforcement and problem solving skills were related to child academic and social skills.

These parent skills are thought to have causal status because they are the variables that have served as the goals for the parent training studies. Although the data for the outcome studies have shown significant reductions in antisocial behavior (Patterson et al., 1982) and persistence of treatment effects over 12 months (Patterson & Fleischman, 1979), no systematic study demonstrating that the changes are produced because the parents successfully altered their family-management practices has been completed, nor has it been demonstrated that maternal rejection is reduced following successful parent training.

The third area explored consisted of two sets of variables thought to determine maternal rejection. Measures of discipline confrontations, target child and sibling conflicts observed in the home, and mother's daily reports of recently occurring problem behaviors defined the daily hassles. The multiple R of .69 showed that the discipline and target child-sibling conflict scores were strongly correlated with maternal rejection. The next hypothesis examined was that the mother's perception of her failures to socialize the child would correlate with the measure of rejection. Her perception of the child as being aggressive and a composite measuring his academic competence both contributed significantly to a multiple R of .49. The daily hassles and maternal perception of failure to socialize the child are reasonable condidates for status as significant determinants for maternal rejection.

There is another aspect of this report that bears some comments. It would seem that there are problems other than antisocial behavior in children or maternal rejection that could be addressed by an interactional approach. The focus on multiple agent and multiple modes of assessment to define important constructs is certainly not a novel idea, nor is the inclusion of field observation data and sequential analysis, but it is felt that the illustration of their employment is one useful function served by the present report.

There is another methodological note that is reflected in the pattern of findings presented here. Most clinical phenomena, such as disrupted parent child relationships, are reflected by a myriad of accompanying correlations. For example, parental rejection correlates significantly with many, or even most, child clinical problems. Most problem children are rejected or ignored by their peer groups, and many of them are academic failures, too. The literature often ascribes any or all of these accompanying variables to a causal status (e.g., it is the child's lack of social skills that causes him or her to be antisocial, and it is the mother's rejection that causes him to act out). Only properly designed longitudinal and treatment manipulation studies can decide whether these variables determine the problems or not. The fact that they are correlated does not mean they are casually related. In fact, as shown in the present report, it is just as reasonable to believe they are accompaniments or products of the process that produced the problem behaviors. The present set of findings point to the definite possibility that the mother's rejection may be largely determined by a lack of parenting skills. The lack of skills sets up a process that gets out of control and disrupts the affection and commitment of an otherwise attached mother.

ACKNOWLEDGMENT

The preparation of the chapter was supported in large part from grant 1 RO1 MH 33067 from the National Institute of Mental Health, Section on Crime and Delinquency. The author gratefully acknowledges the contributions of R. Loeber, T. Dishion, M. Stouthamer-Loeber, and J. Reid to the development of many of the ideas presented here.

REFERENCES

Achenbach, T. M., & Edelbrock, C. S. (1981). Behavioral problems and competencies by parents of normal and disturbed children aged four through 16. *Society for Research in Child Development Monograph, 188.*

Ageton, S. S., & Elliott, D. S. (1982). The incidence of delinquent behavior in a national probability sample of adolescents. MTT 27552 project report for *The Dynamics of Delinquent Behavior,* Behavioral Research Institute, Boulder, Colorado.

Bandura, A. (1977). *Social learning theory.* New York: General Learning Press.

Bentler, P. M. (1980). Multivariate analysis with latent variables and causal modeling. *Annual Review of Psychology, 31,* 419–436.

Bijou, S. W., & Baer, D. (1961). *Child development. Vol I. A systematic and empirical theory.* New York: Appleton-Century Crofts.

Dodge, K. (1980). Social cognition and children's aggressive behavior. *Child Development, 51,* 162–170.

Eron, L. (1982). Parent-child interaction, television violence, and aggression of children. *American Psychologist, 37,* 197–211.

Fagan, O. S., Langner, T. S., Gersten, J. C., & Eisenberg, J. (1977). *Violent and antisocial behavior. A longitudinal study of urban youth: Interim report.* New York: Division of Epidemiology, School of Public Health, Columbia University.

Forgatch, M. (1984). *Poor problems solving: Concomitant for psychopathology in families.* Manuscript in preparation.

Glueck, S., & Glueck, E. (1950). *Unraveling juvenile delinquency.* Cambridge MA: Harvard University Press.

Glueck, S., & Glueck, E. (Eds.). (1972). *Identification of predelinquents.* New York: Intercontinental Medical Book Corporation.

Hartup, W. W. (1978). Children and their friends. In H. McGurk (Ed.), *Child social development.* London: Methuen Press.

Hartup, W. W. (1982). Symmetries and asymmetries in children's relationships. In J. deWit & A. L. Benton (Eds.), *Perspectives in child study,* Lisse, Netherlands: Ziwets & Zeitlinger.

Hetherington, E. M., Cox, M., & Cox, R. (1978). Aftermath of divorce. In J. H. Stevens, Jr. & M. Matthews (Eds.), *Mother-child, father-child relations.* Washington, D.C.: National Association for the Education of Young Children.

Hetherington, E. M., Cox, M., & Cox, R. (1979). Family interaction and the social, emotional, and cognitive development of children following divorce. In V. Vaughn & T. Brazelton (Eds.), *The family: Setting priorities.* New York: Science and Medicine.

Hirschi, L. (1969). *Causes of delinquency.* Berkeley: University of California Press.

Holleran, P., Littman, D., Freund, R., Schmaling, K., & Heeren, J. (1982). A signal detection approach to social perception: Tracking of negative and positive behavior by normal and distressed parents. *Journal of Abnormal Child Psychology, 10,* 447–457.

Lorber, R. (1981). *Parental tracking of childhood behavior as a function of family stress.* Unpublished doctoral dissertation, University of Oregon.

Lorber, R., Reid, J. B., & Simard, K. (1979, December). *Parent perception: Behavioral tracking skills in distressed and nondistressed environments.* Paper presented at the meeting of the Association for the Advancedment of Behavior Therapy, San Francisco.

McCord, J. (1978). A 30-year follow-up of treatment effects. *American Psychologist, 33,* 284–289.

McCord, J. (1979). Some child-rearing antecedents of criminal behavior in adult men. *Journal of Personality and Social Psychology, 9,* 1477–1486.

McCord, W., McCord, J., & Zola, J. K. (1959). *Origins of crime.* New York: Columbia University Press.

Patterson, G. R. (1976). The aggressive child: Victim and architect of a coercive system. In E. Mash, L. Hamerlynck, & L. Handy (Eds.), *Behavior modification and families.* New York: Brunner/Mazel.

Patterson, G. R. (1979). A performance theory for coercive family interaction. In R. Cairns (Ed.), *Social interaction: Methods, analysis, and illustrations.* Hillsdale, NJ: Lawrence Erlbaum Associates.

Patterson, G. R. (1982). *A social learning approach, Vol. 3: Coercive family process.* Eugene, Oregon: Castalia Publishing Company.

Patterson, G. R. (1983a). Stress: A change agent for family process. In N. Garmezy & M. Rutter (Eds.), *Stress, coping, and development in children.* New York: McGraw Hill.

Patterson, G. R. (1983b). Microsocial process: A view from the boundary. In J. C. Masters & K. L. Yarkin (Eds.), *Boundary areas in psychology: Social and developmental psychology.* New York: Academic Press.

Patterson, G. R., Chamberlain, P., & Reid, J. B. (1982). A comparative evaluation of a parent training program. *Behavior Therapy, 13,* 638–650.

Patterson, G. R., Dishion, T. J., & Bank, L. (1984). Family interaction: A process model of deviancy training. *Aggressive Behavior, 10,* 253–267.

Patterson, G. R., & Fleischman, M. J. (1979). Maintenance of treatment effects: Some considerations concerning family systems and follow-up data. *Behavior Therapy, 10,* 168–195.

Patterson, G. R., & Forgatch, M. S. (1975). *Family living series audio cassette tapes.* Champaign, IL: Research Press.

Patterson, G. R., Hops, H., & Weiss, R. L. (1975). Interpersonal skill training for couples in early stages of conflict. *Journal of Marriage and the Family,* 295–303.

Patterson, G. R., Reid, J. B., Jones, R. R., & Conger, R. (1975). *A social learning approach to family intervention, I.: Parent training.* Eugene, Oregon: Castalia Publishing Company.

Patterson, G. R., & Stouthamer-Loeber, M. (1984). The correlation of family-management practices and delinquency. *Child Development, 55,* 1299–1307.

Reid, J. B., & Patterson, G. R. (1976). The modification of aggression and stealing behavior of boys in the home setting. In A. Bandura & E. Ribes (Eds.), *Behavior modification: Experimental analyses of aggression and delinquency.* Hillsdale, NJ: Lawrence Erlbaum Associates.

Reid, J. B., Patterson, G. R., & Loeber, R. (1982). The abused child: Victim, instigator, or innocent bystander? In D. J. Bernstein (Ed.), *Response structure and organization.* Lincoln: University of Nebraska Press.

Robins, L. N. (1966). *Deviant children grown up: A sociological and psychiatric study of sociopathic personality.* Baltimore: Williams & Wilkins.

Roach, J. L. (1958). Some social-psychological characteristics of a child guidance clinic caseload. *Journal of Consulting Psychology, 22,* 183–186.

Rutter, M. (1976). Parent-child separation: Psychological effects on the children. In A. M. Clarke & A. D. B. Clarke (Eds.), *Early experience: Myth and evidence*. New York: The Free Press.

Schmaling, K. B., & Patterson, G. R. (1984, November). *Maternal classification of deviant and prosocial child behavior and reactions to the child in the home*. Paper presented at American Association for the Advancement of Behavior Therapy, Philadelphia.

Sears, R. R., Maccoby, E., & Levin, H. (1957). *Patterns of child rearing*. New York: Harper & Row.

Sullivan, J. L. (1974). Multiple indicators: Some criteria of selection. In H. M. Blalock (Ed.), *Measurement in the social sciences*. Chicago: Aldine.

Wahler, R. G., & Dumas, J. E. (1983, June). *Stimulus class determinants of mother-child coercive exchanges in multidistressed families: Assessment and intervention*. Paper presented at Vermont Conference on Primary Prevention, Bolton Valley, Vermont.

Walter, H. I., & Gilmore, S. K. (1973). Placebo versus social learning effects in parent training procedures designed to alter the behavior of aggressive boys. *Behavior Research and Therapy, 4,* 361–377.

West, D. J., & Farrington, D. P. (1973). *Who becomes delinquent?* London: Heinemann.

West, D. J., & Farrington, D. P. (1977). *The delinquent way of life*. London: Heinemann.

Wilson, H. (1980). Parental supervision: A neglected aspect of delinquency. *The British Journal of Criminology, 1980, 20,* 203–235.

Wiltz, N. A., & Patterson, G. R. (1974). An evaluation of parent training procedures designed to alter inappropriate aggressive behavior in boys. *Behavior Therapy, 1974, 5,* 215–221.

Youniss, J. (1980). *Parents and peers in social development*. Chicago: University of Chicago Press.

5 Continuities and Transformations in Social Relationships From Childhood to Adulthood

Robert S. Weiss
University of Massachusetts and Harvard Medical School

Studies of adults suggest that there are several different emotional bases on which relationships are formed and maintained (Henderson, Byrne, & Duncan-Jones, 1981; Weiss, 1974). In this paper I offer speculation regarding the possible developmental history of different relational bonds.

A typology of adult bonds I have found useful was developed from work with members of a Parents Without Partners chapter on the relational needs of these recently separated or widowed individuals. Six distinct bonds make up the typology.

The initial observation of this study was that most members of the organization remained lonely despite forming close friendships with other members. The exceptions were members who were "going with" someone, i.e., who had established a relationship that resembled marriage in that it provided them with a sense of sharing their emotional lives (Weiss, 1973a, 1973b). This observation suggested that the relational provisions necessary for protection from the distress of loneliness, once obtained by organization members from their marriages, could not be obtained from the new friendships fostered by the organization but *could* be obtained from at least some "dating" relationships.

Marriages and marriage-like relationships apparently make provisions not to be found in friendships. But is the converse also true? Elizabeth Hartwell and I interviewed a small sample of married couples who had moved in very recent months from two or three states away: far enough away so that their former communities were now inaccessible to them. We found that for a time after their move the wives, but not the husbands, reported distress as a result of the loss of their previous communities. The husbands, it appeared, had been absorbed into the community of their fellow workers. To be sure, their membership in this community was not secure; they were still being evaluated by their fellows. But

95

having yet to prove themselves made the workplace even more engaging for them.

The wives of these men either did not work or, if they did, treated work as an activity of secondary importance. In either event, they required friends or family to provide them with a social community. Having moved away from the friends and family in their previous communities, they now felt isolated. These new-comer wives demonstrated that adults may require for their well-being not only the provisions made by marriages but also the provisions of friendships or family ties or work relationships.

The identification of two relational bonds distinct from one another in their provisions suggested asking how many distinct relational bonds there might be, and what might be their provisions. Examination of field materials and interview transcripts in the Parents Without Partners study led to the surmise that the organization attempted to provide or to strengthen several distinct bonds (Weiss, 1973a). In a subsequent study of the life organization of single parents, it appeared that this set of bonds, with a single addition, could account for all the bonds maintaining the relationships that together constituted the respondents' social worlds. (The additional bond, characterized as "help-obtaining," did not seem to have been a concern of Parents Without Partners.) One conclusion is that the loss of marriage can disturb virtually every linkage an individual has to others. Another conclusion is that we now had a list of relational bonds.

The six bonds and their specifications are:

1. *Attachment.* This bond is based on feelings of enhanced security linked to the presence of the person to whom there is attachment. In the presence of that figure, individuals feel "at home" and comparatively free from anxiety. The inaccessibility of that figure makes individuals vulnerable to separation distress and loneliness. Naming this bond "attachment" expresses a belief that the bond is based on a development of the emotional system Bowlby identified as linking children to parents (Bowlby, 1974, 1979, 1982). The system in adults, it is hypothesized, has changed from its childhood configuration, especially in that it is directed toward a new kind of figure. But the presence or at least accessibility of the attachment figure still fosters feelings of security, and the inaccessibility of the figure, especially if combined with conditions of threat, produces symptoms of separation distress.

2. *Affiliation.* This bond is based on recognition of shared interests that may develop through belief that situations and their challenges or outlooks or aims are shared. From this sharedness can develop a sense of mutuality, feelings of affection and respect, and loyalty.

3. *Nurturance.* This bond seems to be based on a sense of commitment, investment, responsibility for, or desire for responsibility for, someone perceived as weak and needful. There can develop investment in the well-being of the other.

4. *Collaboration.* This is a bond based on a feeling of shared commitment to the achievement of a goal. The other is seen as a colleague, teammate, or partner with whom one's own efforts are coordinated. Associated with this bond is a sense of mutual respect from which may be derived support for feelings of personal worth.

5. *Persisting alliance.* This is a bond that appears to be based on feelings of identification or overlapping identities independent of aims or goals. Strongly associated with it are feelings of obligation to help the other as needed and of rights to the help of the other. Also associated are feelings of lives permanently associated. It is this bond that seems fundamental to kinship ties although it seems also to be one of the bonds of marriage and a bond that communal groups may attempt to foster.

6. *Help Obtaining.* This is a bond to someone perceived as more knowledgeable and wiser, who is looked to for trustworthy support and who is felt to be a legitimate source of guidance. It is a bond especially likely to be established by adults who have come to doubt their own abilities to deal with the challenges confronting them.

This category system has now been used in several investigations. Henderson, Byrne, and Duncan-Jones (1981) found that the perceived adequacy of both attachment and affiliation independently predicted the likelihood of surmounting adversity without succumbing to neurosis. Cutrona (in press), in a study of a small sample of pregnant women, found that before subjects gave birth their well-being seemed most strongly related to the accessibility of an attachment figure, but after they gave birth their well-being was most strongly related to the accessibility of affiliative relationships. Brown and Harris (1978) while not considering the category system as a whole, found that irrespective of relationships' formal characteristics, "confidant" relationships—essentially, what are here termed relationships of attachment—provided a defense against depression.

Other category systems for relational bonds may be preferable, at least for some purposes, to the one I offer. Harlow and Harlow (1965) in attempting to characterize what seemed to them to be distinct "affectional systems" in primates, provide a different category system, including a distinction between maternal and paternal bonds to infants. Henderson et al. (1981) found it useful to treat collaboration, alliance and affiliation as making the same provisions. The category system I offer, while I believe it to be useful, may not in every case identify fundamentally distinct emotional processes, may not be exhaustive, and may fail to make distinctions that should be made. The extent to which it is entirely satisfactory may be clarified as more work is done in the area.

If the bonds I identify do, indeed, provide bases for linking adults to others, it is reasonable to inquire into their development: What is their origin, how do they display themselves in the life of the child and how are they changed as the child moves toward adulthood? In what follows I offer some speculations regarding answers to these questions.

Attachment

Infants appear to be responsive to their mothers' voices at birth and perhaps before. "A newborn infant younger than three days of age cannot only discriminate its mother's voice but also will work to produce her voice in preference to the voice of another female." (DeCasper & Fifer, 1980. The work required of the baby was sucking on a pacifier.) Babies not yet 4-months-old show marked separation distress when left by their mothers (Slayton, Ainsworth, & Main, 1973). It would seem that humans are born with some level of attachment to their mothers or, if they are not actually attached at birth, then they are at least prepared to form this bond and are attached not long thereafter.

The properties of the mother that elicit an infant's response have been shown to include both her appearance and the sound of her voice. Quite possibly stimuli in other sense modalities may also become integrated in the perceptual component of the child's bonding: the mother's tactile qualities, her odor, even the tempo of her movements. It is an appealing idea that figures who will later elicit attachment responses from the child-grown-into-adult will reproduce in one or more of the sense modalities the primary attachment figure of infancy. Yet there are so many different kinds of similarity that might exist—appearance, voice, energy level, tempo, and so on—that any experimental or correlational attempt to link attachment objects of adults with earlier objects might find itself swamped by possibilities.

The attachment bond appears to be the central relational system—indeed, the central emotional system—of the young child's life. Children's behavior is compatible with the idea that for the young child attachment figures are seen as intimately linked to the self whereas other individuals in the environment are seen as quite distinct and so to be explored, played with, or feared. The fundamental environmental distinction for the young child may be not between the animate and the inanimate or the human and the nonhuman, but rather between attachment figures and all else. (See Ainsworth, Blehar, Waters, & Wall, 1978).

As children become older they are steadily less needful of their parents' presence. Bowlby (1982) described the decreasing frequency of attachment behavior in the developing child:

Other interests and activities attract him and occupy his time, and there is less that alarms him. Not only is his attachment less frequently and less intensely activated, but it can be terminated in novel ways, thanks to his increasing cognitive competence, especially a greatly improved capacity to think in terms of space and time. Thus, for spells of increasing duration, a child may feel content and secure even in his mother's absence, simply by knowing where she is and when she will return, or by being assured that she is available whenever he really wants her. (p. 356)

It may be worth noting that Bowlby's treatment of attachment (Bowlby 1974, 1979, 1982) emphasizes the activation of the emotional system of attachment by perceptions of threat or fears of abandonment. For Bowlby, as the child moves on in its development, the attachment system is less frequently elicited. In my view the bond of attachment remains but less frequently is expressed in behavior. It is this bond, however, that holds children in the relationship with their parents.

Although there is an extensive literature on the nature of attachment in children, many questions remain. These include whether, in the usual situation of two parents, one parent is a primary attachment figure. In most families it seems unquestionably the case that attachment of some sort develops for each parent, and often for siblings as well. But whether these attachments are equally strong—or even what such a question would mean and how it might be decided—seems still to be unsettled.

Another question that seems still to be open is whether there is a sensitive period in a child's development after which attachment to parents or parent figures is not likely to form. It appears to be common experience that children who first enter a relationship with a step-parent or adoptive parent when the children are latency aged or older seem to learn to relate to the adult as a kin figure but not as an attachment figure. There may be affection and loyalty, but there is likely not to be a sense of security-fostering augmentation. These reports are as yet entirely unsystematic; here, though, systematic examination of the matter might prove feasible.

As the child moves on in development, the bond of attachment is less powerful as a determinant of behavior. Bowlby suggests that the older child's ability to tolerate the temporary inaccessibility of a parent stems from the child's increased understanding of the meaning of time and distance and, perhaps, increased ability to take the parent's promise of return as a token for the parent's presence. Another factor may be the child's increased self-confidence which makes new situations less likely to produce alarm. Furthermore, identification processes may provide the child with an internalized image of the parent which constitutes a source of security.

Older children do, of course, continue to experience the separation distress that Bowlby associates with the activation of the attachment system. However, they do so only under unusual circumstances. One such circumstance for many children is a first night away from home at summer camp. The "homesickness" that children may then experience is, of course, separation distress produced by the distance from the child's parents. Attachment behavior, in the form of need for reassurance of the parent's presence, is also likely to be displayed by an older child who has become seriously ill. The child is then in a threatening situation and at the same time aware of a less capable self.

With the exception of occasions such as these, older children seem to assume the reliability of the attachment bond and to direct their energies toward relationships outside their homes. At the same time their relationships with their parents increasingly express bonds other than attachment: Much of older children's interaction with parents is a consequence of their collaboration (sometimes reluctant on the children's part) in the management of the children's personal programs and their shared living situations.

Nevertheless, even while collaborative bonds increasingly dominate the relationship of parents and children, the persisting bond of attachment may ensure even an older child's continued linkage to the parent. This would be made evident by the reaction of the child to the parent's departure from the home, as might happen in parental separation. Indeed, it has frequently been observed that college students, presumably beginning to assume control of their own lives, experience feelings of abandonment on learning of a parental separation (Judith Wallerstein, personal communication).

If children are eventually to form their own households, their bonds of attachment to the parents must become attenuated and eventually end. Otherwise, independent living would be emotionally troubling. The relinquishing of attachment to parents appears to be of central importance among the individuation-achieving processes of late adolescence and early adulthood.

I am not aware of systematic investigations into the processes by which attachment to parents becomes attenuated and, eventually, relinquished. Some observations may, however, be offered, based on interviews with high school seniors undertaken by my colleagues and myself in an exploratory study of the transition to adulthood. Some of these young people were interviewed a second time a year after their senior high school year.

First, the timing of the relinquishing of parents appears to be influenced by situational factors. Some youngsters, required by their household situations to display early autonomy (because of parental absence or inaccessibility), seem by not much more than their mid-teens no longer to treat their parents as attachment figures. They say that they are not at all uncomfortable when their parents are away from home overnight. They may also form, earlier than most of their peers, the kind of relationship with someone of the other sex that will provide an adult version of attachment. (See, for further discussion of the impact on adolescents of the disruption of the parents' marriage, Wallerstein & Kelly, 1980; Weiss, 1979.) At the other extreme, some young people appear to continue into their twenties to relate to parents as attachment figures. A development of this sort may be fostered by the parents having learned to view the children as their own attachment figures, perhaps because of their otherwise isolated situations.

The relinquishing of attachment does not proceed in a steady course of ever-diminishing intensity, nor does it move only in a single direction. Instead, there seem to be abrupt changes followed by halts and regressions. Among young people in their first year of college whose relationships with their parents were not remarkable for particular developments (the parents' marriages remained intact, the young peoples' relationships with the parents were good), it seemed often the case that young people who had felt themselves to be emotionally independent of their parents before leaving for college would in their first weeks at college find themselves painfully lonely. They would then be able to interrupt their loneliness by telephoning the parents or planning a return home for a visit. The reassurance they experienced on hearing their parents' voices on the telephone demonstrated that the attachment bond to the parents remained, although it required the anxiety of the new situation to elicit it.

Cutrona and Russell (1982), in a small-scale study of college students, found that when students in the freshman year described themselves as lonely, they were more often lonely for a place in a network of relationships—for community—than they were for someone who might function as an attachment figure. Students in the senior year, in contrast, when they reported themselves as lonely were more often lonely for someone who might function as an attachment figure. One possible interpretation of this finding is that many young people experience a kind of latency of late adolescence in relation to attachment. To give too much energy to the bond to parents would impede their movement toward independence. To become attached to an other-sex peer would remove them from the communities within which their adult identities will be formed. And so, although they may vaguely yearn for a special other person, they direct their energies to finding a place for themselves within a community of others.

During this phase in their lives young people may make close friendships, but only infrequently do these friendships seem to involve the emotional reliance on the other's accessibility that signals attachment. The late adolescent may also experience the excitement associated with attachment in formation, but only rarely is this permitted to continue to a well established, taken-for-granted bonding. An entirely accepted emotional relationship in which attachment is an element seems more to be dreamed about and enjoyed vicariously in movies, television and books than experienced in life. None of this seems to be the result of the absence of appropriate partners: The same figure who is felt as not right in late adolescence may be accepted a few years later. Rather, it appears to be a result of the young person's self-appraisal as not yet ready. How this appraisal is made and how it changes seem to be specific questions within the larger puzzle of the process by which the attachment system of children transmutes itself into the attachment system of adults.

Is "attachment" in the pair relationships of adults a development of the attachment system of children? The two bonds resemble each other in that each provides a sense of well-being in the presence of the individual to whom it is directed. Furthermore, very much the same sort of separation distress is displayed should that individual become inaccessible. And it does seem to be the case that attachment to peers becomes a possibility only as attachment to parents fades.

Nevertheless, the bond of attachment in adults is in significant respects different from that in children: There has taken place a change in object, from parent to peer, ordinarily of the other sex; and with this, there has taken place a change in the character of the object from the awesomely powerful, usually protective, parent of childhood to a peer whose frailities, once the relationship has passed its initial idealizations, are apt to be well recognized. Furthermore, in the adult version there is usually an intermeshing of sexual desire with attachment. The extent to which this also occurs among children is unclear, but if it does occur it seems likely that it is quite different in character: weaker, more diffuse, more likely to be disguised; certainly, to use Freud's phrase, aim-inhibited.

My own belief is that the attachment system in adults is a development of the earlier childhood attachment system in the senses that the same perceptual mechanisms and the same biochemical pathways are utilized and the first system modifies itself to become the second. I believe this to be the case because interruption of attachment seems to give rise in adults to the same feelings (despair, loss, anger) and the same behavioral expressions (vigilance, sleeplessness) that occur in children, and because the system in its form in children does seem to fade before the system in its adult form appears. (For further supporting argument, see Weiss, 1982.) Deciding whether the proposition is true, however, and if it is, working out the processes by which the adult system emerges from the earlier childhood system, seem to me among the most intriguing problems in the field of human development.

Affiliation

The affiliative bond is a linkage which seems to be formed from a sense of parallel concerns permitting mutual assistance and understanding. Such bonds seem often to be initiated by perceptions of shared situation or background or aims. A sense of complementarity in skills or knowledge is compatible with feelings of essential commonality and can contribute to the linkage. The relationships that eventually develop are often strengthened by feelings of sympathy, affection and loyalty.

To restate the argument of an earlier section, there is evidence that the provisions of affiliative bonds do not ameliorate separation distress or loneliness and therefore cannot be seen as making the same provisions as attachment bonds. This would seem to be the case among children as well as among adults. Some parents of 6-year-olds report that their children are unwilling to sleep over at the homes of close friends because of separation anxiety. To be sure, under sufficiently severe stress and in the absence of other possible attachment figures, peers with whom previously there had been only affiliative bonds may be accepted as attachment figures. To give an example from adult life, under combat conditions men seem to become attached (in the sense given the term here) to buddies (Little, 1964). Something similar may happen among children who have been virtually abondoned by the world of adults (Freud & Dann, 1951).

Affiliative bonds can be helpful to individuals in distress by reducing their sense of being alone and marked for misfortune. Relationships with peers developed around affiliative bonds can be helpful, too, in providing information, counsel, and help. None of these provisions should be confused with the greatly enhanced sense of security that is a provision of the bond of attachment.

It seems a reasonable guess that affiliative impulses are a development of exploratory impulses. Bowlby (1982), drawing on Harlow and Harlow's work with young monkeys (1965), writes, "Play with peers seems to begin as an extension of exploration and play with inanimate objects" (p. 239). Awareness that these others are significantly different from inanimate objects seems to develop extremely early: Hartup, in his comprehensive review of research (1983), notes that "smiles and vocalizations" are reported in the contacts of 6-month infants.

There is much evidence that from the first the content of an infant's affiliative relationships is different in character from that of the infant's relationship with its mother. Hartup reports that "When mothers and other babies are both available, looking and vocalization are more commonly directed to the baby; touching is more commonly directed to the mother." Furthermore, "Even though year-old babies smile and laugh at each other, the vast majority of their interactions are emotionally neutral."

It may be added that children are at first relatively indifferent regarding the identity of the other children with whom (or alongside whom) they play. Only as children become older do they develop the steeply graded hierarchy of preference for possible playmates that resembles the attachment system's sharp distinction between those to whom bonds of attachment are directed and all others.

It has been noted that infants whose relationships with their parents are more secure are likely to be more sociable than other infants (Lieberman, 1977; Sroufe & Fleeson, this volume; Hartup, 1983). Secure attachment appears to make for confidence in exploration, including exploration that takes the form of social initiative. Securely attached children, compared to other children of the same age, can be more trusting of their parents' commitment to them as well as more confident of their personal effectiveness. That it is the more securely attached children that are the more sociable is still further evidence that the aim of sociability is not the achievement of still further security.

Affiliative ties seem to assume greater priority as children move on in development. By three years, some children are severely distressed by the loss of a friend. Most children, however, seem able at this age and even later to make and break affiliative linkages with facility and to accept the loss of a particular friend without persisting upset. More upsetting might be the loss of a play-group, as would be produced by a move to a new community.

The increasing salience of affiliation as children become more mature may be due to their greater tolerance of distance in time and space from attachment figures. There may be a turning away from attachment in order more effectively to establish autonomy. Children now can give a larger proportion of their energies to the world outside the family. Peers become both allies in the effort to deal with the challenges of independence and themselves potential sources of gratification.

The groups to which adolescents belong through their high school years, important as they then are, tend to disintegrate as members leave for college or for distant jobs. We do not know very much about the emotional impact on young people of this loss of their high school friendship group, but my interviews suggest that young people often are buffered from its full impact by not entirely recognizing its occurrence. While the social group may lose some members during the summer after the senior year of high school, enough of a membership remains to prevent feelings of isolation. For the young person still in the home community with the coming of fall, there usually are a few other members of the group also remaining. For the young person who has gone away to college or a job, the social group may be imagined as continuing even though its members are now separated. Only on return home, perhaps at the Christmas break, will there be recognition that what had earlier been a sustaining social network no longer exists. And by then the young person is likely to have established membership in a new social group in the new community.

Young people entering residential college indicate that their feelings of comfort in their new settings depend on having a place in a network of others. Affiliative bonds seem to provide the basis of these network relationships. The possibility of a more intense relationship with someone of the other sex is likely to be much thought about by a young person in this situation, but initially it appears to be linkages to the new community that engage the young person's energies.

One of the developments of the young adult years, the years from 18 or 19 to 22 or 23, appears to be a shift in primacy between establishing new bonds of affiliation and establishing new bonds of attachment. At first, ties to community have primacy with the linkages to parents available as a source of relief from loneliness; later, new attachments have primacy. Cutrona and Russell, as was noted earlier, found that among college freshmen loneliness generally meant marginality to community, whereas among college seniors it generally meant the lack of someone with whom life might be shared. Affiliative ties appear to be of greatest importance as young people seek to find their bearings in independent life.

Persisting Alliance

Persisting alliance, a sense of a bond based on commitment by each to the well-being of the other as an end in itself, without reference to community of interests, is found above all in kin ties. Indeed, when individuals not actually kin attempt to establish such bonds they are apt to say they are like kin or to designate their relationships in the terms of kin ties.

Although kin ties provide adults with community just as do friendships, the bond of persisting alliance in kin ties results in a relationship that responds differently to personal reversals such as marital separation. Friends tend at first to be solicitous but friendships fade as lives take different courses; in contrast, kin may initially be supportive or critical or simply confused, but the relationship with them persists (Weiss, 1975). Whereas it seems to be nearly essential to the continuation of a friendship that there be mutual respect, if not actually liking, kin may be highly ambivalent towards one another without the relationship ending: mutual obligations for each to assist the other, all else equal, can be expected to continue, no matter what.

The examination of sibling ties would seem to be a useful place to begin the attempt to understand the development of kin ties. We might guess that bonds to cousins and to collatorals of the parents—aunts and uncles—are similar in character. In any event, sibling relationships are the most important of collatoral kin ties.

My current work with adults suggests that sibling relationships, although frequently peripheral to current life, retain much of the emotional character they had while individuals were growing up and remain emotionally important to them. Individuals seem to carry as an aspect of their own identity an awareness that they have siblings and, when in touch with their siblings, to continue to express toward them their childhood themes of identification, competition, solicitude and resentment.

The work of Dunn and Kendrick (1982) provides evidence that sibling relationships are almost from the very first different from relationships of both attachment and affiliation. Often a child of only 8 months seems able to enjoy a certain measure of joint activity with an older sibling. Even at 8 months there can be enough basis in common understanding for jokes. Dunn and Kendrick report:

> It may well be that even at eight months the younger child's sensitivity to the communicative signals of the elder is so much greater than that of the observer that the nature of the exchange is completely misunderstood by the observer. We were baffled by several of the sibling interactions, such as incidents where there was simply a mutual gaze across the room and both siblings laughed. . . . Shared expectations and routines can become grounds for allusions and jokes, and neither a parent nor still less an observer can be party to all such shared expectations and jokes. (p. 150)

Contrast the nature of this relationship with the affiliative ties being formed by children of the same age. Instead of the very limited mutuality there displayed, here is enough density of mutual experience to furnish a rich vocabulary of looks and sounds and gestures. Nevertheless, the relationship is not entered into for purposes of play; instead play occurs, and takes meaning, from the continuing relationship.

Part of the link to siblings would seem to derive from their being always around, always a part of life. For the younger child this must seem the way it always has been. For the older child the advent of the younger sibling may have taken some getting used to. As Dunn and Kendrick demonstrate, there are great differences from child to child in the intensity of distress on the birth of a sibling, but it is quite common for there to be serious disturbance. Yet both younger and older siblings seem in time to develop a family feeling about each other, a sense of shared membership in an identity-establishing, caring unit.

Of importance may be siblings' recognition that they are each recipients of their parents' emotional investments and so can each count, more or less equally, on their parents' protection. But this means that when in dispute with each other neither child can be sure of the parents' aid. And this, in turn, means that disputes with siblings have a unique potential for triggering separation distress, for the parents may side with the sibling and against the self. Here is strong motivation for avoiding disputes with siblings. And yet, because siblings are always around, and absorb so much of parents' attention, disputes with them become almost inescapable.

One resolution of the resulting dilemma may be some degree of identification—fostered by parents' even-handedness as well as by shared understandings developed through continuing interchange—along with persisting feelings, perhaps muffled, of resentment. Identification would then produce a bond between the siblings. There might, further, be an element of attachment in their relationship, as a second distinct bond. Siblings seem able to augment each other's sense of security simply by their presence. This is suggested by siblings' increased reliance on each other when away from home after parents separate (this is accompanied by increased rivalry within the home) and, also, by the distress of children on extended separation from siblings.

The relationships with their parents of adult children appear to be maintained largely by the kin bond here described, once the earlier bonds of attachment, on the children's side, and of nurturance, on the parents', have faded. Children and parents display the same commitment to support each other, no matter what, that is displayed by many adult siblings, long after the parents' presence has stopped being essential to the children's security and the children's well-being has moved nearer to the periphery of the parents' concerns. Yet even among fully mature adults and their parents, earlier feelings of attachment and emotional investment may be elicited by threat to either, or by either's loss. Attachment to parents and investment by parents in their children can then be seen only to have been latent, unexpressed, until called upon by the threat or loss.

Collaborative Relationships

To enter and continue in relationships whose aim is the accomplishment of some task seems to require both the ability to perform in roles and the ability to understand how others may perform in complementary roles. There is a great deal of theory and empirical research on these issues of role-taking and understanding the perspectives of others. The work of Mead (1934) and Piaget (1955) provided both initial concepts and early research directions. More recent empirical work has established the progression of role-taking from the fantasy (and fantastic) roles in the play of nursery school children through adolescents' actual activities (Gottman & Parkhurst, 1980; see also the review of research in Damon, 1983). Ability to understand the perspective of role partners seems to require long development through childhood and may be insecure until adolescence (Damon, 1983, p. 119).

While the usefulness of play as a vehicle for learning role relationships has been much explored, the motivations for play seem still largely speculative. These motivations may, in part, have to do with expressing and mastering fears and anxieties, as may be the case in the very early peek-a-boo game, but they seem also to have to do with taking joy in developing competencies. Furthermore, among adults, performance within purely collaborative relationships has enormous impact on self-esteem; might this not also be the case among children? It seems fairly common, among latency aged boys at least, for a child to practice a skill in a sport while simultaneously providing a sports announcer's description of how marvelously he is doing.

Investigators of children's play tend to link play with relationships of friendship. Yet even small children seem to understand how to establish narrowly limited play relationships with children whom they do not know. Such relationships may provide a basis for the formation of a friendship, but this need not be their intent. By adolescence children seem able to fill positions on sports teams with the understanding that their linkage to others is narrowly goal-oriented.

Ability to form nonplayful collaborative linkages is sometimes thought to be high on the list of things learned in school. Yet recent research suggests that the ability may be well in place by the time children first enter school. Indeed, there is evidence that children only 18-months-of-age can begin to grasp the distinction between play and work and can enter a work-oriented partnership with a parent or another adult. Rheingold (1982) reports, "As very young children follow their parents through a round of everyday activities, they often spontaneously execute behaviors that if performed by older persons would be labeled as helping." Their "help" may not contribute much to the actual room-straightening or meal-preparing, but the impulse to participate in a productive relationship seems very much present.

Other societies seem more than our own to utilize this impulse in children toward productive contribution (Whiting & Whiting, 1975). In societies more rural and familistic than our own, small children are often assigned such household tasks as babysitting and the preparation of food.

Other Bonds

In relation to the origins and development of other bonds I have identified in adults—nurturance and help-obtaining—there seems less available material. Care of younger siblings and care of pets, along with play with dolls, offer opportunities for display of nurturant behavior. Undoubtedly such behavior is associated with investment in its object just as is nurturant behavior in adults. Undoubtedly, too, there are important differences in the sexes in early display of nurturant behavior. The Whitings found that small girls everywhere display impulses toward nurturance but found variations from society to society in the extent to which small boys displayed such impulses (Whiting & Whiting, 1975). The questions of how such nurturance is produced, what relationships are formed as a result, and how nurturance develops over time seem to me as yet not well explored.

There also seems to me to be as yet little data available for understanding help-obtaining relationships among children. It is evident that adults confronted by challenges such as serious illness or moral dilemma often look for support and guidance to individuals seen by them as possessing special capabilities: physicians or priests, for example. Their bonds to these individuals often contain the security-seeking motivations that children bring to relationships of attachment. Help-obtaining bonds thus appear to involve transferences of a sort. But at what age such bonds first appear and what development, if any, they undergo are issues in relation to which I know of no data. Yet surely, as Zick Rubin points out (personal communication) these must be present in children's relationships to their parents.

Conclusion

Despite what seem to me to be gaps in the research literature, there has been a great deal of work on children's relationships. Yet still lacking may be systematic attention to the origin, emotional importance and development of the bonds that underlie them, with the exception of the bond of attachment in children who are small. That children's relationships change over time is evident; such work might provide a way of explaining, as well as describing, the changes.

The same sorts of issues which have proven important in work with adults might deserve exploration in children. One such issue is the emotional meaning of deficit: the absence of a needed social tie. What does it mean to children to be without affiliative relationships, or opportunities to experience collaboration or to display nurturance?

Individuals do not sequester the feelings produced in their various relationships. Among adults problems in collaborative relationships frequently give rise to tension, and familial relationships are then looked to for support; is this true among children as well? In general, what is the interplay of children's behaviors and feelings in their various relationships?

An ultimate aim in the study of children's relationships might be full understanding of the processes by which the relationships of adulthood are reached. With such understanding it would be possible not only to identify developmental problems but to be more capable of judging the likely worth of interventions designed to help children move more effectively toward satisfactory adult lives.

ACKNOWLEDGMENT

Work on this paper was supported by the National Institute of Mental Health Grant MH31716, "Single Parent Influences on Transitions to Adulthood." The author gratefully acknowledges the editorial help of the volume's editors and of Carolyn Bruse.

REFERENCES

Ainsworth, M. D., Blehar, M. C., Waters, E., & Wall, S. (1978). *Patterns of attachment.* Hillsdale, NJ: Lawrence Erlbaum Associates.

Bowlby, J. (1974). *Separation: Anxiety and anger.* New York: Basic Books.

Bowlby, J. (1979). *Loss: Sadness and depression.* New York: Basic Books.

Bowlby, J. (1982). *Attachment* (second Edition). New York: Basic Books.

Brown, G., & Harris, T. (1978). *Social origins of depression: A study of psychiatric disorders in women.* New York: Free Press.

Cutrona, C. E., & Russell, D. (1982). Transition to college: Loneliness and the process of social adjustment. In L. A. Peplau & D. Perlman (Eds.), *Loneliness: A sourcebook of current theory, research and therapy.* New York: Wiley-Interscience.

Cutrona, C. E. (in press). Social support and stress in the transition to parenthood. *Journal of Abnormal Psychology.*

Damon, W. (1983). *Social and personality development.* New York: Norton.

DeCasper, A. J., & Fifer, W. P. (1980). Of human bonding: Newborns prefer their mothers' voices. *Science, 208,* 1174–1176.

Dunn, J., & Kendrick, C. (1982). *Siblings: Love, envy and understanding.* Cambridge, MA: Harvard University Press.

Freud, A., & Dann, S. (1951). An experiment in group upbringing. *Psychoanalytic Study of the Child, 6,* 127–189.

Gottman, J., & Parkhurst, J. (1980). A developmental theory of friendship and acquaintance processes. In W. A. Collins (Ed.), *Minnesota Symposia on Child Psychology: Development of cognition, affect and social relations.* Hillsdale, NJ: Lawrence Erlbaum Associates.

Harlow, H., & Harlow, M. (1965). The affectional systems. In A. Schrier, H. Harlow, & F. Stollnitz (Eds.), *Behavior of nonhuman primates* (Vol. 2). New York: Academic Press.

Hartup, W. W. (1983). Peer relationships. In P. H. Mussen (Ed.), *Handbook of child psychology (Vol. 4). Socialization, personality and social development.* New York: Wiley.

Henderson, S., Byrne, D., & Duncan-Jones, P. (1981). *Neurosis and the social environment*. New York: Academic Press.

Lieberman, A. F. (1977). Preschoolers' competence with a peer: Relations with attachment and peer experience. *Child Development, 48*, 1277–1282.

Little, R. (1964). Buddy relations and combat performance. In M. Janowitz (Ed.), *The new military*. New York: Russell Sage.

Mead, G. H. (1934). *Mind, self and society*. Chicago: University of Chicago Press.

Piaget, J. (1955). *The language and thought of the child*. Cleveland: World Publishing.

Rheingold, H. L. (1982). Little children's participation in the work of adults, a nascent prosocial behavior. *Child Development, 53*, 114–125.

Slayton, D. J., Ainsworth, M. D., & Main, M. B. (1973). Development of separation behavior in the first year of life: Protest, following, and greeting. *Developmental Psychology, 9*, 213–225.

Wallerstein, J., & Kelly, J. (1980). *Surviving the breakup*. New York: Basic Books.

Weiss, R. S. (1973a). The contributions of an organization of single parents to the well-being of its members. *The Family Coordinator 22*, 321–326.

Weiss, R. S. (1973b). *Loneliness: The experience of emotional and social isolation*. Cambridge, MA: MIT Press.

Weiss, R. S. (1975). *Marital separation*. New York: Basic Books.

Weiss, R. S. (1979). *Going it alone: The family life and social situation of the single parent*. New York: Basic Books.

Weiss, R. S. (1982). Attachment in adult life. In C. M. Parkes & J. Stevenson-Hinde (Eds.), *The place of attachment in human behavior*. New York: Basic Books.

Whiting, B., & Whiting, J. (1975). *Children of six cultures: A psychocultural analysis*. Cambridge, MA: Harvard University Press.

6

The Temporal Course of Close Relationships: Some Thoughts About The Development of Children's Ties

George Levinger
University of Massachusetts, Amherst

Ann Cotton Levinger
Swift River School
New Salem, MA

Friendships and other intimate relationships are central to human existence. When adults are surveyed about what is most important in their lives, they generally mention the people they feel closest to (Klinger, 1977). There is reason to believe that children's priorities are no different. We still remember how our 2-year-old son, shortly after our family had moved away from his birthplace and his first playmates, found a large doll in our new house; announcing its name to be "Friend," he carried it with him everywhere. Older persons also carry their friendships around with them, but are better able to do so symbolically and to maintain relationships over a long distance and a long time.

This chapter discusses development and change in close relationships. Two sorts of models, originally employed for analyzing adult relationships, are considered in regard to children's relationships. One model concerns the interplay between the microanalytic interpersonal events and the macrolevel causal conditions that shape a long-term bond; both domains of variables affect the closeness of an interpersonal relationship. The second model offers a sequential perspective for conceiving of temporal changes in a relationship. Extending these perspectives to children's relationships may help illuminate problems that have hitherto been ignored.

DEFINING A PAIR RELATIONSHIP

To say that two persons have a "relationship" means that each one can and does influence the other. Different theorists have considered such actual or potential interdependence in terms of goals (Lewin, 1948), behavioral exchange (Homans, 1979), and personal outcomes (Kelley, 1979). According to our present conception, the closeness of a relationship between any two persons refers to the degree to which their respective strings of action, thought, and affect are ''causally interconnected'' (Kelley, Berscheid, Christensen, Harvey, Huston, Levinger, McClintock, Peplau, & Peterson, 1983). For example, two former strangers are said to have developed a ''close'' relationship if they have moved from total *independence* (no causal connections at all) to a large amount of *interdependence* (strong, diverse, and durable interconnections) in their actions, thoughts, and feelings. In other words, a relationship consists not only of the individual partners' behaviors and cognitions, but also of the patterns in which each member's strings of events are woven into those of the other.

This conception was first used in the context of adult relationships. Here we explore its implications for children's relationships. Consider, for example, two different pairs of toddlers playing in a sandbox. One pair might play simultaneously but show little influence between its members; the second pair may exchange objects, imitate each other's actions, and build things together. In the first pair, one can observe few ''causal interconnections'' between the children's ''chains of events.'' The second pair, however, exhibits noticeable interdependence; one child's actions trigger responses in the other, which in turn call forth new responses. Observers would therefore surmise that the second pair has a closer relationship than the first.

Microlevel Events

Defining a relationship between two individuals as the existence of causal connections between their chains of events highlights the role of interactive sequences of events and the meshing of each member's intrapersonal happenings (i.e., thoughts or feelings) with those of the partner. This perspective emphasizes that a pair's degree of closeness is indicated by the frequency, diversity, and strength of the influence that flows between the members' chains: How often do the partners interact? How varied are the domains of their interaction? How strongly do they affect each other? The nature of those interchanges—friendly or hostile, nurturant or uncaring, hierarchical or equalitarian, facilitative or interfering—suggests additional defining qualities.

This perspective emphasizes the ''microlevel'' events and interconnections of a pair's relationship. A complementary view, discussed below, emphasizes ''macrolevel'' causal conditions, which include the two partners' personal characteristics, their respective physical and social environments, and their shared relational history (Kelley et al., 1983, Chapter 2). Such contextual conditions continually influence and are influenced by the specific and immediately observable events. Before we examine these general conditions, let us look at some examples of children's interactions at the microlevel.

By the end of their first year, babies begin to relate to one another less as mere physical objects and more as persons who have a potential for responsiveness. It appears that social interchanges—i.e., chains of two or more socially directed behaviors with obvious connections among them—do not usually occur between children until early in their second year (Mueller & Lucas, 1975; Rubin, 1980). Such interaction is a prerequisite for building any substantial relationship.

By the age of three, we can find many examples of children's ability to maintain interaction sequences of considerable length and complexity. In his systematic observations of how children become friends, Gottman (1983) has recorded verbal interactions of pairs from 3- to 9-years-old who played together in the home of one pair member. He observes numerous instances of information exchange, positive reciprocity, the establishment of "common ground," conflict resolution, and self-disclosure (pp. 18–32). He also finds interesting oscillations between high and low mutual responsiveness in such interactions:

> Children continually escalate and deescalate the play, thereby managing both the level of amity and conflict. Coloring side by side, for example, requires little responsiveness from each child and the risk of conflict is low; unfortunately, the chances of amity and self-exploration are also low. Play is both more exciting and more risky when it demands more social responsiveness. Children's progress toward friendship can be described, in part, by the way they handle this complex problem of social management. (Gottman, 1983, p. 74)

In addition to making such precise moment-to-moment analyses, it is possible to study more molar segments of interaction. For instance, one may conclude that two friends have built a relationship with a high amount of closeness if they see each other often, do a wide variety of things together, and have known each other for a long time. In other words, the frequency, diversity, intensity, and duration of interaction are all meaningful dimensions for estimating the extent of a relationship.

A relationship low on all four dimensions—e.g., one between two strangers talking on the playground—is usually considered superficial. One high on most of these dimensions would be considered close, especially if the impact that partners have on each other is intense.

Macrolevel Conditions

We can now see how microlevel interchanges fit into the broader context of a relationship. Figure 6.1 illustrates our basic conceptual model (from Kelley et al., 1983). The bottom part shows a brief segment of an interaction sequence between two persons, P and O. The top part depicts the continuing presence of stable causal conditions—i.e., the interactants' personal characteristics (P and O), influences from their physical and social environments (E_{soc} and E_{phys}), and

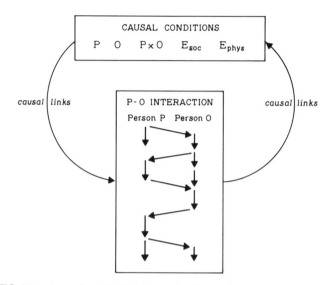

FIG. 6.1.   A causal model of pair interaction. Person-Other interaction is affected by, and in turn affects relatively stable causal conditions, which include P's and O's personal characteristics (P and O), their relationship's attributes (P $\times$ O), and their environmental characteristics (E_{soc} and E_{phys}). Adapted from Kelley et al. (1983, p. 57).

the cumulative characteristics of their relationship (P$\times$O). These causal conditions persist over a much longer time than does any particular interaction sequence but, as Fig. 6.1 suggests, they are causally linked with immediate interaction events in a continuous circular loop. For example, a pair's environment may be conducive to pleasant and rewarding interaction; in turn, the occurrence of such positive interaction often leads partners to seek out suitable environments where they can play together without distraction from others.

Note that Fig. 6.1 is an extension of Lewin's (1951) well-known dictum that "behavior is a function of personality and of environment." To extend that dictum, behavior *in a pair relationship* is a function of the partners' personal characteristics, of their environment, *and* of their previous relationship. This model further emphasizes the circular causal linkage between immediate behavior and long-term conditions. We now discuss each of the three basic types of causal conditions—personal, environmental, and relational characteristics.

Personal Characteristics.   Let us consider three sorts of individual characteristics that are likely to affect one child's interactions with another: (1) the other child's looks or "stimulus attributes," (2) the first child's understanding of the other and the relationship, and (3) the first one's skills at communicating and interacting constructively. All are relatively stable personal dispositions; if changeable, they change only gradually.

1. Stimulus attributes include such personal characteristics as sex, race, physique, attractiveness, commonness of first name, and academic status. Studies of school children have found that each of these attributes is in some way associated with sociometric choice (Asher, Oden, & Gottman, 1977; Hartup, 1983)—i.e., with one child's desire to interact with another. For instance, another's sex or race may be a criterion for merely talking with him or her. Physical attractiveness and commonness of first name frequently affect how children are treated. High grades may increase a child's popularity in school. Temperament and activity level also are attributes that affect social choice.

2. Conceptions about social relationships are a second type of important personal characteristic. Obviously, young children differ greatly from older children in how they *understand* other people. Selman (1981) has formulated a stage model of children's conceptions of close friendship. At Stage 0—at an age period that Selman locates from three to seven, but which may start even earlier—he suggests that children conceive of a friend as a "momentary playmate," defined largely by proximity and interaction. At Stage 0, children have great difficulty differentiating their own viewpoint from another child's. Selman proposes that children later pass through Stage 1 of "one-way assistance" (roughly ages 4 to 9), Stage 2 of "fairweather cooperation" (ages 6 to 12), Stage 3 of "intimate-mutual sharing" (ages 9 to 15), and eventually Stage 4 of "autonomous interdependence" (age 12 to adulthood). Each of these successive stages implies an expanded understanding of what friendship signifies. In other words, Selman proposes that the age of a child—a personal characteristic—sets limits on his or her ability to conceive of pair mutuality.

Other researchers (e.g., Gottman, 1983) have questioned the applicability of Selman's stages for describing real world peer interaction. Children much younger than the ages Selman has specified often show signs reciprocal play and mutual concern. Nevertheless, it is unquestionable that there are important developmental components in the growth of children's understanding of pair bonds. For instance, Lickona (1974) has argued that "a child cannot develop a specific attachment to a particular person until he develops a cognitive representation that fits that person but no other" (p. 35). Thus infants do not show stranger anxiety until they have developed schemas that differentiate between familiar parents and unfamiliar adults; boys do not identify especially with their father until they possess a cognitive representation of father as a model and self as masculine (Lickona, 1974).

3. Interpersonal skills are another type of personal characteristic that is linked to developmental level. Children differ greatly, both across and within age levels, in their abilities to communicate, to listen, and to empathize with others. Such skills affect, of course, their capacity to build and maintain stable peer relationships. Relevant skills may range from a capacity for empathy and communication to athletic prowess prized by their peers, such as the ability to help one's team win consistently at kickball.

Environmental Conditions.   Environmental conditions pertain to the physical environment around Person-Other interaction (e.g., physical space or
noisiness) and to the social surround (e.g., cultural norms or interpersonal ties)
that affect either or both partners. Interaction is affected greatly, for example, by
the physical crowdedness of a situation and by social factors such as whether two
persons share mutual friends or belong to groups that differ in social norms.

Like fish swimming in water, individuals are rarely aware of the influence of
their environment unless it is altered from its usual state. Nevertheless, people's
most "personal" choices are affected by the constraints and the opportunities
offered by their environments. Let us consider instances of how the physical and
the social environment affect interaction.

Inside the home, sheer physical space and material resources govern a significant part of parent-child interaction; whether children have a private room or
share it with siblings, parents, or others affects family relationships in significant
ways (see Bronfenbrenner, 1979). Outside the home, the availability of daycare
and school facilities exert an impact. After children build a friendship, their
ability to meet and continue seeing the friend depends on the distance between
homes and the availability of transportation.

Research on social attraction among adults has repeatedly shown that sheer
physical proximity is highly associated with the choice of friends; the same
seems true among children. For example, our recent interview study (A. C.
Levinger & G. Levinger, unpublished) found that all first graders in a rural
school named as their best friend either a classmate, a neighbor, or a nearby
relative. Striking evidence of the effects of *current* propinquity comes from
pupils' friendship choices in two adjoining fifth/sixth grade classes in the same
school. Almost all the fifth graders had been in the same fourth grade room
during the previous year, as had nearly all the sixth graders a year earlier. Now
these children were divided into two separate fifth/sixth grade classes, but all
were still together at breakfast, lunch, and recess. When asked to "name three
people in the fifth or sixth grades in this school whom you especially like," 83%
of their choices were within their present classroom. Although the children's
interactions were not observed systematically in this study, it is evident that their
most important interchanges occurred primarily with others from their own current classroom.

Another important environmental variable is class size. A study done in an
English nursery school (Connolly & Smith, 1978) found that, when grouped into
small classes of ten, children interacted as a single group with few exclusive
pairings. When three such groups were later merged into one class of 29, children tended to interact in small clusters and to form exclusive buddy relationships. In their initial groups, it had been possible for them to build interactive
chainings within the entire cluster. In the large class, that was less feasible; the
previously established ties maintained themselves and resisted change in the new
context. One wonders what would have happened to their interaction had

these children first been all together in the larger unit? Or how much these findings were due to the young age of these children?

Consider now the effects of the social environment. Research on adults has shown that even private aspects of interaction—e.g., how far people stand from each other and how much they look in each other's eyes—are governed by sociocultural norms (e.g., Hall, 1959). We would wonder at what age such influences become noticeable in children's interaction.

Some research has focused directly on the importance of children's social context. For instance, it has been found that the range of preschoolers' conversations is more restricted in a laboratory context than in the home (Gottman, 1983). More dramatic is the finding of profound upset when a young child is left by the mother, who is replaced for a few moments by a strange adult. Sroufe and Fleeson (this volume) have observed striking differences in an infant's willingness to reach out and explore depending on whether the mother is present or absent.

The social environment also exerts effects in combination with personal conditions. For example, having an ordinary first name or being high in achievement—mentioned earlier as affecting popularity with peers—is mediated by environmental conditions. What is an "ordinary" name depends on place and time: In one school we surveyed recently, there was not a single Jack or Jill but many Jasons and Stephanies. And, although in many schools academic achievement is a source of high status, in others it can be a social impediment.

Relational Conditions.   P×O conditions refer to a variety of interpersonal characteristics, from the match between the Person's and the Other's personal characteristics to their shared goals, jointly built pair norms, and patterns of interlocking role behaviors, all of which emerge out of a pair's previous interactions. Thus, two longstanding friends can enjoy each other's company regardless of either their environment or their individual moods; because they both prize their shared memories and their ability to have fun, they overcome physical, social, and personal obstacles so as to spend time together.

Aside from a pair's relational history, other examples of relational conditions are P-O similarity and complementarity, such as in maturity or temperament. Among children, similarity in age is a strong correlate of friendship (see Hartup, 1983), associated as it is with the ability to interact at a mutual level of interest and skill.

Given similar age, similarity in sex is a potent predictor of friendly interaction through elementary school. For example, Schofield (1981, p. 62) found even fewer "cross-sex adjacencies" than "cross-race adjacencies" in her observations of lunch time seating patterns among sixth and seventh graders in an interracial school. We ourselves recently studied friendship choices of children in different school grades: Among first graders asked to name up to three people they especially liked, only seven out of 55 choices were cross-sex nominations;

among fifth and sixth graders, only three out of 129 choices were directed toward children of the other sex.

Relational conditions often combine with personal and environmental conditions either to maintain or to change a given pairing. In other words, it may take *both* personal and relational readiness for a relationship to progress from one stage to a new one. Or it may take an environmental change—such as the departure of another friend—to transform a formerly casual friendship into a deeper one. Here we can only touch on the countless possibilities that variations in the personal, environmental, and relational conditions noted in Fig. 6.1 can have for Person-Other interaction over either the short or the long run. Having looked at the components of closeness in relationships, though, we are now ready to consider aspects of change over time.

THE TEMPORAL COURSE OF PAIR RELATIONSHIPS

In considering the development and change of close relationships, one becomes aware of the wide variety in type, intensity, and meaning of pair relations. For instance, at the beginning of a relationship, two persons may meet each other's casual wants for novelty and sociability; later, if their relationship should grow, it may fulfill these same people's deepest needs for identity and emotional security. In that case, the relationship will have changed from a mainly affiliative or instrumental tie to a bond characterized by high emotional attachment. Whereas casual affiliations are broken easily and find substitutes readily, attachment relationships "augment the self" in essential ways (Weiss, this volume) and are not broken without some damage to the partners' selves. The breakup of a close relationship not only would cut the interpersonal bond, but also would rupture each individual member's deeply grained *intra*personal chains of action, thought, and feeling (Berscheid, this volume). Such effects need not, of course, be the same for both partners. A relationship may be crucial for one but not for the other partner; one friend may be far more disturbed than the second by the loss of a friendship.

A Hypothetical Sequence

Given the wide variety of relationship types, can one generalize about any normative developmental course? Although the course of a relationship depends on its social and personal functions, some generalizations are possible. All relations have beginnings, middles, and endings. The vast majority of interpersonal relations are superficial, their maintenance takes little effort, and their ending occasions little sense of loss. In other words, most human contacts are weakly connected and have little prospect of becoming very strong. Close relationships, in contrast, are often marked by the partners' concern about buildup and continuation, a desire to prevent deterioration, and distress at the idea of breakup. The partners' interconnections are strong.

The following sequence of potential phases in the course of an extended close relationship can be postulated (Levinger, 1983):

A. Acquaintance with another person.
B. Buildup of a relationship.
C. Continuation and consolidation.
D. Deterioration or decline of the bond.
E. Ending, either voluntary or involuntary.

Although all relationships start with phase A, the later phases are only potential. Few of one person's relationships actually travel in turn over all five phases. For example, of the fraction of one's acquaintanceships that enter the buildup phase (B), many are likely to end before they go farther. And of those few of one's pairings that enter a mature consolidation phase (C), not all necessarily show later deterioration (D). Regarding phase E, the causes, the meaning, and the timing of endings all take many different forms.

This five-phase sequence is a normative conception that enables one to look for processes within phases, as well as transitions between adjacent phases. For instance, one can ask what are the determinants of a move from a casual acquaintance to meaningful buildup (A→B)? Or, after the buildup of strong pair connections, what factors either impel partners toward a more enduring commitment (B→C) or inhibit such a development? Or, during the more stable phase C, what events or ongoing conditions maintain the relationship, and what factors contribute to its decline (C→D)? Finally, if formerly close interconnections have indeed deteriorated, what are the forces that either encourage repair or lead to the ending of the relationship (D→E)?

Adult Love Relationships

Although the development of love relationships differs widely across cultures and across couples in the same culture, the A-to-E sequence applies most readily to this form of pairing. We start therefore by examining changes in adult pairs.

A. *Acquaintanceship.* A major portion of the research on interpersonal attraction has been conducted on this beginning phase, particularly on people's initial impressions and first encounters (Huston & Levinger, 1978). Casual acquaintance is, by definition, superficial. Its interdependencies either have a very short history or they have been limited to a narrow range. Acquaintanceships are usually dominated by the members' external environment. For example, two neighbors carry on their mutual relationship only as long as they continue to live nearby. Or, at work, social norms dictate who eats lunch with whom. The continuity of acquaintanceships depends greatly on the stability of such influences in the individuals' physical and social environment. At this phase, pair interconnections are too weak to survive the impact of geographic separation or of major changes in either member's social norms or social context.

B. *Buildup.* Some relationships progress beyond the surface. The members develop connections that are unique to their own particular pairing. For example, a relationship between neighbors may go beyond casual greetings to sharing some special experiences. Or two coworkers may discover that they really enjoy their lunch time conversations and begin to sit together regularly in the company cafeteria.

The farther advanced a relationship, the more its development resists external monitoring. Whereas it is fairly easy to design research on initial meetings of strangers, it is difficult to trace the establishment of strong and durable pair connections. Thus there are few good studies of mate selection processes. Some accounts (e.g., Altman, Vinsel, & Brown, 1981; Bolton, 1961) emphasize the cyclic nature of the buildup process—an alternation between superficial and deep exchanges, between advances and retreats. Few relationships advance in a clear linear progression.

Nonetheless, theoretical analyses suggest that the building of a relationship is accompanied by a transformation from I-centered to we-centered criteria for judging outcome satisfaction (Kelley, 1979; Levinger & Snoek, 1972). In an acquaintanceship, one typically evaluates the consequences of events or outcomes purely for oneself: What are my own personal preferences, regardless of the other's? Casual acquaintances are often unaware of the nature of each other's needs or preferences.

As a relationship grows, however, partners become increasingly disposed to evaluate their actions with regard to each other's needs. In a recent study of intimate couples, Borden (1983) found that pair members were greatly affected by their partner's outcomes, not only by their own. When each partner was asked to rate his or her preferences for engaging in a series of everyday activities with or without the other, it appeared that pair members' preferences converged in ways that showed mutually oriented transformations. Such convergences appeared to keep conflict at a fairly low level. The more satisfied that partners were with their relationship, the more they behaved so as to maximize the other's as well as their own personal outcomes.

In exclusive partnerships, the transition from Buildup to Continuation generally entails a clear statement of mutual intent that is rare in other types of relationships. Processes of dyadic commitment are a fascinating area for theory and research (see Kelley, 1983); they are essential to the future stability of a pair's continuing interconnections.

C. *Continuation.* Whereas the formation of relationships is marked by instability, novelty, and cognitive arousal, the middle period is accompanied by relative stability, familiarity, and emotional tranquility. Nevertheless, the difference is relative rather than absolute. An established dyad generally faces new, often supradyadic problems. For example, two newly married partners soon face issues of dealing with a household, with in-laws, or with the advent of children; as the "environment" of a relationship expands, so do its challenges. The spouses' previously established interconnections are subjected to new demands; many new connections are likely to be created. The partners' resourcefulness and compatibility in meeting those demands will determine whether their interdependence during this middle phase continues to grow or starts to decline.

D. *Deterioration.* If a relationship begins to decline, how likely is its deterioration to become progressively worse? Although there is little empirical research to answer that question, studies of conflict in close relationships (see Peterson, 1983) suggest that the avoidance of conflicts often contributes to further problems. Blaming or attacking the partner is also associated with difficulties in a relationship (Madden & Janoff-Bulman, 1981), as is a "win-lose" approach to solving interpersonal conflicts.

Deterioration of a long-term relationship is not only linked to the partners' inability to *interact* constructively; it also stems from significant changes in either member's personal or external circumstances. For example, a marriage may be radically affected by either spouse's debilitating illness, by the loss of a job, or by a child's difficulties in school. Earlier coping skills may thus be inadequate to meet the new demands.

If a relationship seems to worsen, there are at least three major ways of dealing with its difficulties—avoiding them, blaming the partner for the problems, or trying to solve the difficulties jointly (see Rands, Levinger, & Mellinger, 1981). Although there has yet been no adequate longitudinal research on processes of deterioration, the former two modes seem to offer little prospect for improvement. The latter mode of coping with conflict is associated with higher degrees of pair satisfaction (Rands et al., 1981), although the precise circumstances under which improvement is feasible require further study.

The repair of a deteriorated relationship may require a combination of personal, environmental, and relational changes, but it can begin with an improvement in just one of these areas that spills over into the other domains. Conversely, as Jaffe and Kanter (1976) pointed out in their analysis of the separation process, strains in a couple's relationship often exert a negative effect on the environments they live in, which in turn worsens their personal dispositions, which then contribute to a further deterioration in their mutual relationship. Eventually such a negative process, especially if it pulls in third parties, can lead to separation and pair termination.

E. *Ending.* Close relationships may end through interpersonal separation or through a partner's death. Either type of ending is likely to leave wounds whose healing requires time. The extent of the pain is associated with the sense of interconnectedness one feels with the other, the extent to which one feels insufficient without him or her. As Weiss (1975; this volume) has noted, the breakup of a close relationship often requires the realignment of a large variety of personal and environmental connections, as well as the building and rebuilding of alternative relational bonds.

Adult Friendships

The course of friendships can also be conceived according to the sequential model used to discuss love relationships. Friendships develop after acquaintance. They build up over time, usually gradually but sometimes dramatically, and they continue on a stable plateau of mutual appreciation and support. Sometimes friendships deteriorate and end through quarrels or abrupt changes; more often, it seems that friends drift slowly, even imperceptibly, out of each other's lives.

One major difference between friendships and romance is in the exclusivity and formality of commitments. In a study of college student relationships, Purdy (1978) found that almost all respondents rated their love relationships high in exclusivity and carried on only one serious romantic relationship at any one time. These same individuals hardly ever rated their friendships as exclusive and found little difficulty in maintaining numerous concurrent friendships. This difference was especially large for males, whose same-sex friendships are generally less intimate than those of females (Dickens & Perlman, 1981).

A second major difference between friendships and romantic attachments may be a function of the first: At their peak, romantic relationships tend to be higher in interdependence and emotional involvement (e.g., Rubin, 1973, p. 221). The rise of friendships generally follows a flatter trajectory than that of love relationships; both their advances and their retreats are less noticeable (Purdy, 1978).

Given the lesser intensity and exclusivity of friendship, how able are observers or the participants themselves to judge the "phase" of a friendship? To what degree can they specify its comparative goodness at different points in time? Purdy's study, in which respondents graphed the magnitude of their involvement over the entire course of several close relationships, found that they were indeed able to make such retrospective judgments, and that members of the same pair generally agreed fairly well in their recollections. Even school children as young as eight or nine are capable of graphing temporal change in their friendships, although their criteria for judging progress and regress appear rather different from those of older people (A. C. Levinger, unpublished data).

THE DEVELOPMENT OF CHILDREN'S RELATIONSHIPS

Looking at temporal changes in a child's relationships entails thinking both about the child's own personal development—physiological, psychological, and social—and about the relationships themselves. Temporal changes in two contrasting types of relationships are examined here: (1) a child's ties to parents, and (2) a child's friendships with peers.

Parent-Child Relationships

A child's first relationships in life are with adults, not with peers. These relationships are characterized by an immense inequality in power, knowledge, skill, and other capacities, that make them qualitatively different from more egalitarian relations. Furthermore, children's relationships with their biological parents carry with them an expectation of permanence. These relationships begin before the child's birth, both in the parents' anticipations and in the physical sensations of a child living in utero; they continue until, and in some ways beyond, a parent's death. Thus their beginnings, middles, and endings differ in meaning from those of peer relationships. Nonetheless, some parallels do exist, especially in children's relations to stepparents or parent surrogates, an increasingly frequent phenomenon. The following two sections consider two different kinds of parent-child relationships: (1) an attachment with a biological mother, and (2) a relationship with a noncustodial parent and with a stepparent.

A Mother's Relationship with Her Biological Child.   The initial acquaintance between mother and child begins with a high degree of attraction and interdependence. Consider an illustration:

> When Sara first saw her son Josh in the delivery room, her initial impressions were influenced not only by her previous experience of his presence in utero, but also by her prebirth anticipations and aspirations. Josh, in contrast, connected mainly with his mother's breast; he had only a fuzzy awareness of her existence, linked largely to the warmth and nourishment she provided him. If, during the first days of his life, his mother were to have left him and had been replaced by a competent substitute, he would probably have been affected only minimally. Even for Sara, had another infant been substituted in those early moments, her maternal attraction could have been transferred to him.

Both child and parent usually experience a "buildup" in their mutual attachment early in the child's life. Within a short time, they establish strong interconnections so that later separation would have traumatic consequences for either of them (Parkes & Stevenson-Hinde, 1982). Each of them, though in very different ways, becomes dependent on the persistence of the bond.

Thus from the early months of infancy, continuation (Phase C) is the normally expected condition of parent-child relationships. Barring family breakup, parents and dependent children are expected to stay together through the child's adolescence. Strong personal, societal, and even legal pressures support the continuance of parent-child relationships at this period.

Although there is more social pressure to maintain familial than peer relationships, deterioration and endings (phases D and E) do, of course, occur. Temporary deterioration of parent-child relations is considered normal at times when childen are trying to emancipate themselves from their earlier dependency.

Especially during adolescence, and again when grown children are establishing their own career or household, they are likely to reduce the quantity and often the quality of their interactions with their parents. Such deterioration, difficult as it may be for parents desiring to maintain the former closeness, does not generally portend breakup or ending; there is the expectation of future continuity and of restoration of former ties.

Endings of parent-child relationships do occur, either through death or through discord. In previous eras, it was not uncommon for a parent to die while a child was young; today, it is far more common that endings occur through parental separation or divorce (Bane, 1979). In the United States today, a large proportion of children—a percentage approaching 40%—will not live out their childhood in the same household with both biological parents (Furstenberg, Nord, Peterson, & Zill, 1983). And more than a fourth of these same children will later, after the remarriage of their custodial parent, experience the subsequent breakup of their new family (Furstenberg et al., 1983).

How children experience the ending of parental relationships is a relatively unstudied topic. For example, a recent volume on human attachment considers some of the implications of early parental loss for children's later feelings of depression (Parkes & Stevenson-Hinde, 1982), but the long-term effects of parental loss or the breakup of parents' marriages are exceedingly difficult to evaluate (Levitin, 1979). There is a need for solid prospective longitudinal research to study the processes of adaptation beyond the near-term crisis period.

Relationships to Noncustodial Parents or Stepparents.   If a child's biological parents separate, the child and the noncustodial parent will have a markedly different relationship than if they were living together. Consider the following case, where a little girl's relations with her father changed markedly after the end of her parents' marriage, and where she also developed a new attachment to a stepfather.

Jenny, age three, had rarely had any long periods alone with her father before he and her mother were divorced. After the divorce, Jenny had dinner alone with her birth-father every week and stayed at his house every second weekend. During this time, her relationship with him progressed from their earlier more superficial contacts to a fairly solid sense of continuity and mutual regard. A year later, when Jenny was four, her father was transferred to another state. Frequent visits were no longer possible and Jenny's mother objected to Jenny's spending long periods far away from her home. For these and other reasons, Jenny now has not seen her father for over two years, and their ties to each other seem to have declined.

In this case, the father has tried to maintain contact through writing and telephoning, and the relationship is likely to continue; at a future time, their ties may be reestablished. However, in the national survey of families by Furstenberg and his collaborators (1983) at least half of the children in divorced mother-custody families reported no contact at all with their absent father during the year prior to the survey. Such children have to deal not only with the ending of their parents' marriage, but also with the ending of their own paternal contacts.

Overlooked until recently (see Spanier & Furstenberg, in press) has been the development of new relationships with surrogate parents. The literature on childhood attachment (e.g., Parkes & Stevenson-Hinde, 1982) so far appears silent on that topic. Here the previously discussed phases of acquaintance and relational buildup, germane to deepening relations among former strangers, are especially appropriate. Before considering them abstractly, let us examine Jenny's experience a year later.

> Jenny is now in the process of developing a relationship with Mark, the man her mother is living with. Jenny likes Mark, and likes having him live with her mother and her. It is Mark who fixes her breakfast and takes her to nursery school each day. The two of them have become good friends.

> When her mother and Mark began planning to get married, however, Jenny became noticeably worried. "If you get married, then Mark will leave," she finally told her mother. That had, of course, been Jenny's previous experience of what happens after marriage. After accepting Mark's and her mother's reassurance about this, Jenny spent weeks exploring the meaning of such a change in the parental relationship: For example, could she be sure that, when Mark becomes her stepfather, he can still be her friend?

In other words, Jenny, who had progressed through the acquaintance and buildup phases with Mark, wanted to be sure that his marriage to her mother would mean continuation, and not a decline and ending of her relationship with him.

There are often major changes in a child's relationship with a new adult when the relationship moves from early acquaintance and buildup into a continuation phase. This person, in his or her early acquaintance with the child's natural parent, is likely to be more indulgent toward the child than after the formal relationship becomes one of stepparent and stepchild. In the absence of systematic research data on the processes of adaptation between children and their stepparents, we merely mention the following case.

> After Derek and Daniel's mother moved away, they found great comfort in going next door to the neighbor's house. The neighbor, Carolyn, was concerned about the boys. She kept a cookie jar available, and she tried to take time to listen to the boys' troubles. About a year later, Carolyn and the boys' father became seriously interested in each other. After they finally decided to get married, Carolyn's role with Derek and Daniel changed. She began to feel responsible for such things as their table manners and how their clothes looked. When there was a call from school, she became more likely to answer the phone than their father. She also began to

expect help with household chores. All of these things introduced drastically new behaviors and responses into her relationship with the boys.

In a recent book on stepfamilies, Einstein (1982) urges stepparents to leave issues of discipline to the birth parents, largely so as to facilitate the building of new ties between self and stepchild. But even if such advice is followed, living with a stepchild—or with a stepparent—is very different from just spending a Sunday together. The transition from a casual relationship to a more committed one is large indeed.

Traditional schemas applied to children's relations with their birth parents do no easily fit those with surrogate parents. For example, an older child begins a relationship with a stepparent with far less dependence and more equality than does a younger child. And the presence or absence of stepsiblings would also make an important difference. Since we lack systematic evidence concerning the formation and maintenance of relationships between children and surrogate parents, we here raise some questions for future study.

For instance, are there general processes by which stepchild-stepparent relations move from early acquaintance to later attachment? What are common temporal changes in each one's knowledge about and feelings toward the other? How are these changes affected by the child's and the adult's personal characteristics—e.g., by their age or gender? How are the changes affected by their social environments—especially the child's birth parents, siblings, and possible stepsiblings, and the adult's relations to the child's parents? How do other relational variables enter the equation—e.g., the strength of the adult's commitment to the new family?

Answers to such questions, even if they are only partial answers, will help illuminate the dramatic differences between attachments to biological parents and those to sociological parents. In some instances, the course of children's relations with their stepparents may more nearly aproximate that of peer relationships.

Children's Friendships

Let us now look at the development of children's relationships with their peers. For children, as for adults, few relationships pass through all five phases. The large majority of acquaintanceships stay at that level, although a portion of them do progress to intimacy and later become subject to deterioration and breakup.

If we wish to consider whether two children are likely to develop a fully mutual relationship of considerable durability, though, we must also take account of each individual child's degree of personal development. For example, it is widely believed that young children are unable to empathize with another person's outcomes, one of the criteria for forming a deeply mutual pairing (e.g., Lickona, 1974; Selman, 1981). A cognitive-developmental perspective suggests that the building of intimate relationships requires greater capacities than young children normally possess. Nevertheless, other observers (e.g., Gottman, 1983) suggest that children as young as four may construct long-lasting friendships that resist geographic separation.

Our own contacts with 3- and 4-year-olds, and even 2-year-olds, confirm that they are often able to provide substantial emotional support to one another. Here are several instances; all of them refer to children from the same preschool group.

> Joey's mother reports that, by age two, children from his group would get very excited whenever they saw each other in town or at a park. They would run over and greet each other eagerly.

> When Steve, just turned three, was at home on weekends, he would repeatedly speculate (in less than full sentences) about what he thought Cara, his best friend in daycare, might be doing just then. And, whenever Cara and he met again after a long weekend or a vacation, they would hug each other enthusiastically.

> Jason's parents were divorced when he was not yet four. At that point he turned for help to one of his friends at daycare. Jason's father had left, and his mother was in no shape to reassure him, but Sara—only two months older than he—provided ongoing solace and support.

These examples suggest that rather young children may become quite interdependent with one another and may be capable of caring for each other in surprisingly mature ways. On the other hand, we can find examples of older children and adults whose relations are marked by a seeming *in*capacity to care for or empathize with each other. Thus Lickona (1974), in commenting on the concept of "mutuality" as a characteristic of deep interpersonal relationships, has suggested that only a minority of adults are capable of conducting relationships beyond the norms of "role-bound conventional morality" (p. 47). Nonetheless, it is clear that children's abilities to build or maintain close relationships do grow with age. The following discussion, however, does not attempt to account for age differences.

A. *Acquaintance.* The large majority of children's relations remain at the level of acquaintance. Classmates work and play together, but a child's departure from the class is not felt as a great loss by most of the other children; the connections are too weak and too limited for such a disruption to have much effect.

Acquaintanceship is determined mainly by proximity, by the mere opportunity to get to know someone. Young children rarely have the opportunity to seek out acquaintances among a broad range of alternative partners. In one of our interviews with elementary school children about their friendships, a 6-year-old boy described such an acquaintanceship very simply: "I met Mike when I was five and he was four. He lives next door."

Among schoolmates or neighbors, children tend to interact most with those who are most like themselves. Similarity in choice of activities, in energy level, and in skills affect choice of playmates.

B. *Buildup of a friendship.* Given that proximity and similarity help to establish the field of potential friends, the strengthening of a relationship may occur in a variety of ways. Our field research, in which we interviewed elementary school children and asked them to write essays about friendship, yielded numerous examples of the beginnings of friendship.

A 10-year-old boy, recounting the start of his friendship with his current best friend, said: "I got to be good friends with Terry in kindergarten. He spilled paint on me, so I spilled paint on him, and then we started dumping paint on each other. That's how we got to be good friends."

In this case, their strong initial effect on each other led to an expansion of further interactions.

Two 11-year-old girls, Liz and Mandy, wrote independently about the beginnings of their friendship two years earlier. Liz said: "Mandy came to this school in fourth grade. Nobody wanted to play with her. They called her names and she felt bad. I knew how she felt. People never called me those names, but they used to call me others. So I decided to be her friend."

Mandy wrote as follows: "When I came to this school, everyone hated me. They called me names and only one person understood how I felt. Her name was Liz."

Whether suddenly engaging in a shared activity or recognizing mutual sympathies, the move from mere acquaintance to the beginning of friendship is furthered by evidence that one's presence has special significance for the other.

C. *Continuation.* In children's friendships, as in those of adults, changes are often gradual and little attended to by those involved. The Continuation phase could refer to the continuation of any sort of friendship that entails interconnections of moderate closeness over an extended period of time. Here, though, we consider mainly "best friend" relationships.

When asked about the difference between "friends" and "best friends," a 10-year-old girl answered as follows: "A friend is someone you just like. A best friend you like better than a friend; you play together at recess, you go out together, you have sleepovers—you do a lot of things together." In other words, this phase is marked by high diversity and frequency of interaction, and an ability to affect one another very strongly.

This phase is also marked by expectations of high duration. Eight-year-old Amy says of her friendship with Stephanie: "She is my best friend and probably will still be when I get to tenth grade." For some children this phase is signaled by a stated commitment—such as 6-year-old Joseph's "good buddy" pledge, or the formal promise to be "best friends forever" made by Marcia and Sue, aged 11. Most elementary school children appear to think that their present best friendship will last indefinitely.

Some relationships begun in childhood do indeed continue into adulthood. Best friends in nursery school do occasionally become college roommates. A grade school romance does once in a while become a marriage. And kids who play kickball together at school recess may play in the same adult softball league. Although the objective probabilities are small, children at this age often believe they are high.

Deterioration.   There are difficulties, of course, in maintaining a close friendship over time. Friends may move apart either geographically or psychologically. Children's relations are affected by such changes even more than those of adults.

Geographic changes—to another neighborhood or school district, or even to another state—are usually decided on by parents. And, if there is such a move, children find it more difficult to keep in touch with old friends than do adults.

Psychological changes are also beyond their deliberate control. As children grow older, their abilities, interests, and even values change. It often occurs that friends develop in a different direction or at a different pace. As one older girl explained, "Sometimes a kid grows up and sometimes the friend doesn't. So then all of a sudden you find you don't have anything in common. You like boys and she's still interested in dolls" (Selman & Jaquette, 1977, p. 172). Writing about a past friendship, a 12-year-old girl in our study said: "That year was the best year we had together. Even though I was in third grade and she was in sixth grade, we still got along great. The next year was the worst year; she went to junior high; and I didn't see her any more."

When children move to another town, it is difficult for them to maintain their old friendships, although some do continue at a lessened level of intensity. A 10-year-old girl speaks of a friend who now lives a thousand miles away:

She's been a great friend since nursery school. I met her and loved her. She did a lot for me, 'cause I was going through a rough time. We used to fight, but that just got us to like each other even more. I wrote to her and sent her a Christmas present this year. I don't get letters from her, but I called her two weeks ago.

Another 10-year-old child, whose friend moved about 30 miles away, says:

I was sad when Nadine moved, but mostly it was something else. I was afraid she would make new friends and like them better than me. But I've visited her on weekends and she's visited me, and that's fun.

E. *Endings.* Some relationships withstand moves and are maintained despite them. Others break apart. At the end of an essay describing her friendship with

Julie, a 10-year-old girl writes: "My friendship broke up when Julie moved away and I didn't call or see her any more. Soon she had other friends to go rollerskating and have sleepovers with, and then she forgot about me." A 9-year-old boy writes: "When I went to Scotland I met a boy who was my best friend in all my life. We would still be friends, but I had to leave Scotland."

Breakups occur also for other reasons, of course. An 11-year-old girl writes: "When we broke up, it was because another girl came into school and my friend became good friends with her. She started palling around with the new girl and forgot about me."

A more sudden instance was communicated by a 7-year-old boy: "Mike was my best friend. But, one day, he threw around my baseball cap when we were playing ball. We had a fight and now we aren't friends any more."

The last two examples, both from elementary school children, suggest that the terminated friendships had been highly unstable. Such instability appears less probable with children's increasing age (Lickona, 1974). Lickona suggests that at least two reasons may account for the increasing stability of friendships at older ages. One is that children's interests, which lie at the base of many friendships, are less likely to fluctuate as they grow into adolescence. A second is that "cognitive-structural changes in the experience of emotion and the self" (p. 49) permit adolescents to absorb quarrels without suffering damage to their relationships.

The intensity of distress at a breakup depends on both the importance of the friendship and the availability of alternative friends. Although many friendships end with little pain or trauma, during the course of childhood most boys and girls do experience pain over the loss of one or more good friends.

CONCLUSION

Children's relationships, like those of adults, undoubtedly differ widely and progress along varied paths. This chapter goes only a small distance toward illuminating the development of children's connections with parents or with peers. To go much further will require systematic descriptive data from prospective longitudinal research.

Nonetheless, we believe that such research can benefit from a focus on both specific, transient interactive events and general, enduring causal conditions— i.e., partners' personal characteristics, their social and physical environments, and the cumulative properties of the relationship itself. Figure 6.1 shows the circular loop that describes the causal interplay among both the immediate and the long-lasting factors in a relationship.

This chapter has also considered examples of the interconnections between partners and the ways that such connections develop over the course of a relationship. Both parallels and differences between adults' and children's relationships have been noted at each of the major phases—at acquaintance, buildup, continuation, deterioration, and the ending of a pair's ties.

Numerous issues that we have touched upon deserve fuller treatment elsewhere. Here we mention only two.

It remains uncertain how children's cognitive and emotional capacities limit their abilities to form stable, long-lasting interpersonal ties. Gross differences across wide age gaps are easily noted, but most generalizations seem to suffer from numerous exceptions. For example, Selman's (1981) model of the successive social-cognitive stages of friendship seems to be a good fit for his interview data from the "child philosophers" in his cross-age research population. As others (e.g., Gottman, 1983; Rubin, 1980) have previously suggested, however, it does not necessarily describe the actual interaction that takes place outside of the interview room. Also relevant is the fact that adults' relationships—and ways of thinking about them—are also likely to be limited. Adults frequently show limitations in empathy and imaginative reciprocity, and an inability to move beyond conventional morality (Lickona, 1974). Such issues blur contrasts between children's and adults' orientations and thus pose a challenge for comparative research.

Another issue that we considered in this chapter concerned the increasing frequency of today's children having to form relationships with new parent figures who enter their family life after the breakup of their parents' marriage. Such new relationships differ markedly from those between children and their birth parents. They put into question earlier norms and generalizations about child-parent ties. This topic now deserves intensive research attention.

REFERENCES

Altman, I., Vinsel, A., & Brown, B. A. (1981). Dialectic conceptions in social psychology: An application to social penetration and privacy regulation. *Advances in Experimental Social Psychology, 14*, 108–160.

Asher, S. R., Oden, S. L., & Gottman, J. M. (1977). Children's friendships in school settings. In L. G. Katz (Ed.), *Current topics in early childhood education* (Vol. 1). Norwood, NJ: Ablex.

Bane, M. J. (1979). Marital disruption and the lives of children. In G. Levinger & O. C. Moles (Eds.), *Divorce and separation: Context, causes, and consequences* (pp. 276–287). New York: Basic Books.

Bolton, C. D. (1961). Mate selection as the development of a relationship. *Marriage and Family Living, 23*, 234–240.

Borden, V. M. H. (1983). *Transformations in married and cohabiting couples*. Unpublished master's thesis, University of Massachusetts, Amherst.

Bronfenbrenner, U. (1979). *The ecology of human development*. Cambridge, MA: Harvard University Press.

Connolly, K., & Smith, P. (1978). Experimental studies of the preschool environment. *International Journal of Early Childhood, 10*, 86–95.

Dickens, W. J., & Perlman, D. (1981). Friendship over the life cycle. In S. Duck & R. Gilmour (Eds.), *Personal relationships: 2. Developing personal relationships* (pp. 91–122). London: Academic Press.

Einstein, E. (1982). *The stepfamily.* New York: Macmillan.

Furstenberg, F. F., Jr., Nord, C. W., Peterson, J. L., & Zill, N. (1983). The life course of children of divorce. *American Sociological Review, 48,* 656–667.

Gottman, J. M. (1983). How children become friends. *Monographs of the Society for Research in Child Development, 48* (3, Serial No. 201).

Hall, E. T. (1959). *The silent language.* New York: Doubleday.

Hartup, W. W. (1983). Peer relations. In P. H. Mussen (Gen. Ed.), *Handbook of child psychology,* Vol. 4, E. M. Hetherington (Ed.), *Socialization, personality, and social development.* New York: Wiley.

Homans, G. W. (1979). Foreword. In R. L. Burgess & T. L. Huston (Eds.), *Social exchange in developing relationships* (pp. xv–xxii). New York: Academic Press.

Huston, T. L., & Levinger, G. (1978). Interpersonal attraction and relationships. *Annual Review of Psychology, 29,* 115–156.

Jaffe, D. T., & Kanter, R. M. (1976). Couple strains in communal households: A four-factor model of the separation process. *Journal of Social Issues, 32* (1), 169–191.

Kelley, H. H. (1979). *Personal relationships.* Hillsdale, NJ: Lawrence Erlbaum Associates.

Kelley, H. H. (1983). Love and commitment. In H. H. Kelley et al., *Close relationships* (pp. 265–315). San Francisco: W. H. Freeman.

Kelley, H. H., Berscheid, E., Christensen, A., Harvey, J. H., Huston, T. L., Levinger, G., McClintock, E., Peplau, L. A., & Peterson, D. R. (1983). *Close relationships.* San Francisco: W. H. Freeman.

Klinger, E. (1977). *Meaning and void: Inner experience and the incentives in people's lives.* Minneapolis: University of Minnesota Press.

Levinger, G. (1983). Development and change. In H. H. Kelley et al., *Close relationships* (pp. 315–359). San Francisco: W. H. Freeman.

Levinger, G., & Snoek, J. D. (1972). *Attraction in relationship: A new look at interpersonal attraction.* Morristown, NJ: General Learning Press.

Levitin, T. E. (Ed.). (1979). Children of divorce. *Journal of Social Issues, 35* (4), Special Issue.

Lewin, K. (1948). *Resolving social conflicts.* New York: Harper.

Lewin, K. (1951). *Field theory in social science.* New York: Harper.

Lickona, T. (1974). A cognitive-developmental approach to interpersonal attraction. In T. L. Huston (Ed.), *Foundations of interpersonal attraction* (pp. 31–59). New York: Academic Press.

Madden, M. M., & Janoff-Bulman, R. (1981). Blame, control, and marital satisfaction. *Journal of Marriage and the Family, 43,* 663–674.

Mueller, E., & Lucas, T. (1975). A developmental analysis of peer interaction among toddlers. In M. Lewis and L. A. Rosenblum (Eds.), *Friendship and peer relations* (pp. 223–258). New York: Wiley-Interscience.

Parkes, C. M., & Stevenson-Hinde, J. (1982). *The place of attachment in human behavior.* New York: Basic Books.

Peterson, D. R. (1983). Conflict. In H. H. Kelley et al., *Close relationships* (pp. 360–396). San Francisco: W. H. Freeman.

Purdy, T. F. (1978). *Perceptions of involvement in close relationships.* Senior honors thesis, University of Massachusetts, Amherst.

Rands, M., Levinger, G., & Mellinger, G. (1981). Patterns of conflict resolution and marital satisfaction. *Journal of Family Issues, 2,* 297–321.

Rubin, Z. (1973). *Liking and loving.* New York: Holt, Rinehart, & Winston.

Rubin, Z. (1980). *Children's friendships.* Cambridge, MA: Harvard University Press.

Schofield, J. W. (1981). Complementary and conflicting identities: Images and interaction in an interracial school. In S. R. Asher & J. M. Gottman (Eds.), *The development of children's friendships* (pp. 53–90). Cambridge: Cambridge University Press.

Selman, R. L. (1981). The child as friendship philosopher. In S. R. Asher & J. M. Gottman (Eds.), *The development of children's friendships* (pp. 242–272). Cambridge: Cambridge University Press.

Selman, R. L., & Jaquette, D. (1977). *The development of interpersonal awareness.* Draft of manual, Harvard-Judge Baker Reasoning Project, Harvard University.

Spanier, G. B., & Furstenberg, F. F., Jr. (in press). Remarriage and reconstituted families. In M. B. Sussman & S. K. Steinmetz (Eds.), *Handbook of marriage and the family.* New York: Plenum.

Weiss, R. S. (1975). *Marital separation.* New York: Basic Books.

7 Emotional Experience in Close Relationships: Some Implications for Child Development

Ellen Berscheid
University of Minnesota

An individual's first close social relationship long has been believed to have a deep and fundamental impact upon his or her later relationships (e.g., Freud, 1933; Bowlby, 1973). Although contemporary views of the developmental effects of early relationships increasingly recognize the plasticity of behavior and the reversibility of certain behavior patterns (e.g., see Cairns, 1979), a person's earliest relationships continue to be regarded as importantly implicated in the patterns of emotional experience and behavior exhibited in subsequent relationships. (For a sampling of hypotheses concerning the impact of early relationships upon emotional experience in marital relationships, see Breger, 1974; Klimek, 1979; Saul, 1979.) Precisely how they are implicated, however, remains poorly understood (e.g., see Strongman's review of the "emotional development" literature, 1978; Izard, 1982; Lewis & Rosenblum, 1978).

Among the many reasons that the effects of early relationships upon later emotional experiences are not yet well defined is the fact that the association between social relationships and human emotional experience itself remains poorly understood. That there is such an association, that relationships with other people are the singlemost important source of an individual's experience of emotion throughout the life cycle, is widely recognized and well documented (e.g., Fitz & Gerstenzang, 1978). As clinicians Albert Ellis and Robert Harper succinctly put it, other people are "the most highly emotogenic stimuli in our civilized environment" (1961, p. 20). Or, as the cognitive psychologist Herbert Simon observes:

In human behavior, situations involving interaction with other human beings are characteristically more heavily laden with emotion than are other situations. A theory of emotional behavior, to be satisfactory, must explain this connection of emotion with social interaction (1967, p. 37).

In this chapter, we briefly describe a theoretical framework (Berscheid, 1983) that attempts to do just that. It relates the causal antecedents of emotion to the properties of close relationships and argues that:

a. Close relationships satisfy the necessary, but not sufficient, conditions for the experience of intense emotion within the relationship, and satisfy both the necessary and sufficient conditions for the experience of intense emotion upon the irrevocable separation of the partners from one another;

b. Participants in a close relationship are "emotionally invested" in the relationship, whether they are consciously aware of it or not and whether or not they frequently experience emotion—positive or negative, intense or mild—within the relationship.

Because this theory represents a synthesis and extension of the conceptual framework for viewing relationship phenomena developed by Kelley, Berscheid, Christensen, Harvey, Huston, Levinger, McClintock, Peplau, and Peterson (1983) and George Mandler's (1975) theory of emotion, we shall first briefly discuss each of these. After doing so, we present the emotion-in-relationships model and discuss some implications it may have for delineating the role early close relationships play in a child's socioemotional experiences.

CLOSE RELATIONSHIPS

Attempts to explicate the "connection of emotion with social interaction" have been hindered by a wide variety of obstacles. Perhaps the most troublesome of these has been the tendency, both within the social scientific literature and within the popular literature, to define a close relationship with reference to the emotions the participants typically experience within it, particularly their positivity and intensity. It is not unusual, for example, for an adult close relationship to be defined with reference to the "love" or "attraction" the principals feel for one another. Indeed, many persons would not consider a relationship to be close unless there exist "strong, positive affective ties" between the participants.

Nevertheless, despite the popular association between strong positive emotional experiences and the closeness of a relationship, there are several reasons why the frequency, intensity, and hedonic sign (positive or negative) of the emotions two people experience in their relationship with one another is not only an inadequate classificatory variable of the closeness of that relationship, but one that obscures an understanding of the emotional phenomena that occur within that relationship as well (see Berscheid, 1983). Among these reasons is the now well-documented fact (e.g., see Straus & Hotaling, 1980) that family relationships—such as those between husband and wife, parent and child, and sibling and sibling, often considered to be the very prototypes of a close relationship—are the most usual setting for the most intensely *negative* emotions people commonly experience. Thus, if relationships characterized by negative affect were eliminated from the investigative domain of "close" relationships, that domain would be suspiciously small.

In addition, classification schemes that depend on observations of the intensity and the hedonic sign of emotions experienced in the relationships must confront the fact that many relationships one would classify as "close" on other grounds are not infrequently characterized by little or no emotional experience, positive or negative, at all. Often, in fact, such emotionally quiescent relationships reveal the fact of their closeness only upon the partners' irrevocable (or perceived to be so) separation from each other and by the severe emotional reactions such separations may precipitate.

Although emotional reaction to separation may itself constitute a useful classificatory variable to distinguish "close" from "non-close" relationships, it presents numerous problems. In adult relationships, for example, the use of an emotional-reaction-to-irrevocable-separation indicant permits the closeness of the relationship to be assessed only posthumously, after the relationship has dissolved. For young children, for whom even the momentary disappearance of a person or object may be perceived to be irrevocable and forever, emotional reaction to separation may be, and has been, more easily assessed and profitably used in a variety of relationship classification schemes. Nevertheless, such an indicant appears to be useful only at certain developmental stages (e.g., before proximity to the other may be symbolically maintained and various temporal continuities learned; see Cohen, 1974). More importantly, however, it is emotional reaction to separation that many investigators of both child and adult relationships seek to predict *before* the fact of its occurrence. Thus, the understanding and prediction of emotional reaction to separation, as well as other emotional phenomena, require the identification and investigation of the variables of which such phenomena are a function.

For these and other reasons, we (Kelley et al., 1983) sought to conceptualize the term "relationship," and the qualifier "close," on grounds other than the emotions and feelings precipitated by, directed toward, or otherwise associated with the relationship partner. Consideration of the meaning of the word "relationship," along with a distillation of its numerous conceptions and usages, revealed that at the core of the term is the notion that two entities are in a relationship with one another to the extent that they have *impact* on each other, or are *interdependent* in the sense that a change in the state of one causes a change in the state of the other (and vice versa). The basic data of human relationships thus concern the ways in which two people influence each other. Specifically, such data allow: (a) identification of the activities (e.g., the thoughts, feelings, actions, etc.) of each person that affect and are affected by the activities of the other; and (b) specification of the nature of the effects of each person's activities on those of the other. Thus, the descriptive analysis of a relationship (which, of course, necessarily precedes the classification of a relationship as "close" or as anything else) focuses upon describing the number, nature, and temporal patterning of the causal interconnections between the activities of two people.

This view of the basic data of relationships is congruent with the views of many psychologists especially interested in social development, beginning most notably with the views of Robert Sears (1951) who emphasized the necessity of interactional analysis for the study of social development, or, the necessity of focusing upon the sequential nature of social interchanges in order to discover how the activities of one person in the relationship influence the activities of the other. It also, more contemporaneously, is compatible with the approach taken by Robert Cairns (e.g., 1977, 1979) to questions of social development. These approaches, like our own, which has focused primarily upon adult relationships, emphasize that the pattern of causal interconnections between two people *is,* at base, the relationship. Nevertheless, recognition of the need "to take into account simultaneously information from both members of the relationship and the context in which it occurs," to use the dyad as the unit of analysis rather than the responses of individuals taken separately, is, as Cairns observes (1977, p. 2), relatively recent within developmental psychology. It is also recent within those branches of psychology (e.g., social, counseling, clinical) that commonly address adult relationship phenomena.

Since it is the causal interconnections between two people that form the substance of their relationship, classification of that relationship presumes not only the observation and description of a time-series of such interconnections, but it also presumes an assessment of certain of their properties. For purposes of classifying a relationship as "close," we (Kelley et al., 1983) have argued that certain properties of the interaction pattern are especially important. Specifically we propose that a relationship may be profitably described as *close* if the two people are *highly interdependent* upon each other, where interdependence is revealed in four properties of their interconnected activities: (1) the individuals have *frequent* impact on each other; (2) the degree of impact per each occurrence is *strong;* (3) the impact is upon *diverse* kinds of activities for each person; and (4) all of these properties characterize the causally interconnected activity series for a relatively long *duration* of time.

Thus, and to use a child friendship relationship as an example, Joe's relationship with Tom might be classified as "close" if:

a. First, Tom's activities *frequently* influence Joe's. Physical proximity is probably a necessary condition for frequent impact, especially when one of the relationship partners is a child; thus, if Joe and Tom are physically together day and night, a probable necessary (but not sufficient) condition for Tom's activities to frequently influence Joe's is established.

b. Second, Tom's activities have a *strong* impact on Joe's activities (e.g., produce responses of large amplitude; numerous responses, etc.). For example, if Tom's new acquisition of a "Cowboy and Indians" video game leads Joe to beg and plead with his parents for one of his own, to take a daily job mowing lawns in order to earn enough money to buy one, to dream about cowboys, to watch TV programs that feature cowboys, to abandon his Hardy Boys novels in favor of Zane Grey, and to refuse to bathe until he gets one, then the change in Tom's activities has had a strong impact on Joe's activities.

c. Third, the impact upon Joe's activities has clearly been to *diverse* kinds of activities; it has caused a change in Joe's interchanges with his parents, as well as changes in his reading activities, his working activities, his TV watching habits, and his bathing habits.

d. Fourth, this kind of frequent, strong, and diverse impact of Tom's behavior upon Joe's behavior has gone on for some time—so much so, in fact, that Joe's parents may be able to predict much of Joe's future behavior simply from observance of Tom's current behavior.

It should be noted that the pattern of interdependence between Joe and Tom may be symmetrical or asymmetrical; that is, changes in Tom's activities may cause frequent, strong, and diverse changes in Joe's activities but the reverse may not be true. Tom may be merely tolerating Joe's perpetual presence (as in the case of an older and younger brother) and may be behaving independently of what Joe is or is not doing. To even get Tom's attention, in fact, Joe may have to shout at him, push him, or otherwise exert a great deal of effort to achieve even a weak impact upon Tom (e.g., a mild disinterested verbal response of "*Now* what do you want?" as he continues to go about his business). Such severe asymmetry is probably atypical of adult relationships (apart from those that develop and are maintained in "closed" field situations [Murstein, 1970]) for a variety of reasons, including the fact that at some point the individual may prefer to interact (where there is a choice, in an "open" field) with persons more "responsive." The question of symmetry or asymmetry of influence has, of course, been of interest even in parent-child relationships, which have been revealed to be not as asymmetrical as was traditionally assumed (e.g., Bell, 1971).

Although this conceptualization of the properties of a relationship that qualify it for the designation "close" has a number of implications for investigating the effect of early relationships on a child's socioemotional development, it shall have to suffice here to underscore that this scheme for classifying a relationship as "close" or "not close" does not depend on the frequency, intensity, or hedonic sign of the emotions the participants typically experience in the relationship. Theoretically, at least, two individuals may be highly interdependent, as evidenced by frequent, strong, and diverse interconnections, and yet typically experience frequent negative emotion, frequent positive emotion, or even little emotion at all within their close relationship. We shortly shall argue, however, that such interdependence satisfies the necessary, although not sufficient condition, for the experience of intense emotion within the relationship.

EMOTION

An understanding of the connection between the experience of emotion and close relationships not only has been hindered by the tendency to define the latter in terms of the former, but also by the conceptual ambiguity and diversity within the emotion literature with respect to its central construct. The term "emotion," along with its legions of synonyms, qualitative modifiers, and adjectival transformations, currently has an extraordinarily wide variety of referents. The myriad problems that result from this state of affairs are exacerbated by the fact that these referents are frequently left unspecified, with only contextual discourse suggesting their nature.

As Hinde (1972) has discussed, the concept of emotion has been used by both scientists and laypersons to: (a) refer to a "category of input" (e.g., "emotional stimuli," although, as Hinde notes, it is seldom stated whether this category is to be defined in terms of the subjective feelings, the physiological state, or the behavior of the actor, or even in terms of the person who presents the stimuli); (b) to refer to "subjective experience" (and, here, the nature of the experience referred to may range from simple pleasant or unpleasant sensory sensations, such as pain, to cognitively elaborate constructions and interpretations of external and internal events, or even to such sensations and constructions only insofar as they are associated with overt molar actions [e.g., Bowlby, 1969]); (c) to refer to a "phase of a process" (e.g., feeling as a phase of a physiological process rather than a product of it); (d) to refer to a "bodily state" (e.g., to a particular configuration of visceral, neurophysiological, and/or motor events that, variously, may be assumed to be relatively brief or to be a state of longer duration, as in an emotional "mood"); (e) to refer to an "intervening variable" (e.g., "anxiety") that helps account for a variety of behavioral patterns, but with no assumptions made about the individual's physiological state or subjective experiences; and (f) to refer to a "response" or pattern of responses (e.g., agitated bodily movement, certain facial expressions, etc.).

Even this listing, and the many possible combinations and permutations of these conceptualizations, does not exhaust the ways in which the term "emotion," and the more generic word "affect," has been, and is, used. The phrase "affective behavior," in fact, currently covers the broadest conceivable range of behaviors and events (including thoughts, sensations, and actions) that are perceived by someone (usually, but not always, the individual doing the thinking, feeling, or acting) as being located somewhere on a "good/bad" continuum (or, are perceived to be good/bad, pleasant/unpleasant, favorable/unfavorable, preferred/nonpreferred, rewarding/punishing, to be approached or avoided, or are otherwise perceived to carry a positive or negative hedonic tone). For example, a preference for vanilla over chocolate is sometimes referred to as an "emotional" preference, and the most dispassionate and lackluster cognitive evaluation of an event as "bad" may be referred to as an "affective" appraisal. As a consequence, the phrase "affective behavior" or "emotional behavior" is not only denotatively useless, it often is also misleading (as discussed elsewhere, see Berscheid, 1982).

Thus, it should be empahsized at the outset that we shall here focus exclusively on a constellation of behavioral events, occurring over a relatively short duration of time within an individual, that include: (a) a change in the individual's internal physiological state (especially the occurrence of autonomic nervous system discharge); (b) the individual's perception that such a change has occurred, along with his or her subsequent "emotional" interpretation of the event of change, an interpretation usually made with reference to the external context in which the event has occurred; (c) overt external changes in behavior, both verbal (e.g., self-report) and nonverbal, often associated with "emotional" states.

It might be noted that the constellation of behaviors outlined above is generally congruent with Lewis and Rosenblum's (1978) delineation of the "essential elements" involved in "affect" for the purpose of exploring questions of affective development. It also might be noted, however, that this particular constellation of behaviors is increasingly referred to as "hot" emotion, in an attempt to distinguish this type of event from others that contain one or more, but not all, of the above elements, including: "cool" feelings (e.g., appraisals of an event or stimulus as "good" or "bad" unaccompanied by physiological arousal); attitudes (e.g., predispositions to respond in a "favorable" or "unfavorable" way toward an object, in the absence of the other events outlined above); moods (e.g., relatively long periods of thinking good or bad thoughts [see Clark & Isen, 1982]); alterations of physiological state, including ANS discharge, unperceived by the individual, or uninterpreted as an "emotional" event, or otherwise unaccompanied by the other elements in the constellation.

All of these other behaviors—feelings, moods, predispositions to approach or avoid certain objects, appraisals of events as good or bad, agitated physiological states, and so on—are important in themselves, rightly belong under the rubric "affective behavior," and thus may be of concern to anyone interested in an individual's "affective development." Feelings, preferences, attitudes, moods, and so on, however, are beyond the scope of the present chapter, and the reader stands warned that the behavioral events of concern here are of the circumscribed nature indicated above.

Antecedents of Emotional Experience: The Mandlerian View

The causal antecedents of this constellation of behavioral events, or of hot emotion, is, of course, the focus of many theories of emotion. The present model of emotion-in-relationships draws upon Mandler's theory of the antecedents and dynamics of emotion, as presented in *Mind and Emotion* (1975) and in *Mind and Body* (1984). Like many other contemporary theories of emotion, Mandler's: (a) takes an *evolutionary perspective,* and thus makes the assumption that the experience of emotion has served, and probably continues to serve, a vital function in the survival of humans; (b) emphasizes the role of *peripheral physiological arousal,* specifically discharge of the autonomic nervous system (ANS), in emotional experience; (c) emphasizes the role of *cognition* in emotional experience, particularly with respect to the individual's assessment of the *meaning* of a stimulus situation in terms of its implications for his or her welfare, in identifying and reporting the emotional state experienced, and in selecting appropriate action alternatives in response to the stimulus event; (d) takes a *continuous loop perspective* of the temporal patterning and action of physiological and cognitive components of emotional experience, and thus makes the assumption that each of these is both stimulus and response to the other, each very rapidly feeding back upon and modifying the other during the duration of the emotional experience.

As suggested above, peripheral physiological arousal, specifically that associated with the ANS, plays a central role in Mandler's theory. In accord with Schachter (1964), Mandler assumes that ANS discharge is a necessary condition for the experience of emotion. The ANS is concerned with those bodily functions that are generally termed "visceral." Its functions are largely involuntary, or "autonomous" of the individual's control. The physiological symptoms so often associated with emotion—the pounding heart and dry mouth, the perspiring hands and clammy skin, the butterflies in the stomach and the flushed face and tremulous hands—are all products of ANS discharge, particularly of the sympathetic nervous system.

ANS arousal has long been considered to be of *physiological adaptive significance* to humans. Cannon (1929) proposed that the responses of the sympathetic nervous system were part of a bodily "emergency reaction," and the notion of a "general adaptation syndrome" of responses that facilitate the individual's "fight or flight" from harmful stimuli was later developed by others. Selye (e.g., 1974) and many other physiologists believe, for example, that the body reacts adaptively with a single general syndrome of physiological responses to stress (or change in its internal or external environment), whether that stress be a severe loss of blood, a snarling dog in our path, or a threatening spouse or parent. This set of physiological responses appears to prepare the individual's body to cope with the stress (e.g., increase in blood sugar level gives the individual an extra boost of energy to fuel the "flight" or the "fight" against the stressor).

Mandler believes that ANS arousal has *psychological adaptive significance* as well. Specifically, he hypothesizes that our perception that we are experiencing ANS arousal warns us, if we are not already aware of it, that there is some stimulus in our external environment to which we must pay attention in order to initiate appropriate action if it should prove that our well-being is at stake. ANS arousal is thus conceived to be a psychological alarm bell that tells us: "Something important is going on out there that may affect your well-being! Pay attention! Something needs to be done!"

Thus, it is proposed that the ANS acts as a "secondary support system" for directing attention to the stimulus situation in which we find ourselves in order to discover its meaning and thus its implications for our welfare. The ANS is only a "back-up" warning system that something has happened that may have implications for our welfare because the ANS is relatively slow; it may not respond until 1 to 2 sec after the stimulus event has been perceived and, thus, we may have already determined the meaning of the external event and have selected an appropriate action in response to it (e.g., we may feel our heart pound only after we have swerved our car out of the way of an on-coming truck). However, if we have not already determined the meaning of the external stimulus event and taken action in those few seconds, then our perception of the secondary and internal event of ANS discharge provides a back-up signal which alerts us that the situation demands that we turn our attention to it to try (or continue to try) to determine its meaning. The psychological adaptive significance of ANS arousal is, then, to ensure that we will attend to, and cognitively evaluate, stimuli for which appropriate action in the interest of personal well-being and survival might need to be taken. At the same time, and as previously mentioned, ANS discharge is physiologically ensuring that should our analysis of the situation lead us to decide or pursue or fight or to take flight, our bodies will be prepared to do so.

As the above illustrates, Mandler conceives of emotion to be integrally related to the functioning of the "mind," a theoretical fiction that cannot be directly observed but whose existence and workings are believed by cognitive psychologists to be revealed through observation of the relationship between the sensory input the individual receives (any and all perceptible events, whether they take place inside or outside the skin of the person) and the individual's observable outputs (e.g., verbal reports, measurable physiological arousal, actions, etc.). It is the "mind" that presumably intervenes between the two and helps us determine, in the light of our past experiences stored in memory, the meaning of a stimulus input to us and, thus, the output we exhibit in response to it, including ANS discharge and the actions we subsequently take. Mandler's theory underscores the old saying that "It is not what happens to a man that causes emotion, but what he *thinks* is happening to him."

If ANS arousal is necessary to emotional experience, and if it also is functionally related to the workings of the mind in terms of prompting further attention and cognitive analysis of a stimulus situation, what kinds of stimulus inputs cause ANS arousal? Mandler argues that the occurrence of events that *interrupt* some ongoing activity or plan is a sufficient, and possibly necessary, condition for ANS arousal. Interruption is thus a sufficient and possibly necessary condition for the experience of emotion; when an individual experiences emotion, an interruption of some ongoing activity has probably occurred.

From the evolutionary point of view, interruption is an important event to any organism. It signals that important changes have occurred in the environment. These environmental changes often lead to altered circumstances of living, adapting, and surviving. The fact that arousal occurs whenever current activity is interrupted has important survival value for, as previously noted, it has preparatory flight and fight functions which will help the organism adapt to the changed environment and it may also serve as an additional signal system which leads to increased attention and information seeking when the environment has altered.

What kinds of stimuli, then, are interruptive? Some stimulus events tend to be interruptive regardless of who the individual is or what he or she is doing at the time. A sudden blinding light, an unexpected flash of pain, a surprising loud noise; novel, unexpected, incongruent, or intense stimuli have long been known to be associated with arousal and attention (e.g., Berlyne, 1960). Mandler's theory, however, calls special attention to the fact that, apart from these universals, what is interrupting to whom and when depends very much on the individual and their on-going plans and activities.

Among these activities often will be *highly organized action sequences of behavior.* An organized action sequence is a series of actions that are emitted as a whole, or as a single unit; when the first action in the sequence is made, the others in the series tend to follow. In addition to their inevitability of completion once started, the individual does not give full conscious attention to the behaviors as they are being executed; the performance of each bit of behavior in organized behavior sequences tends to be "thoughtless," "automatic," or relatively "unconscious." An important antecedent condition for the development of organized behavior sequences is the frequency of use of the sequence, with organization developing gradually. The continuing exercise or execution of a particular action system tends to generate a more tightly organized and invariant structure. Thus, to discover an individual's organized action sequences, the frequency with which a series of actions are performed is a good clue, as are the invariability of the nature of the actions performed and the smoothness of their performance. Another useful clue is a decrease in the actor's conscious attention to the behavioral acts during their performance, and, relatedly, the actor's superior reaction time to extraneous stimuli (e.g., Keele, 1968) and ability to conduct a second activity simultaneously with the series of acts (e.g., Schmidt, 1968).

Many organized action sequences are parts of other organized action sequences, some of which may be parts of *higher order plans.* A child's tightly organized behavior sequence of delivering newspapers each morning, for example, may be a part of the much higher-order plan of buying a new bike. Plans thus involve "goals," or objects and/or events that an individual not only values but also is committed, at least in some degree, to striving for (see Klinger, 1977). Like organized behavior sequences that have been performed in the past, plans also probably vary in their degree of organization and detail (e.g., the vague plan to buy a bike *some day* versus a well thought out step-by-step series of actions that will culminate in buying a bike in 6 months). Higher-order plans, then, may be viewed as response sequences initiated and in some state of completion.

Mandler theorizes that the subjective experience of emotion, and the occurrence of so-called "emotional behavior," generally occurs between the time a highly organized response sequence or plan is interrupted and the time in which either the interrupting stimulus is removed or the individual has found an available substitute response which allows the sequence to be completed. During the "no response" emotional period initiated by the onset of an interrupting stimulus: (a) ANS discharge occurs; (b) attention is likely to be focused upon the interrupting stimulus or a search for it; (c) the interrupting stimulus is likely to undergo a cognitive analysis of its meaning with the aim of selecting an appropriate action, one that allows completion of the sequence or plan that was interrupted. During the period in which the meaning-analysis is occurring, ANS arousal should be increasing. When an action that permits completion is found, ANS arousal should disappear and, with it, the subjective experience of emotion.

In addition to subjective emotional experience, another consequence of interruption is assumed to be a tendency to try to complete the organized response sequence as long as the situation remains essentially unchanged, perhaps by more vigorously performing the actions previous to the blockage (e.g., when the key that has always unlocked the front door in the past now unexpectedly fails to open it, we most likely will persist for some time in twisting the key harder and harder, finally kicking and pounding on the door and perhaps simultaneously showing such *emotional behaviors* as crying and cursing). Or, as Mandler puts it, "Organized sequences tend to follow the dictum: 'If at first you don't succeed, try again'" (1975, p. 156). During the period of redoubled effort, however, the individual should be experiencing emotion as a consequence of the interruption and the failure to complete the sequence. Still another possible consequence of interruption is response substitution, or the completion of the sequence or plan by other organized sequences or plans that are more or less specific to the one that has been interrupted (e.g., if upon driving to work we find that our usual route is blocked, an alternative route we have used in the past may be quickly substituted to complete the sequence). If and when completion occurs, by whatever means, ANS arousal should be "turned-off" and emotional behavior should cease.

To summarize, then, the prime preprogrammed, "wired into the species" releasor of ANS arousal is conceived by Mandler to be unexpected interruption of an on-going activity, especially highly organized behavior sequences and higher-order plans. Interruption is thus conceived to be a sufficient, and possibly necessary, condition for emotional experience. ANS arousal has the effect of constricting attention to the stimulus situation in order to discover the stimulus that is the source of the arousal and its nature and meaning. ANS arousal initiates a cognitive meaning analysis of the stimulus situation (if one has not already been initiated), which is directed toward determining whether action should be taken and, if so, identifying the nature of an action that will protect the individual's interests. During the meaning-analysis, and before an action alternative is determined (if one is available), ANS arousal should be increasing. Thus the interruption of an organized behavior sequence or higher-order plan produces a state of arousal that, in the absence of substitute responses to complete the sequence or plan, then develops into one or another emotional experience depending upon the occasion of the interruption. Interruption, then, may lead to the experience and report of fear, anger, or another emotion, depending on factors (e.g., learned emotional "labels" and interpretations suitable to this particular situation) other than the interruption itself. The resumption of an organized response sequence or plan is one "stop-rule" for ANS arousal and the meaning analysis of the stimulus event; thus, it is also a stop-rule for the emotional experience.

EMOTION IN CLOSE RELATIONSHIPS

Within most relationships, some of the partners' activities that are causally interconnected can be identified as emotional ones; that is, the change in the state of the individual occasioned by a change in the state of the partner will include certain changes in thoughts, changes in physiological state, and changes in overt behaviors such that all of these, when viewed together, will lead an observer to conclude that: (a) the individual is experiencing an "emotion"; and (b) this emotion has occurred "in" the relationship (i.e., a change in the state of the partner, rather than some other change in the physical or social environment, has directly precipitated the emotion). It is, of course, the prediction and understanding of these *emotional events* that occur within relationships that relationship investigators and laypersons alike seek to understand.

Berscheid (1983) argues that if the substance of a relationship lies in the causal interconnections that exist between the individual and the other, and if ANS discharge is a necessary condition for the experience of emotion, and if we entertain the proposal that interruption is a sufficient, and possibly necessary, condition for the occurrence of ANS discharge, then it follows that for the individual to experience emotion "in" the relationship, some event in the other's (O's) series of activities must interrupt something in the individual's (P's) series of activities. And, following Mandler, what it probably must interrupt is a highly organized behavior sequence and/or a higher-order plan. Or, what it must interrupt is an *intrachain sequence;* that is, a sequence of events within P's series of activities in which one event is causally connected to the next event. Further, since this intrachain sequence must be interrupted by an event in O's series, it is clear that for P to experience physiological arousal as a result of an interchain causal connection (and thus for emotion to occur "in" the relationship), some of the events in O's chain must be causally connected to an intrachain sequence within P's series of events (see Fig. 7.1). Thus, the existence of *inter*chain causal connections to *intra*chain sequences may be regarded as a necessary condition for emotion to occur within the P–O relationship.

The existence of interchain causal connections to intrachain event sequences is a necessary but not sufficient condition for arousal (and thus emotion). For emotion to occur, the interchain causal connection must interrupt, or *interfere* with, the occurrence of the remainder of the events in the intrachain sequence (see Fig. 7.2). That is, the events that would have occurred in P's event chain (had O *not* performed O_1 and had O_1 not been causally connected to P_2) do *not* occur (or they occur more weakly, in distorted form, or otherwise show significant variance in strength or form from what would have been expected on the basis of P's previous performance of this intrachain sequence).

For example, the $P_1 \rightarrow P_2 \rightarrow P_3 \rightarrow P_4 \ldots P_n$ intrachain sequence may represent P's laboriously prepared, carefully honed, eagerly anticipated piano recital of "The Volga Boatman" for her parents and grandparents at her birthday party (the performance itself part of her secret higher-order plan to favorably impress her grandparents so that they will finance her attendance at a summer piano camp with her friends). O_1 may represent her brother's application of a transparent film of "Super Glue" to a piano key prominently featured in the second bar of the piece. When O_1 impacts upon P_2, P's response constituting the remainder of her performance ($P_3 \rightarrow P_4 \ldots P_n$) undoubtedly will not be executed as flawlessly as they have so many times before in the past few weeks; in fact, an emotional display (e.g., tears, anger, etc.) is likely to result.

In the context of this example it might be noted that, first, O's behavior is not in itself interfering and interruptive; it is cause for emotion only in association

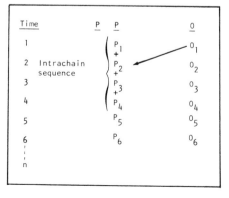

FIG. 7.1. Illustration of an interchain causal connection to an intrachain sequence.

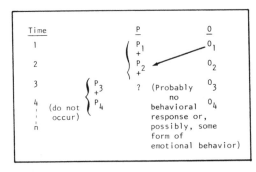

FIG. 7.2. Illustration of an interchain causal connection interrupting an intrachain sequence.

with the fact that the events in P's chain to which they are causally interconnected are highly organized (intrachained) and also part of an important higher-order plan. If O had performed the same behavior somewhat later in the party, immediately before his younger brother's attempted recital of the same piece, his brother (who has feared that his lack of interest, practice, and general ineptitude was about to be revealed) might: (a) show little emotional reaction to the interruption, since there was not much of an organized action sequence, and no higher-order plan, in the process of execution; or (b) might even find the unexpected interruption of his dreadful performance to be hilariously funny—an occasion for a positive emotional experience, since it allows premature and unexpected completion of *his* secret higher-order plan (e.g., to vacate the piano, the party, and the house as soon as possible to go swimming). (See Berscheid, 1983, for a discussion of predicting the hedonic sign of the emotion experienced.[1]) Thus, the same behavior performed by O may be interruptive in one relationship, noninterruptive (or even facilitative) in another, and, further, if the event has been interruptive, the fact of interruption itself does not dictate the hedonic sign of the emotion subsequently experienced.

Interchain causal connections to intrachain event sequences are not always interruptive. Sometimes they *facilitate* and augment the performance of the next event in the individual's sequence. Many relationship interactions are instances where one person's intrachain sequence could not be performed well, if at all, were it not for the occurrence and appropriate timing of the other person's

---

[1]Positive emotion, it is argued, is associated with events that are interrupting but are, at the same time, perceived by the individual not only to be benign but *enhancing,* rather than destructive, of his or her welfare. At least three classes of stimulus events have these properties: (a) Events which, although they are unexpected and interrupting while occurring, may be terminated by the individual at will (e.g., an exciting carnival ride); (b) Events that suddenly and unexpectedly remove the presence of a stimulus that has previously interrupted an action sequence or plan; and (c) Events that produce the unexpected and sudden *completion* of highly organized sequences of behavior or higher-order plans that have not been previously interrupted, but which have been proceeding "on schedule" as expected. This last is congruent with Carr's (1929) contention that "Joy is awakened by the sudden and unexpected attainment of a highly desired end."

response that helps stimulate and make possible the next response in the individual's sequence. In adult marital relationships, these may include sexual activities, getting the kids ready for school, and so on.

Often, of course, especially in long-term close relationships, *both* P and O are simultaneously executing highly organized intrachain sequences, and events in each person's chain facilitate the performance of the other's sequence. In such cases, the two intrachain sequences are meshed, as contrasted to: (a) *unmeshed* sequences, where there are no causal connections between the two intrachain sequences simultaneously occurring (when they are "disengaged," so to speak); and (b) *nonmeshed* sequences, where the causal connections between the two intrachain sequences interfere with the enactment of one or both (See Fig. 7.3).

Meshed event sequences show all the characteristics of other highly organized behavior sequences: (1) Given the initial stimulus, the full chain of responses, on both P's and O's side, tends to run off, thereby revealing their character as a single unit rather than discrete responses; (2) Little variation in the nature of the sequence, the form and timing of the responses, is observed; (3) The behaviors are performed smoothly, rapidly, and without a great deal of conscious thought, sometimes allowing other activities to be pursued simultaneously. These characteristics, as well as their repetitive occurrence in P and O's event chains, permit their identification as meshed event sequences. Meshed sequences also often can be identified as having existed when one person, through sickness or absence or for other reasons, fails to do "their part" and the partner's sequences become disorganized. On these occasions, the failure of one person to provide the appropriate responses at the appropriate time in sequence are interruptive of the other person completing the sequence and probably constitute a sufficient condition for emotional behavior.

If the relationship is characterized by a great number of meshed intrachain sequences, however, and if they stay meshed, there should be little occasion for the experience of emotion in the relationship. Further, participants in such relationships may be unaware of this property of their relationship. Events (and people) who interrupt us not only are the source of our physiological arousal, and

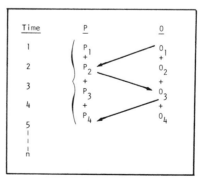

FIG. 7.3.   Illustration of a meshed causally interconnected intrachain sequence.

thus our subjective experience of emotion, but they can successfully compete for our attention and can command and dominate our thoughts. Since the emotional system largely appears to be a "trouble-shooting" system, where there is no trouble—where there are only meshed facilitative interactions—there also should be relatively little attention to, and conscious awareness of, the interactions. Over time, and as an interaction pattern becomes increasingly integrated and organized, it should recede from awareness and become "automatic" and unthinking. Berscheid (1983; Berscheid, Gangestad, & Kulakowski, 1984) hypothesizes, therefore, that while participants in relationships characterized by non-meshed intrachain sequences may be acutely conscious of the relationship overall and of the partner as well, those in well-meshed relationships may not be so aware. They may, in fact, be seduced by the emotional tranquility of the relationship to discount their emotional investment in it, only to discover, when the relationship is dissolved, how much the relationship means to them, as evidenced by their severe emotional upheaval upon the termination of the relationship.

It is thus not difficult to see why emotional reaction to dissolution of a relationship (or to irrevocable separation) may be a good index of the "closeness" of the relationship. Upon separation, all of the hidden and long forgotten meshed interconnections are unmasked to wreak their emotional vengeance upon the individual. Myriad facilitative interconnections are interrupted, and each interruption should cause the absent partner and the former relationship to painfully surge into the surviving partner's conscious awareness.

In brief, this model argues that while close relationships probably should not be defined in terms of either the magnitude or the hedonic sign of the affect that is typically experienced within the relationship by the participants, such relationships *are* generally characterized by emotional investment; that is, there is considerable *potential* for emotional experience within a close relationship, whether or not that potential has been actualized and whether or not the participants themselves are aware of it. The proposition that close relationships are also emotionally invested relationships rests upon the assumption that as the number, strength, and diversity of the interchain causal connections between the participants in a relationship increases, the probability that a significant number of these are facilitative to intrachain event sequences also increases.

The emotional investment of each partner thus is defined by the number and strength and diversity of the facilitative interchain connections to that individual's intrachain event sequences. The emotional investment of each individual in the relationship may be unrelated to the frequency, intensity, and quality of the emotion the individual typically experiences in the relationship, or to the frequency, intensity, and quality of emotion the individual has *ever* experienced in the relationship (e.g., where facilitative interconnections have imperceptibly grown over a long period of time without conscious effort). Thus the absence of frequent or intense emotion in a relationship is a poor index of either closeness of the relationship or the degree of emotional investment of the participants. Relationships may be emotionally quiescent because: (a) there are no interchain connections to intrachain event sequences (and thus there is no emotional investment in the relationship); and (b) there are many interchain connections to intrachain events, and the relationship is highly emotionally invested, but the interconnections are facilitative. In the latter case, the full degree of the partners' emotional investment in the relationship is most likely to become evident upon dissolution of the relationship.

SOME IMPLICATIONS FOR CHILD DEVELOPMENT

The present framework suggests that what is developing in an early relationship that has implications for later emotional experience include, at minimum:

a. Organized action sequences and plans whose execution require the participation of another person (i.e., facilitative interchain interconnections are required to complete these intrachain sequences), which, if these sequences are later interrupted, satisfies a sufficient condition for emotional experience;
b. Expectancies, whether capable of being verbalized or not, about the probable sequences of events, including those that occur in relationships with other people of certain characteristics, which later may be disconfirmed;
c. Substitute responses that may permit previously or currently facilitated sequences and plans to be completed through the individual's own effort and without the need of external facilitation.

We shall use a broad brush to sketch how these may engage, first, the question of with whom a child is likely to develop a close relationship; second, emotional reactions to relationship dissolution; and, third, some cognitive consequences of interruption.

Relationship Development

With whom the individual is likely to develop a relationship, and the properties of that relationship (e.g., "closeness"), obviously depend on a number of factors, many of which have been discussed by Cairns (1979). Here, we shall mention only a few of these, highlighting similarities between the development of child–adult and adult–adult relationships.

First, in children's relationships, as well as in adult relationships, the development of a close relationship that is characterized by many facilitated and/or meshed interaction sequences probably depends importantly on the number and nature of the individual's preexisting organized behavior sequences (some of which may be given at birth) and higher-order plans, the number and nature of the partner's sequences and plans, the degree to which these "spontaneously" mesh (i.e., immediately mesh without special effort on the part of the individual and the partner) and, when they don't: (a) the degree to which each individual is *capable*, through effort, of making them mesh; and (b) is *motivated* to expend that effort.

Thus, for example, the development of a relationship with another human (e.g., infant) or animal (e.g., a pet cat) who possesses only a limited repertoire of responses, as well as limited motor and cognitive abilities to develop new responses (e.g., brief attention spans, primitive cognitive structures, poor motor coordination) usually requires that the more capable partner carry the burden of developing the relationship, with the less capable partner's limitations dictating the terms. Where there is no spontaneous meshing, and where the able partner does not have a behavioral repertoire that allows him or her to quickly make facilitative connections (e.g., perhaps because such responses have not been previously learned through interaction with other infants or cats), the development of these is no easy task even under the best of circumstances and even for extraordinarily capable humans. As the columnist Ellen Goodman observes in the case of parents who delayed having children until they believed they were optimally capable of coping with the experience:

> Even successful people who deal with large problems efficiently have to learn new skills to deal with little people. Goals, five-year plans, five-hour plans, all pale in the face of a six-month-old with his own agenda. Parents of newborns, willy-nilly, live in The Now, and The Now is a 3 a.m. feeding. Whether they are 40 or 25, they experience the same stress. . . . (*St. Paul Dispatch,* January 7, 1983).

The "stress," of course, results from the interruption of many of the sophisticated partner's sequences and plans, which also satisfies a sufficient condition for a variety of emotional experiences on this partner's part.

Whether the more capable partner will expend the necessary effort to develop the relationship (or, in the case of an infant-adult relationship, will quickly call in an experienced nanny, grandmother, child-care center, etc.) probably depends on a number of factors, including where the development of a relationship of a particular nature with this specific individual fits into this person's hierarchy of higher-order plans (e.g., to be a *good* mother; to avoid arrest for child-neglect; to prevent conflict with the spouse) and the resources available to them. Sometimes a close relationship is possible, but one or both persons are not motivated to make it so, perhaps because of the demands of other relationships or alternative activities necessary to the achievement of other higher-order plans. For example, it may be within an adult's capacity to engage in a great deal of facilitative interaction with a child, but to do so would be interruptive of the execution of other sequences and plans (e.g., to earn a living, to maintain relationships with other children, the spouse, etc.).

In other cases, of course, the potential relationship partners may similarly possess limited repertoires, and if these do not spontaneously mesh, then no relationship may be possible (e.g., as in an infant-infant pair). This holds true in adult relationships as well. It requires, for example, an extraordinarily skilled and motivated partner to "play" tennis with a person who has never played before; while the sophisticated partner may manage a semblance of meshing their responses with the individual's, two novices may spend their entire time chasing balls and soon weary of the endeavor. Thus, motivation without ability isn't enough, and some pairs, involving both children and adults, are undoubtedly like the pot and the kettle floating down the river in Aesop's fable. While both would *like* to be close companions on their journey downstream, the properties of the kettle make interaction injurious and interruptive to the pot, and since it is not within the capacity of the pot to make itself less breakable nor within the capacity of the kettle to make itself less hard, a close relationship simply is not possible however much it is desired. For this reason, even in some adult relationships no amount of "working on the relationship" produces the desired result; one or both partners simply are not capable of developing the requisite responses (e.g., poor hand-eye coordination precludes their becoming an acceptable tennis partner, limited intellect precludes their making facilitative responses on the chess board; and physical pain and ill health may preclude their performing a wide variety of responses needed to facilitate the partner's sequences and plans).

Even when a close relationship has developed, people, even adults, grow and change and, so, not infrequently "out-grow" relationships. The behaviors of the other person that were once facilitative may now be interruptive. For example, the child who returns from nursery school with new shoe-tying and clothes-buttoning skills may find his partner's formerly facilitative acts now get in the way of his performing these sequences himself; similarly, while a marital mate's solicitous aid to a novice in the culinary arts may be welcome for a while, until these skills are learned, if they continue ever after, they may become a source of interference and irritation. When one person in the relationship is rapidly changing, for maturational reasons or due to outside influence (e.g., schooling, the development of third-person relationships, etc.), the chances of the individual outgrowing the original relationship should be maximized. Partners in child relationships, as in adult relationships, may differ in the extent to which they encourage the development of new behavior sequences and plans (e.g., through encouraging the person to expose themselves to external influences and develop new relationships), as well as the extent to which they encourage the development of responses that allow the individual to substitute for the partner's facilitative responses and so perform sequences and achieve plans without external aid. Some, of course, actively try to prevent and inhibit these to protect and maintain their own relationship with the individual.

In any event, the question of with whom, and why, a child develops a close relationship encompasses a wide variety of questions (see Cairns, 1977, 1979), all of which have implications for later emotional experience. This may be most easily seen when later reactions to dissolution of a specific relationship are considered.

Emotional Reactions to Relationship Dissolution

Emotional investment in the relationship, it will be recalled, is conceived to be a function of the partner's facilitative causal connections to the individual's organized action sequences and plans. With respect to relationships involving infants, this view is compatible with that of Cairns who hypothesizes that "To the extent that environmental events become synchronized with and supportive of the ongoing activities of the young, a 'bond' or preference tends to evolve" (1979, p. 55), and ". . . preferences evolve when the infant's activities become organized around or dependent on some property or properties of the other animal" (1979, p. 73). Thus, Cairns proposes that "*Response systems,* not organisms, become 'attached' to stimuli . . ." (emphasis added) (1979, p. 56). Like adults, then (see Berscheid, 1984), infants are hypothesized to prefer to interact with (e.g., as revealed through approach tendencies, etc.) people who facilitate the execution of their organized behavior sequences (and, in the case of older children, higher-order plans as well).

It will also be recalled that, at least in adult relationships, emotional investment in a relationship is often revealed when the partners are irrevocably separated and suffer the interruption of numerous sequences and plans whose completion depended upon their partner's responses. It has been hypothesized (see Berscheid, 1983) that even in adult relationships, the partners are often unaware of, and cannot accurately report, their degree of emotional investment because: (a) well-meshed interaction sequences are often "automatic," "unconscious," and are not subject to awareness; (b) the meshing may have occurred "spontaneously" or have developed so gradually that it *never* was a matter for conscious deliberation, effort, and thought; (c) interfering, nonmeshed, interruptive interactions *do* command attention and awareness, leading participants to overestimate the extent to which they interfere with each other (and at the same time, because of [b] above, *under*-estimate their degree of meshing). Thus (and apart from substitution possibilities, to be discussed shortly), emotional distress upon separation is conceived to be a better index of emotional investment than self-report, even in adult-adult relationships.

Emotional distress, as evidenced by vocalization and agitation, to a relationship dissolution perceived to be irrevocable has, of course, been of great interest to those who have focused upon the caretaker-child relationship and, indeed, has been taken as a good index of the "emotional bond" or "affective attachment" of the child to the caretaker. Although various explanations have been offered for the observation that infants cry when they are interrupted, and that this is an important class of events antecedent to symptoms of emotional distress (along with hunger and pain, which themselves may also be interruptive), the framework of emotion offered by Mandler and extended here argues that the human organism is constructed in such a way that interruption, at *any* stage of development, frequently signals a change in the environment, is attended to, results in ANS discharge (or "arousal"), and leads to responses whose function often is to remove the interruptive stimulus. Again, this view is eminently compatible with Cairns' contention that ". . . separated-induced crying is one aspect of a more general process; hence one does not need to propose a special mother-infant motivational system to explain the effect" (Cairns, 1979, p. 104).

However, to predict the severity and duration of the interruption-inspired emotional responses, the present framework calls special attention to the necessity of considering the availability of *substitute responses* that permit the completion of the interrupted sequences. In the case of infants, of course, these undoubtedly are few, and, in fact, vocalization and agitation may be the *only* responses available to remove the interruption. For example, the infant whose feeding is interrupted by the mother (who herself may have been interrupted) cannot walk over to the table and recapture the bottle. An older child often can, however, and so the interruption, and the emotional distress, may be only momentary in the latter case. Thus, as the child grows older, he or she learns substitute ways to complete organized sequences of behavior without the necessity of facilitative responses from others.

Much of early child-rearing is directed toward helping the child become independent of others' facilitative responses (e.g., teaching the child to feed himself). How much, and how fast, the child moves toward such independence from the relationship probably depends on a wide variety of factors, including the capabilities of the child to make the necessary responses as well as the extent to which others encourage these either by default (i.e., simple failure to continue to make facilitative responses) or active promotion of independence. An example of the latter is described by Berscheid and Fei:

> The lengths to which parents will go to foster the American ideal of independence in their children is described by former chief medical consultant to Project Head Start, Robert S. Mendelsohn (1975). The father of a three-year-old boy told Mendelsohn that, because he had lost his job, his wife would be going to work at the same day-care center that his child was currently attending. Mendelsohn remarked that this would be a good arrangement, for it would be reassuring to the child to have his mother close by. Mendelsohn's response horrified the father. He and his wife did not want their boy to be *reassured,* he protested; they wanted him to be *independent!* In fact, to encourage their three-year-old's self-reliance, they had already planned for the child and his mother to take separate buses to the day-care center (1977, p. 108).

The point here is simply that whatever interruption the loss of a mother for 3-year-olds generally occasions, for this little boy, disruption of his daily routine of getting himself to the day-care center isn't going to be one of them! And, so, other things being equal, his emotional reaction to such a loss should be less.

In the beginning, however, responses to disruption appear to be limited to vocalization and agitation, these increasing with the extent of the disruption (see Cairns, 1979), with few or no substitute responses in the behavioral repertoire present or possible. Vocalization and agitation undoubtedly continue throughout the life cycle to be useful responses to partner-inspired interruptions; even in adult-adult relationships where the individual is interrupted by the failure of the other to perform their accustomed facilitative responses, and even where substitute responses are possible, vocalization and agitation are frequently used first (as any spouse can testify) since they often serve to prompt the inattentive and negligent partner to do their part.

Vocalization and agitation not only serve to bring the individual's situation to the attention of the partner, but they also bring the individual's distressing situation to the attention of others who, if they can make the necessary facilitative responses (i.e., these exist in their repertoire) and they are also willing to do so, may permit completion of the interrupted response sequences or plans. Thus completion may be achieved through the substitution of responses or the *substitution of partners*. The availability of a third person who can and will immediately substitute for the partner—who can and will facilitate the performance of the interrupted sequences and plans—ought to quickly quell the emotional distress, if the "stop-rule" for emotion is the completion of interrupted sequences and plans.

These hypotheses are generally compatible with the results of Spitz and Wolf (1946) who found that children who were judged to have the "closest" relationship with their mothers showed the most disruption after separation, and with Cairns' interpretation of these and similar findings:

> These results should not be too surprising. Those children whose responses are dependent upon the unique cues provided by their mothers should be the ones who would be most seriously disrupted by her absence, because they have the most to lose. Rather than protecting the child from the traumatic effects of separation, the focalized relationship could make subsequent social adaptations even more difficult for the child (1979, p. 135–136).

They *could*. But the present approach also emphasizes that whether or not they *will* depends on the nature of the child's social environment. Specifically, it depends importantly on whether alternative relationships are available to the interrupted individual and whether these relationship alternatives will permit the interrupted sequences to be completed. The more unique the sequences are to the pair, however, it is probably true that the less likely suitable substitute partners are present in the environment. In the case of long-term adult relationships, for example, partner substitution is often difficult because the meshed sequences developed over a long period of time are both numerous and highly idiosyncratic (e.g., it is difficult, if not impossible, to find a single other person who enjoys backgammon as well as bird-watching, who is also a vegetarian, who also . . . , etc.).

Thus, the present framework calls special attention to the child's social environment in predicting the impact of current relationships, specifically the behavioral sequences and expectations developed within them, upon later emotional experience; that is, such prediction rests not simply upon the number of facilitative interchain connections to intrachain sequences in the original relationship, but also upon: (a) the extent to which independent substitute responses exist in the individual's repertoire; and (b) the extent to which substitute partners are currently (or will be, given future interruptions) available in the social environment.

The social environment of children usually includes, of course, peers as well as adults and these may constitute able substitute partners for some sequences. For example, the child who played catch with his father every night after school may, given his father's extended absence, start playing catch with the little boy next door, given that he is lucky enough to have such a person in physical proximity who can play catch and who is also willing to do so. For the only child who lives, for example, on an isolated farm, the loss of the father, and the interruption of this and other routines that cannot be completed alone, is a severe loss indeed and ought to occasion, other things being equal, a stronger emotional reaction to interruption than in the former case.

Consideration of the availability of substitute partners thus requires consideration not only of the density of the early social environment, but of the behavioral repertoires and motivations of the people in it, specifically whether others constitute able and willing substitute partners. The facilitative responses in the original relationship may be such that they can be performed by anyone willing to do so in the social environment or they may be highly idiosyncratic in relation to behavioral repertoires represented in the environment. In this connection, Cairns comments that "Margaret Mead (1962) has observed that children who grow up in cultures where several adults share in the caretaking are better able to tolerate separation" (1979, p. 36). (Presumably Mead meant separation from any *one* of them, not all!) This observation, too, is compatible with the present framework, and deserves to be true for several reasons. First, the instance of several caretakers rather than one (just as where there are several spouses rather than one) virtually guarantees that emotional investment in any one relationship will be less. Second, it may be hypothesized that where there are several caretakers, the *kinds* of behavior sequences the individual develops will be more representative of those capable of being performed by other people in the social environment rather than unique, since it may be supposed that each partner's behavioral repertoire represents, first, some overlap with those of others in that same environment and, second, some degree of uniqueness; thus, interaction with multiple partners should assure that sequences with commonality will be learned well and unique ones less well, since they would be performed less frequently, and, so, substitute partners for the well-learned sequences should be more likely to be available.

It should be noted that, like projections of the impact of early relationships upon later emotional experiences, value judgments about the goodness or badness of an early relationship (or constellation of relationships) depend importantly on the conjunction between the early relationship and the individual's later physical and social environment, rather than simply upon the nature of the early relationship(s) alone. In making a similar point, Hinde (SSRC Conference) cites a study by Altmann (1980) of baboon mothers and their infants. High-status mothers were more laissez-faire and permissive with their infants than the less dominant, who tended to be more restrictive of their infants' movements, with the consequence that these infants remained dependent on the mothers longer than their peers. Whether the laissez-faire or the restrictive relationship is *good* or *bad* thus depends, in part but importantly, on the projected probabilities that: (a) predators are likely to be in the environment of the unrestricted infants; (b) the mother will die and leave an infant who cannot fend for himself. If the former probability is high and the latter low, the laissez-faire relationship is *bad* for the infant; it is *good,* however, if the probabilities are reversed.

To take an example closer to home, and to illustrate that adults with whom the child is in early relationship undoubtedly make projections about the future physical and social environment of the child and that these influence the nature of their relationships with the child, consider the following account related by Joseph Persico, Nelson Rockefeller's speech writer. Persico and a number of other aides and officials were summoned to fly through a blinding snowstorm to the Rockefeller residence in up-state New York on a Saturday morning:

The servant took drink orders, Nelson addressing him in French, and we quickly settled into reviewing the latest draft of a budget message from the Governor to be delivered to the state legislature. T. Norman Hurd, then state budget director and a leading authority on public finance, was explaining a passage when a towheaded child bounded into the room. Dr. Hurd stopped as Nelson swept three-year-old Mark, his youngest son, onto his knee. As Dr. Hurd started to speak again, Mark began talking. Nelson stopped to listen, not to Dr. Hurd but to Mark. Hurd stopped too, with a frozen smile. Thus we plodded on, halting whenever Mark had something to say. "Yes, that's right, Marky. That's a two. And that number is a nine. See, we're on page twenty-nine," Nelson patiently instructed his son. Everyone grinned on cue.

I thought of how I was raising my own children. I did not like them to interrupt when I was talking to friends, and I did not enjoy having other people's howling Indians intrude on good conversation. But, little Mark went on happily having his say, while his father responded and we waited. Nelson Rockefeller was passing along an unspoken lesson absorbed from his own father—"These people work for us. Never mind their age, their position, they defer to you." Thus are young princes bred. I was doing it all wrong (1982, pp. 16–17).

Persico wasn't "doing it all wrong." Nor was Rockefeller. Each father was (consciously or not) making different assumptions, and probably correct ones, about the future social environments of their respective children and the likelihood that behavior patterns developed now would later be interrupted (and with what effect) by people in those environments.

To summarize, the present framework suggests that the extent to which dissolution of a relationship is likely to result in emotional distress depends on: (a) the number of highly organized behavior sequences and plans interrupted; (b) the availability of substitute responses that allow the individual to complete the sequences and plans himself or herself and without the aid of another person; and/or (c) the availability of substitute partners, which depends upon the nature of the social environment and the uniqueness of the sequences with the original partner in comparison to those in the repertoires of others in the environment. Further, given that highly organized response sequences recede in awareness and that estimation of the emotional effects of interruption requires consideration not only of the individual's substitute response repertoire but also of the availability of substitute partners in the social environment, this framework also suggests that asking an individual to report (e.g., in child custody cases) how much they would like to maintain a relationship with one person as opposed to another, is as problematic in children's relationships as it is in adult relationships. It is highly unlikely that most individuals can accurately calculate their degree of emotional investment in a relationship before the fact of dissolution.

The view that the emotional system permits the individual, throughout the life cycle, to respond to interruptive events that signal changes in the environment leads us now to briefly consider the role that the emotional system may play in cognitive development.

Cognitive Consequences of Interruption

Interruption of organized behavior sequences and higher-order plans, it will be recalled, is conceived as a sufficient condition for ANS discharge, which, in turn, is generally regarded as a necessary condition for the experience of emotion. Some of the cognitive consequences of interruption have been outlined in the preceding sections, with special emphasis upon constriction of focal attention to the interruptive event and accompanying cognitive processes directed toward interpretation of it, particularly its action implications. Thus, the consequences of interruption are conceived to be both *emotional* and *cognitive,* with each of these inextricably and integrally intertwined in a single process that carries a number of implications not simply for emotional development, but for cognitive development as well.

Piaget (1952, 1981) was perhaps the first to observe that surprise, an essential ingredient of interruption, may play an important role in cognitive development. His views, along with an historical review of the treatment of the construct of surprise in psychological theory, has been presented by Charlesworth (1969), who has himself developed a careful and stimulating analysis of the role of surprise in cognitive development.

Charlesworth begins by discussing the correspondences and discordances between the construct of surprise and the constructs of "orienting reflex" (a term coined by Pavlov), "startle" response, and "novelty," concluding that, "The term surprise implies more than any one term" and that "there is little to be gained from reducing surprise to the OR, novelty, or startle" (1969, p. 277). Surprise is viewed as implying:

(1) a known, and hence potentially manipulable set of external stimulus circumstances that bear a particular relationship to (2) certain measurable dispositional properties of the individual loosely referred to as cognitive structures that are viewed as responsible for the production of (3) expectancies that both aid the individual in responding to the stimulus circumstances at the moment and also determine the total physiological changes and overt responses that occur when the expected outcome of the stimulus circumstances is discordant with the stimulus circumstances themselves. The whole chain of events that entails both structural (cognitive) and dynamic (emotional) systems in the organism properly constitutes the surprise phenomenon and helps distinguish it from such phenomena as startle, the OR, and novelty (1969, p. 278).

Surprise, like interruption, then, is viewed as resulting from a disconfirmed expectancy, which calls attention to the fact that in order to experience surprise, the individual must have some expectancies, or notions about the lawful sequence of events. No expectancies, no surprise:

The capacity to be surprised . . . requires an ability to recognize a signal and anticipate or expect the event the signal signifies; it is a capacity that develops slowly over time and at different rates in different areas of cognitive competence. There is ample anecdotal and observational evidence indicating that a child can be totally insensitive to the implications of a particular stimulus situation not being fulfilled at one age, and then very sensitive a few months later when he shows a pronounced surprise reaction if the sequence is violated (1969, pp. 272–273).

Expectancies thus presuppose cognitive elaboration, which, in turn, presupposes previous experience from which inferences about event contingencies have been formed.

Charlesworth points out that the relationship between the capacity to experience surprise and the existence of cognitive structures it presupposes has rarely been used to *diagnose* an individual's level of cognitive development. Rather, verbal responses and motor behavior in the form of instrumental responses are customarily used to make such assessments, while involuntary overt motor behavior (e.g., facial expressions, postural changes) and autonomically mediated responses (e.g., GSR) in response to violation of expectancies have been neglected in assessment of cognitive competence. These are, however, as Charlesworth emphasizes, directly suggested by the functional links between expectations (cognitive structures), surprise, attention, and subsequent cognitive development:

(From Charlesworth, 1969, p. 259)

Charlesworth goes on to outline a number of interesting questions raised by a consideration of the role of surprise in cognitive development (for example, "Does the surprise reaction actually become more intense over time as the child improves his capacity to make increasingly more precise expectancies, but less frequent as his expectancies prove to become more and more veridical as a consequence of structural development?" (1969, p. 287). Simon (1967), too, asks a similar question with respect to the extent to which social interaction will precipitate emotional responses. Space does not permit discussion of these questions here, and it shall have to suffice to note that surprise is presumed to play an important role in children's further cognitive development (or elaboration) just as it is theorized (Mandler, 1975) to play a crucial role in adult cognitive development (i.e., further cognitive elaboration and/or cognitive reorganization via the cognitive—meaning analyses and information seeking that are precipitated by interruption). Emotional events, then, throughout the life cycle, appear to be associated with cognitive development.

It might be pointed out, however, that while there is an obvious relationship between surprise and interruption, the two concepts are not identical. Interruption always presumes surprise, or the disconfirmation of an expectancy (i.e., an *expected* interruption is, by definition, not interruptive), but surprising events may not necessarily be interruptive (or, at the least, the amount of interruption they generate may be exceedingly small). The concept of interruption thus calls special attention to the individual's ongoing activities at the time the unexpected event occurs and to how the unexpected event impinges on those activities. The difference between surprise and interruption, in other words, is the difference between discovering, on a lazy Saturday morning, that the neighbor's new car has developed a flat tire and discovering that one's *own* new car has developed the same thing on Monday morning when one is already late to an important meeting. In both cases, the event is surprising; in the former, however, nothing much is interrupted, while in the latter, a great deal is. Or, to put it another way, the implications of a surprising event may be impersonal and largely academic; the implications of an interruptive event never are—they are always personal.

Thus, the present framework would suggest that, first: (a) the use of involuntary overt motor behavior and autonomically mediated responses as assessments of cognitive structure are most likely to be useful when the structures involved are representations of the individual's own activities and these structures are currently engaged or in the process of enactment; (b) the use of such involuntary motor and autonomically mediated responses is not only an alternative but preferable to the use of verbal responses in such cases since, with children as with adults, there is no guarantee that the individual is aware of, or can accurately report, these expectations (indeed, if these sequences have been over-learned and have become automatic and unconscious, verbal reports may be especially unuseful).

Second, and as a corollary, the current framework would suggest that further cognitive development is *most* likely to occur when the individual has been interrupted, as opposed to merely surprised. This point is illustrated in the tale of the two farmers in the wagon behind the old balky horse who refused to respond to all signals to proceed left rather than the usual right at the fork in the road. The horse undoubtedly found it surprising that his master was signaling him to turn in a new direction, but no response was evident and the horse was content to remain stationary. Finally, the other farmer said that *he* could teach the old horse the new trick, jumped off the wagon, picked up a board, and whacked the horse forcefully on the head, remarking, "*First,* you have to get his attention!" Interruptive events are attention getting and, by the very fact that they are interrupting of ongoing sequences and plans, they are also "motivating" of cognitive work and remedial action. And since, as Mandler notes, interruptive events more often than not precipitate negative emotions (and see Berscheid, 1983), the oft-heard phrase "No pain, no learning," while not wholly true, of course, does suggest that negative emotion probably does precede new learning quite frequently.

Consideration of the role that interruption plays in inspiring new responses (and the cognitive development and/or reorganization accompanying these), along with the frequent association between interruption and negative emotional experience, suggests, again, how difficult it is to judge the goodness or badness of a relationship simply by considering the hedonic sign of the emotions experienced within it. Interfering interchain connections to intrachain sequences in the relationship may precipitate negative emotional experiences but result in long-term benefits to the individual. In adult–adult relationships, for example, the relationship may be characterized by many facilitative interchain connections (and an absence of negative emotion), and yet the relationship may be unhealthy and destructive to the individual in terms of his or her *immediate* survival and welfare (e.g., as in a relationship between two drug addicts, each of whom facilitates and enables the other's drug dependency) and in terms of the individual's *future* welfare and survival (e.g., a wife whose husband encourages her dependency upon him in all matters, economic, social, etc., but who is likely to die before she does). The latter consideration, of future welfare and survival, is presumably paramount in parents being, often reluctantly, the frequent precipitator of negative emotion in the child (e.g., "You hate me for this now, but you're going to thank me when you're older").

This is, of course, another reason why the individual's verbal report of the goodness or badness of the relationship (if it is based on the hedonic sign of the emotions frequently experienced in it) may or may not correspond to the goodness or badness of the relationship in an absolute sense, if that is taken to be the degree to which the relationship promotes the individual's survival and welfare. Such assessments also may not correspond to the individual's later assessment of the relationship, since children, as well as adults, not infrequently *do* later feel gratitude for others who have precipitated painful, but valuable, learning experiences. But, as previously discussed, whether the facilitation or interference of various behavior sequences and plans is survival enhancing or destructive depends, in part, upon the actual nature of the child's future environment, which, while there are many universals, is undoubtedly somewhat unique to each human. In any event, interruption within a relationship, even a good deal of interruption, may not necessarily be a bad thing. Continual interruption, for an individual, however, may be life-threatening (e.g., see Mandler, 1982), just in terms of the physiological responses it precipitates (e.g., possibly suppression of the immunological system) and, further, constant interruption from the environment may lead to self-conceptions that do not lead to further development of new responses but, rather, lead to negative self-conceptions (e.g., Seligman, 1975; Coopersmith, 1967) that make it even more unlikely that new response repertoires will develop in the future.

SUMMARY COMMENT

In this chapter, we have tried to illustrate how a number of different, but traditionally separate, theoretical concerns and areas of inquiry may be, perhaps must be, integrated with one another. First, we have emphasized that human emotion, as it is most often experienced *in vivo* and *in situ,* occurs within relationships with other people. Thus, an understanding of human emotion ultimately requires an understanding of its functional relationship to the context within which it most frequently occurs. We have presented, then, a model addressed to the antecedents and dynamics of emotion as it occurs in social relationships.

Second, we have tried to underscore the necessity of interactional analysis for an understanding of all phenomena that occur within social relationships, including emotional phenomena. In doing so, we have also tried to emphasize the necessity of interactional analysis for relationship classification (e.g., "close"), as well as some of the difficulties involved in placing value judgments on early relationships.

Finally, and most importantly, in sketching some of the implications of the present model of emotion-in-relationships for child development, we have tried to focus upon those implications which serve to illustrate that matters of social relationship development, of emotional experience, and of cognitive development are integral to one another and, further, that they remain so, and in much the same ways, throughout the life cycle. We have tried to emphasize, then, that the cognitive and emotional apparatus we are born with probably continues to function in much the same way throughout life, with the result that whether the participants in a relationship be adult or child or infant, the general principles that govern the relationship in all its aspects, including emotional ones, probably remain much the same. It thus seems especially lamentable that not only are there relatively sharp divisions between theory and research addressed to emotion per se and emotional development, between emotional development and cognitive development, between relationship development and all of these, but, in addition, between theory and research addressed to adult–adult relationships and to child–adult and child–child relationships. The fact that all of the questions subsumed under each of these investigative endeavors concern one organism, and one biological heritage, ought to permit far more integration of theoretical effort than is currently the case.

REFERENCES

Altmann, J. (1980). *Baboon mothers and infants.* Cambridge, MA: Harvard University Press.

Bell, R. Q. (1971). Stimulus control of parent or caretaker by offspring. *Developmental Psychology 4,* 63–72.

Berlyne, D. (1960). *Conflict, arousal, and curiosity.* New York: Academic Press.

Berscheid, E. (1982). Attraction and emotion in interpersonal relationships. In M. S. Clark & S. T. Fiske (Eds.), *Affect and cognition.* Hillsdale, NJ: Lawrence Erlbaum Associates.

Berscheid, E. (1983). Emotion, In H. H. Kelley, E. Berscheid, A. Christensen, J. Harvey, T. L. Huston, G. Levinger, E. McClintock, A. Peplau, & D. R. Peterson. *Close relationships.* San Francisco: Freeman.

Berscheid, E. (1985). Interpersonal attraction. In G. Lindzey & E. Aronson (Eds.), *Handbook of social psychology* (3rd Ed.). Hillsdale, NJ: Lawrence Erlbaum Associates.

Berscheid, E., & Fei, J. (1977). Romantic love and sexual jealousy. In G. Clanton & L. G. Smith (Eds.), *Jealousy.* Englewood Cliffs, NJ: Prentice-Hall.

Berscheid, E., Gangestad, S. W., & Kulakowski, D. (1984). Emotion in close relationships: Implications for relationship counseling. In S. D. Brown & R. W. Lent (Eds.), *Handbook of counseling psychology.* New York: Wiley.

Bowlby, J. (1969–1973). Attachment and loss. (Vol. 1) *Attachment* (Vol. II) *Separation: Anxiety and anger.* New York: Basic Books.

Breger, L. (1974). *From instinct to identity: The development of personality.* Englewood Cliffs, NJ: Prentice-Hall.

Cairns, R. B. (1977). Beyond social attachment: The dynamics of interactional development. In T. Alloway, P. Pliner, & L. Krames (Eds.), *Attachment behavior: Advances in the study of communication and affect* (Vol. 3). New York: Plenum.

Cairns, R. B. (1979). *Social development: The origins and plasticity of interchanges.* San Francisco: Freeman.

Cannon, W. B. (1929). *Bodily changes in pain, hunger, fear, and rage* (2nd Ed.), New York: Appleton.

Carr, H. A. (1929). *Psychology, a study of mental activity.* New York: Longmans, Green.

Charlesworth, W. R. (1969). The role of surprise in cognitive development. In D. Elkind & J. H. Flavell (Eds.), *Studies of cognitive development.* New York: Oxford University Press.

Clark, M. S., & Isen, A. M. (1982). Toward understanding the relationship between feeling states and social behavior. In A. Hastorf & A. M. Isen (Eds.), *Cognitive social psychology.* New York: Elsevier North-Holland.

Cohen, L. J. (1974). The operational definition of human attachment. *Psychological Bulletin, 81,* 207–217.

Coopersmith, S. (1967). *The antecedents of self-esteem.* San Francisco: Freeman.

Ellis, A., & Harper, R. (1961). *A guide to rational living.* Beverly Hills, CA: Leighton Printing Co.

Fitz, D., & Gerstenzang, S. (1978). *Anger in everyday life: When, where, and with whom?* St. Louis, MO: University of Missouri-St. Louis. (ERIC Doc. Rep. Serv. No. ED 160-966).

Freud, S. (1933). *New introductory lectures on psycho-analysis.* New York: Norton.

Goodman, E. (1983). "New parents, new problems at mid-career." *St. Paul Dispatch,* January 7.

Hinde, R. A. (1972). Concepts of emotion. In *Physiology, emotion and psychosomatic illness.* Ciba Foundation Symposium, Amsterdam: Associated Scientific Publications.

Izard, C. E. (1982). Measuring emotions in human development. In C. E. Izard (Ed.), *Measuring emotions in infants and children.* New York: Cambridge University Press.

Keele, S. W. (1968). Movement control in skilled motor performance. *Psychological Bulletin, 70,* 387–403.

Kelley, H. H., Berscheid, E., Christensen, A., Harvey, J. H., Huston, T. L., Levinger, G., McClintock, E., Peplau, L. A., & Peterson, D. R. (1983). *Close relationships.* San Francisco: Freeman.

Klimek, D. (1979). *Beneath mate selection and marriage: The unconscious motives in human pairing.* New York: Van Nostrand Reinhold.

Klinger, E. (1977). *Meaning and void: Inner experience and the incentives in people's lives.* Minneapolis: University of Minnesota Press.

Lewis, M., & Rosenblum, L. A. (1978). Introduction: Issues in affect development. In M. Lewis & L. A. Rosenblum (Eds.), *The development of affect.* New York: Plenum.

Mandler, G. (1975). *Mind and emotion.* New York: Wiley.

Mandler, G. (1984). *Mind and body.* New York: Norton.

Mandler, G. (1982). The construction of emotion in the child. In C. E. Izard (Ed.), *Measuring emotions in infants and children.* New York: Cambridge University Press.

Mead, M. (1962). A cultural anthropologist's approach to maternal deprivation. In *Deprivation of maternal care.* Public Health Paper No. 14. Geneva: World Health Organization.

Mendelsohn, R. (1975). "Can the American family survive?" *St. Paul Pioneer Press,* December 8.

Murstein, B. I. (1970). Stimulus-value-role: A theory of marital choice. *Journal of Marriage and the Family, 32,* 465–481.

Persico, J. E. (1982). *The imperial Rockefeller: A biography of Nelson A. Rockefeller.* New York: Simon & Schuster.

Piaget, J. (1952). *The origins of intelligence in children.* New York: International University Press.

Piaget, J. (1981). *Intelligence and affectivity: Their relationship during child development.* (Trans. & Ed. by T. A. Brown & C. E. Kaegi). Palo Alto, CA: Annual Reviews, Inc.

Saul, L. J. (1979). *The childhood emotional pattern in marriage.* New York: Van Nostrand Reinhold.

Schachter, S. (1964). The interaction of cognitive and physiological determinants of emotional state. In L. Berkowitz (Ed.), *Advances in experimental social psychology* (Vol. 1). New York: Academic Press.

Schmidt, R. A. (1968). Anticipation and timing in human motor performance. *Psychological Bulletin, 70,* 631–646.

Sears, R. R. (1951). A theoretical framework for personality and social behavior. *American Psychologist, 6,* 476–483.

Seligman, M. E. P. (1975). *Helplessness: On depression, development, and death.* San Francisco: W. H. Freeman.

Selye, H. (1974). *Stress without distress.* New York: J. B. Lippincott.

Simon, H. A. (1967). Motivational and emotional controls of cognition. *Psychological Review, 74,* 29–39.

Spitz, R. A., & Wolf, K. (1946). Anaclitic depression. *Psychoanalytic study of the child, 2,* 313–342.

Straus, M. A., & Hotaling, G. T. (Eds.). (1980). *The social causes of husband-wife violence.* Minneapolis: University of Minnesota Press.

Strongman, K. T. (1978). *The psychology of emotion* (2nd Ed.). New York: Wiley.

8

Girls and Boys Together . . . But Mostly Apart: Gender Arrangements in Elementary Schools

Barrie Thorne
Michigan State University

Throughout the years of elementary school, children's friendships and casual encounters are strongly separated by sex. Sex segregation among children, which starts in preschool and is well established by middle childhood, has been amply documented in studies of children's groups and friendships (e.g., Eder & Hallinan, 1978; Schofield, 1981) and is immediately visible in elementary school settings. When children choose seats in classrooms or the cafeteria, or get into line, they frequently arrange themselves in same-sex clusters. At lunchtime, they talk matter-of-factly about "girls' tables" and "boys' tables." Playgrounds have gendered turfs, with some areas and activities, such as large playing fields and basketball courts, controlled mainly by boys, and others—smaller enclaves like jungle-gym areas and concrete spaces for hopscotch or jumprope—more often controlled by girls. Sex segregation is so common in elementary schools that it is meaningful to speak of separate girls' and boys' worlds.

Studies of gender and children's social relations have mostly followed this "two worlds" model, separately describing and comparing the subcultures of girls and of boys (e.g., Lever, 1976; Maltz & Borker, 1983). In brief summary: Boys tend to interact in larger, more age-heterogeneous groups (Lever, 1976; Waldrop & Halverson, 1975; Eder & Hallinan, 1978). They engage in more rough and tumble play and physical fighting (Maccoby & Jacklin, 1974). Organized sports are both a central activity and a major metaphor in boys' subcultures; they use the language of "teams" even when not engaged in sports, and they often construct interaction in the form of contests. The shifting hierarchies of boys' groups (Savin-Williams, 1976) are evident in their more frequent use of direct commands, insults, and challenges (Goodwin, 1980).

Fewer studies have been done of girls' groups (Foot, Chapman, & Smith, 1980; McRobbie & Garber, 1975), and—perhaps because categories for descrip-

167

tion and analysis have come more from male than female experience—researchers have had difficulty seeing and analyzing girls' social relations. Recent work has begun to correct this skew. In middle childhood, girls' worlds are less public than those of boys; girls more often interact in private places and in smaller groups or friendship pairs (Eder & Hallinan, 1978; Waldrop & Halverson, 1975). Their play is more cooperative and turn-taking (Lever, 1976). Girls have more intense and exclusive friendships, which take shape around keeping and telling secrets, shifting alliances, and indirect ways of expressing disagreement (Goodwin, 1980; Lever, 1976; Maltz & Borker, 1983). Instead of direct commands, girls more often use directives which merge speaker and hearer, e.g., "let's" or "we gotta" (Goodwin, 1980).

Although much can be learned by comparing the social organization and subcultures of boys' and of girls' groups, the separate worlds approach has eclipsed full, contextual understanding of gender and social relations among children. The separate worlds model essentially involves a search for group sex differences, and shares the limitations of individual sex difference research. Differences tend to be exaggerated and similarities ignored, with little theoretical attention to the integration of similarity and difference (Unger, 1979). Statistical findings of difference are often portrayed as dichotomous, neglecting the considerable individual variation that exists; for example, not all boys fight, and some have intense and exclusive friendships. The sex difference approach tends to abstract gender from its social context, to assume that males and females are qualitatively and permanently different (with differences perhaps unfolding through separate developmental lines). These assumptions mask the possibility that gender arrangements and patterns of similarity and difference may vary by situation, race, social class, region, or subculture.

Sex segregation is far from total, and is a more complex and dynamic process than the portrayal of separate worlds reveals. Erving Goffman (1977) has observed that sex segregation has a "with-then-apart" structure; the sexes segregate periodically, with separate spaces, rituals, groups, but they also come together and are, in crucial ways, part of the same world. This is certainly true in the social environment of elementary schools. Although girls and boys do interact as boundaried collectivities—an image suggested by the separate worlds approach—there are other occasions when they work or play in relaxed and integrated ways. Gender is less central to the organization and meaning of some situations than others. In short, sex segregation is not static, but is a variable and complicated process.

To gain an understanding of gender which can encompass both the "with" and the "apart" of sex segregation, analysis should start not with the individual, nor with a search for sex differences, but with social relationships. Gender should be conceptualized as a system of relationships rather than as an immutable and dichotomous given. Taking this approach, I have organized my research on gender and children's social relations around questions like the following: How and when does gender enter into group formation? In a given situation, how is gender made more or less salient or infused with particular meanings? By what rituals, processes, and forms of social organization and conflict do ''with-then-apart'' rhythms get enacted? How are these processes affected by the organization of institutions (e.g., different types of schools, neighborhoods, or summer camps), varied settings (e.g., the constraints and possibilities governing interaction on playgrounds vs. classrooms), and particular encounters?

METHODS AND SOURCES OF DATA

This study is based on two periods of participant observation. In 1976–1977 I observed for 8 months in a largely working-class elementary school in California, a school with 8% Black and 12% Chicana/o students. In 1980 I did fieldwork for 3 months in a Michigan elementary school of similar size (around 400 students), social class, and racial composition. I observed in several classrooms—a kindergarten, a second grade, and a combined fourth-fifth grade—and in school hallways, cafeterias, and playgrounds. I set out to follow the round of the school day as children experience it, recording their interactions with one another, and with adults, in varied settings.

Participant observation involves gaining access to everyday, ''naturalistic'' settings and taking systematic notes over an extended period of time. Rather than starting with preset categories for recording, or with fixed hypotheses for testing, participant-observers record detail in ways which maximize opportunities for discovery. Through continuous interaction between observation and analysis, ''grounded theory'' is developed (Glaser & Strauss, 1967).

The distinctive logic and discipline of this mode of inquiry emerges from: (1) theoretical sampling—being relatively systematic in the choice of where and whom to observe in order to maximize knowledge relevant to categories and analysis which are being developed; and (2) comparing all relevant data on a given point in order to modify emerging propositions to take account of discrepant cases (Katz, 1983). Participant observation is a flexible, open-ended and inductive method, designed to understand behavior within, rather than stripped from, social context. It provides richly detailed information which is anchored in everyday meanings and experience.

DAILY PROCESSES OF SEX SEGREGATION

Sex segregation should be understood not as a given, but as the result of deliberate activity. The outcome is dramatically visible when there are separate girls' and boys' tables in school lunchrooms, or sex-separated groups on playgrounds. But in the same lunchroom one can also find tables where girls and boys eat and talk together, and in some playground activities the sexes mix. By what processes do girls and boys separate into gender-defined and relatively boundaried collectivities? And in what contexts, and through what processes, do boys and girls interact in less gender-divided ways?

In the school settings I observed, much segregation happened with no mention of gender. Gender was implicit in the contours of friendship, shared interest, and perceived risk which came into play when children chose companions—in their prior planning, invitations, seeking-of-access, saving-of-places, denials of entry, and allowing or protesting of "cuts" by those who violated the rules for lining up. Sometimes children formed mixed-sex groups for play, eating, talking, working on a classroom project, or moving through space. When adults or children explicitly invoked gender—and this was nearly always in ways which separated girls and boys—boundaries were heightened and mixed-sex interaction became an explicit arena of risk.

In the schools I studied, the physical space and curricula were not formally divided by sex, as they have been in the history of elementary schooling (a history evident in separate entrances to old school buildings, where the words "Boys" and "Girls" are permanently etched in concrete). Nevertheless, gender was a visible marker in the adult-organized school day. In both schools, when the public address system sounded, the principal inevitably opened with: "Boys and girls . . . ," and in addressing clusters of children, teachers and aides regularly used gender terms ("Heads down, girls"; "The girls are ready and the boys aren't"). These forms of address made gender visible and salient, conveying an assumption that the sexes are separate social groups.

Teachers and aides sometimes drew upon gender as a basis for sorting children and organizing activities. Gender is an embodied and visual social category which roughly divides the population in half, and the separation of girls and boys permeates the history and lore of schools and playgrounds. In both schools— although through awareness of Title IX, many teachers had changed this practice—one could see separate girls' and boys' lines moving, like caterpillars, through the school halls. In the 4th–5th grade classroom the teacher frequently pitted girls against boys for spelling and math contests. On the playground in the Michigan school, aides regarded the space close to the building as girls' territory, and the playing fields "out there" as boys' territory. They sometimes shooed children of the other sex away from those spaces, especially boys who ventured near the girls' area and seemed to have teasing in mind.

In organizing their activities, both within and apart from the surveillance of adults, children also explicitly invoked gender. During my fieldwork in the Michigan school, I kept daily records of who sat where in the lunchroom. The amount of sex segregation varied: It was least at the first grade tables and almost total among sixth graders. There was also variation from classroom to classroom within a given age, and from day to day. Actions like the following heightened the gender divide:

In the lunchroom, when the two second grade tables were filling, a high-status boy walked by the inside table, which had a scattering of both boys and girls, and said loudly, "Oooo, too many girls," as he headed for a seat at the far table. The boys at the inside table picked up their trays and moved, and no other boys sat at the inside table, which the pronouncement had effectively made taboo.

In the end, that day (which was not the case every day), girls and boys ate at separate tables.

Eating and walking are not sex-typed activities, yet in forming groups in lunchrooms and hallways children often separated by sex. Sex segregation assumed added dimensions on the playground, where spaces, equipment, and activities were infused with gender meanings. My inventories of activities and groupings on the playground showed similar patterns in both schools: Boys controlled the large fixed spaces designated for team sports (baseball diamonds, grassy fields used for football or soccer); girls more often played closer to the building, doing tricks on the monkey bars (which, for 6th graders, became an area for sitting and talking) and using cement areas for jumprope, hopscotch, and group games like four-square. (Lever, 1976, provides a good analysis of sex-divided play.) Girls and boys most often played together in kickball, and in group (rather than team) games like four-square, dodgeball, and handball. When children used gender to exlcude others from play, they often drew upon beliefs connecting boys to some activities and girls to others:

A first grade boy avidly watched an all-female game of jump rope. When the girls began to shift positions, he recognized a means of access to the play and he offered, "I'll swing it." A girl responded, "No way, you don't know how to do it, to swing it. You gotta be a girl." He left without protest.

Although children sometimes ignored pronouncements about what each sex could or could not do, I never heard them directly challenge such claims.

When children had explicitly defined an activity or a group as gendered, those who crossed the boundary—especially boys who moved into female-marked space—risked being teased. ("Look! Mike's in the girls' line!"; " 'That's a girl over there,' a girl said loudly, pointing to a boy sitting at an otherwise all-female table in the lunchroom.") Children, and occasionally adults, used teasing—especially the tease of "liking" someone of the other sex, or of "being" that sex by virtue of being in their midst—to police gender boundaries. Much of the teasing drew upon heterosexual romantic definitions, making cross-sex interaction risky, and increasing social distance between boys and girls.

RELATIONSHIPS BETWEEN THE SEXES

Because I have emphasized the "apart" and ignored the occasions of "with," this analysis of sex segregation falsely implies that there is little contact between

girls and boys in daily school life. In fact, relationships between girls and boys—
which should be studied as fully as, and in connection with, same-sex relationships—are of several kinds:

1. "Borderwork," or forms of cross-sex interaction which are based upon
and reaffirm boundaries and asymmetries between girls' and boys' groups;
2. Interactions which are infused with heterosexual meanings;
3. Occasions where individuals cross gender boundaries to participate in the
world of the other sex; and
4. Situations where gender is muted in salience, with girls and boys interacting in more relaxed ways.

Borderwork

In elementary school settings boys' and girls' groups are sometimes spatially set
apart. Same-sex groups sometimes claim fixed territories such as the basketball
court, the bars, or specific lunchroom tables. However, in the crowded, multi-
focused, and adult-controlled environment of the school, groups form and dis-
perse at a rapid rate and can never stay totally apart. Contact between girls and
boys sometimes lessens sex segregation, but gender-defined groups also come
together in ways which emphasize their boundaries.

"Borderwork" refers to interaction across, yet based upon and even strengthening gender boundaries. I have drawn this notion from Fredrik Barth's (1969)
analysis of social relations which are maintained across ethnic boundaries without diminishing dichotomized ethnic status.[1] His focus is on more macro, ecological arrangements; mine is on face-to-face behavior. But the insight is similar:
Groups may interact in ways which strengthen their borders, and the maintenance of ethnic (or gender) groups can best be understood by examining the
boundary that defines the group, "not the cultural stuff that it encloses" (Barth,
1969, p. 15). In elementary schools there are several types of borderwork:
contests or games where gender-defined teams compete; cross-sex rituals of
chasing and pollution; and group invasions. These interactions are asymmetrical,
challenging the separate-but-parallel model of "two worlds."

Contests

Boys and girls are sometimes pitted against each other in classroom competitions and playground games. The 4th–5th grade classroom had a boys' side and a
girls' side, an arrangement that re-emerged each time the teacher asked children
to choose their own desks. Although there was some within-sex shuffling, the
result was always a spatial moiety system—boys on the left, girls on the right—

---

[1] I am grateful to Frederick Erickson for suggesting the relevance of Barth's analysis.

with the exception of one girl (the "tomboy" whom I'll describe later), who twice chose a desk with the boys and once with the girls. Drawing upon and reinforcing the children's self-segregation, the teacher often pitted the boys against the girls in spelling and math competitions, events marked by cross-sex antagonism and within-sex solidarity:

> The teacher introduced a math game; she would write addition and subtraction problems on the board, and a member of each team would race to be the first to write the correct answer. She wrote two score-keeping columns on the board: 'Beastly Boys' . . . 'Gossipy Girls.' The boys yelled out, as several girls laughed, 'Noisy girls! Gruesome girls!' The girls sat in a row on top of their desks; sometimes they moved collectively, pushing their hips or whispering 'pass it on.' The boys stood along the wall, some reclining against desks. When members of either group came back victorious from the front of the room, they would do the 'giving five' hand-slapping ritual with their team members.

On the playground a team of girls occasionally played against a team of boys, usually in kickball or team two-square. Sometimes these games proceeded matter-of-factly, but if gender became the explicit basis of team solidarity, the interaction changed, becoming more antagonistic and unstable:

> Two fifth-grade girls played against two fifth-grade boys in a team game of two-square. The game proceeded at an even pace until an argument ensued about whether the ball was out or on the line. Karen, who had hit the ball, became annoyed, flashed her middle finger at the other team, and called to a passing girl to join their side. The boys then called out to other boys, and cheered as several arrived to play. 'We got five and you got three!' Jack yelled. The game continued, with the girls yelling, 'Bratty boys! Sissy boys!' and the boys making noises— 'weee haw' 'ha-ha-ha'—as they played.

Chasing

Cross-sex chasing dramatically affirms boundaries between girls and boys. The basic elements of chase and elude, capture and rescue (Sutton-Smith, 1971) are found in various kinds of tag with formal rules, and in informal episodes of chasing which punctuate life on playgrounds. These episodes begin with a provocation (taunts like "You can't get me!" or "Slobber monster!"; bodily pokes or the grabbing of possessions). A provocation may be ignored, or responded to by chasing. Chaser and chased may then alternate roles. In an ethnographic study of chase sequences on a school playground, Christine Finnan (1982) observes that chases vary in number of chasers to chased (e.g., one chasing one, or five chasing two); form of provocation (a taunt or a poke); outcome (an episode may end when the chased outdistances the chaser, or with a brief touch, being wrestled to the ground, or the recapturing of a hat or a ball); and in use of space (there may or may not be safety zones).

Like Finnan (1982), and Sluckin (1981), who studied a playground in England, I found that chasing has a gendered structure. Boys frequently chase one another, an activity which often ends in wrestling and mock fights. When girls chase girls, they are usually less physically aggressive; they less often, for example, wrestle one another to the ground.

Cross-sex chasing is set apart by special names—"girls chase the boys"; "boys chase the girls"; "the chase"; "chasers"; "chase and kiss"; "kiss chase"; "kissers and chasers"; "kiss or kill"—and by children's animated talk about the activity. The names vary by region and school, but contain both gender and sexual meanings (this form of play is mentioned, but only briefly analzyed, in Finnan, 1981; Sluckin, 1981; Parrott, 1972; and Borman, 1979).

In "boys chase the girls" and "girls chase the boys" (the names most frequently used in both the California and Michigan schools) boys and girls become, by definition, separate teams. Gender terms override individual identities, especially for the other team ("Help, a girl's chasin' me!"; "C'mon Sarah, let's get that boy"; "Tony, help save me from the girls"). Individuals may call for help from, or offer help to, others of their sex. They may also grab someone of their sex and turn them over to the opposing team: "Ryan grabbed Billy from behind, wrestling him to the ground. 'Hey girls, get 'im,' Ryan called."

Boys more often mix episodes of cross-sex with same-sex chasing. Girls more often have safety zones, places like the girls' restroom or an area by the school wall, where they retreat to rest and talk (sometimes in animated postmortems) before new episodes of cross-sex chasing begin.

Early in the fall in the Michigan school, where chasing was especially prevalent, I watched a second grade boy teach a kindergarten girl how to chase. He slowly ran backwards, beckoning her to pursue him, as he called, "Help, a girl's after me." In the early grades chasing mixes with fantasy play, e.g., a first-grade boy who played "sea monster," his arms outflung and his voice growling, as he chased a group of girls. By third grade, stylized gestures—exaggerated stalking motions, screams (which only girls do), and karate kicks—accompany scenes of chasing.

Names like "chase and kiss" mark the sexual meanings of cross-sex chasing, a theme I return to later. The threat of kissing—most often girls threatening to kiss boys—is a ritualized form of provocation. Cross-sex chasing among sixth graders involves elaborate patterns of touch and touch avoidance, which adults see as sexual. The principal told the sixth graders in the Michigan school that they were not to play "pom-pom," a complicated chasing game, because it entailed "inappropriate touch."

Rituals of Pollution

Cross-sex chasing is sometimes entwined with rituals of pollution, as in "cooties," where specific individuals or groups are treated as contaminating or carrying "germs." Children have rituals for transfering cooties (usually touching someone else and shouting "You've got cooties!"), for immunization (e.g., writing "CV" for "cootie vaccination" on their arms), and for eliminating cooties (e.g., saying "no gives" or using "cootie catchers" made of folded paper) (described in Knapp & Knapp, 1976). While girls may give cooties to girls, boys do not generally give cooties to one another (Samuelson, 1980).

In cross-sex play, either girls or boys may be defined as having cooties, which they transfer through chasing and touching. Girls give cooties to boys more often than vice versa. In Michigan, one version of cooties is called "girl stain"; the fourth-graders whom Karkau, 1973, describes, used the phrase "girl touch." "Cootie queens," or "cootie girls" (there are no "kings" or "boys") are female pariahs, the ultimate school untouchables, seen as contaminating not only by virtue of gender, but also through some added stigma such as being over-weight or poor.[2] That girls are seen as more polluting than boys is a significant asymmetry, which echoes cross-cultural patterns, although in other cultures female pollution is generally connected to menstruation, and not applied to prepubertal girls.

Invasions

Playground invasions are another asymmetric form of borderwork. On a few occasions I saw girls invade and disrupt an all-male game, most memorably a group of tall sixth-grade girls who ran onto the playing field and grabbed a football which was in play. The boys were surprised and frustrated, and, unusual for boys this old, finally tattled to the aide. But in the majority of cases, boys disrupt girls' activities rather than vice versa. Boys grab the ball from girls playing four-square, stick feet into a jumprope and stop an ongoing game, and dash through the area of the bars, where girls are taking turns performing, sending the rings flying. Sometimes boys ask to join a girls' game and then, after a short period of seemingly earnest play, disrupt the game:

> Two second-grade boys begged to "twirl" the jumprope for a group of second-grade girls who had been jumping for some time. The girls agreed, and the boys began to twirl. Soon, without announcement, the boys changed from "seashells, cockle bells" to "hot peppers " (spinning the rope very fast), and tangled the jumper in the rope. The boys ran away laughing.

Boys disrupt girls' play so often that girls have developed almost ritualized responses: They guard their ongoing play, chase boys away, and tattle to the aides. In a playground cycle which enhances sex segregation, aides who try to spot protential trouble before it occurs sometimes shoo boys away from areas

---

[2]Sue Samuelson (1980) reports that in a racially mixed playground in Fresno, California, Mex-ican-American, but not Anglo children gave cooties. Racial, as well as sexual inequality may be expressed through these forms.

where girls are playing. Aides do not anticipate trouble from girls who seek to join groups of boys, with the exception of girls intent on provoking a chase sequence. And indeed, if they seek access to a boys' game, girls usually play with boys in earnest rather than breaking up the game.

A close look at the organization of borderwork—or boundaried interactions between the sexes—shows that the worlds of boys and girls may be separate, but they are not parallel, nor are they equal. The worlds of girls and boys articulate in several asymmetric ways:

1. On the playground, boys control as much as ten times more space than girls, when one adds up the area of large playing fields and compares it with the much smaller areas where girls predominate. Girls, who play closer to the building, are more often watched over and protected by the adult aides.

2. Boys invade all-female games and scenes of play much more than girls invade boys. This, and boys' greater control of space, correspond with other findings about the organization of gender, and inequality, in our society: compared with men and boys, women and girls take up less space, and their space, and talk, are more often violated and interrupted (Greif, 1982; Henley, 1977; West & Zimmerman, 1983).

3. Although individual boys are occasionally treated as contaminating (e.g., a third grade boy who both boys and girls said was "stinky" and "smelled like pee"), girls are more often defined as polluting. This pattern ties to themes that I discuss later: It is more taboo for a boy to play with (as opposed to invade) girls, and girls are more sexually defined than boys.

A look at the boundaries between the separated worlds of girls and boys illuminates within-sex hierarchies of status and control. For example, in the sex-divided seating in the 4th–5th grade classroom, several boys recurringly sat near "female space": their desks were at the gender divide in the classroom, and they were more likely than other boys to sit at a predominantly female table in the lunchroom. These boys—two nonbilingual Chicanos and an overweight "loner" boy who was afraid of sports—were at the bottom of the male hierarchy. Gender is sometimes used as a metaphor for male hierarchies; the inferior status of boys at the bottom is conveyed by calling them "girls":

> Seven boys and one girl were playing basketball. Two younger boys came over and asked to play. While the girl silently stood, fully accepted in the company of players, one of the older boys disparagingly said to the younger boys, 'You girls can't play.'[3]

In contrast, the girls who more often travel in the boys' world, sitting with groups of boys in the lunchroom or playing basketball, soccer, and baseball with

---

[3]This incident was recorded by Margaret Blume, who, for an undergraduate research project in 1982, observed in the California school where I earlier did fieldwork. Her observations and insights enhanced my own, and I would like to thank her for letting me cite this excerpt.

them, are not stigmatized. Some have fairly high status with other girls. The worlds of girls and boys are assymetrically arranged, and spatial patterns map out interacting forms of inequality.

Heterosexual Meanings

The organization and meanings of gender (the social categories "woman/man," "girl/boy") and of sexuality vary cross-culturally (Ortner & Whitehead, 1981)—and, in our society, across the life course. Harriet Whitehead (1981) observed that in our (Western) gender system, and that of many traditional North American Indian cultures, one's choice of a sexual object, occupation, and one's dress and demeanor are closely associated with gender. However, the "center of gravity" differs in the two gender systems. For Indians, occupational pursuits provide the primary imagery of gender; dress and demeanor are secondary, and sexuality is least important. In our system, at least for adults, the order is reversed: heterosexuality is central to our definitions of "man" and "woman" ("masculinity"/"femininity"), and the relationships that obtain between them, whereas occupation and dress/demeanor are secondary.

Whereas erotic orientation and gender are closely linked in our definitions of adults, we define children as relatively asexual. Activities and dress/demeanor are more important than sexuality in the cultural meanings of "girl" and "boy." Children are less heterosexually defined than adults, and we have nonsexual imagery for relations between girls and boys. However, both children and adults sometimes use heterosexual language—"crushes," "like," "goin' with," "girlfriends," and "boyfriends"—to define cross-sex relationships. This language increases through the years of elementary school; the shift to adolescence consolidates a gender system organized around the institution of heterosexuality.

In everyday life in the schools, heterosexual and romantic meanings infuse some ritualized forms of interaction between groups of boys and girls (e.g., "chase and kiss") and help maintain sex segregation. "Jimmy likes Beth" or "Beth likes Jimmy" is a major form of teasing, which a child risks in choosing to sit by or walk with someone of the other sex. The structure of teasing, and children's sparse vocabulary for relationships between girls and boys, are evident in the following conversation which I had with a group of third-grade girls in the lunchroom:

> Susan asked me what I was doing, and I said I was observing the things children do and play. Nicole volunteered, 'I like running, boys chase all the girls. See Tim over there? Judy chases him all around the school. She likes him.' Judy, sitting across the table, quickly responded, 'I hate him. I like him for a friend.' 'Tim loves Judy,' Nicole said in a loud, sing-song voice.

In the younger grades, the culture and lore of girls contains more heterosexual romantic themes than that of boys. In Michigan, the first-grade girls often jumped rope to a rhyme which began: "Down in the valley where the green grass grows, there sat Cindy (name of jumper), as sweet as a rose. She sat, she sat, she sat so sweet. Along came Jason, and kissed her on the cheek . . . first comes love, then comes marriage, then along comes Cindy with a baby carriage . . ." Before a girl took her turn at jumping, the chanters asked her "Who do you want to be your boyfriend?" The jumper always proferred a name, which was accepted matter-of-factly. In chasing, a girl's kiss carried greater threat than a boy's kiss; "girl touch," when defined as contaminating, had sexual connotations. In short, starting at an early age, girls are more sexually defined than boys.

Through the years of elementary school, and increasing with age, the idiom of heterosexuality helps maintain the gender divide. Cross-sex interactions, especially when children initiate them, are fraught with the risk of being teased about "liking" someone of the other sex. I learned of several close cross-sex friendships, formed and maintained in neighborhoods and church, which went underground during the school day.

By the fifth grade a few children began to affirm, rather than avoid, the charge of having a girlfriend or a boyfriend; they introduced the heterosexual courtship rituals of adolescence:

> In the lunchroom in the Michigan school, as the tables were forming, a high-status fifth-grade boy called out from his seat at the table: 'I want Trish to sit by me.' Trish came over, and almost like a king and queen, they sat at the gender divide—a row of girls down the table on her side, a row of boys on his.

In this situation, which inverted earlier forms, it was not a loss, but a gain in status to publically choose a companion of the other sex. By affirming his choice, the boy became unteasable (note the familiar asymmetry of heterosexual courtship rituals: the male initiated). This incident signals a temporal shift in arrangements of sex and gender.

Traveling in the World of the Other Sex

Contests, invasions, chasing, and heterosexually-defined encounters are based upon and reaffirm boundaries between girls and boys. In another type of cross-sex interaction, individuals (or sometimes pairs) cross gender boundaries, seeking acceptance in a group of the other sex. Nearly all the cases I saw of this were tomboys—girls who played organized sports and frequently sat with boys in the cafeteria or classroom. If these girls were skilled at activities central in the boys' world, especially games like soccer, baseball, and basketball, they were pretty much accepted as participants.

Being a tomboy is a matter of degree. Some girls seek access to boys' groups but are excluded; other girls limit their "crossing" to specific sports. Only a few—such as the tomboy I mentioned earlier, who chose a seat with the boys in the sex-divided fourth–fifth grade—participate fully in the boys' world. That particular girl was skilled at the various organized sports which boys played in different seasons of the year. She was also adept at physical fighting and at using the forms of arguing, insult, teasing, naming, and sports-talk of the boys' sub-culture. She was the only Black child in her classroom, in a school with only 8% Black students; overall that token status, along with unusual athletic and verbal skills, may have contributed to her ability to move back and forth across the gender divide. Her unique position in the children's world was widely recog-nized in the school. Several times, the teacher said to me, "She thinks she's a boy."

I observed only one boy in the upper grades (a fourth grader) who regularly played with all-female groups, as opposed to "playing at" girls' games and seeking to disrupt them. He frequently played jumprope and took turns with girls doing tricks on the bars, using the small gestures—for example, a helpful push on the heel of a girl who needed momentum to turn her body around the bar—which mark skillful and earnest participation. Although I never saw him play in other than an earnest spirit, the girls often chased him away from their games, and both girls and boys teased him. The fact that girls seek, and have more access to boys' worlds than vice versa, and the fact that girls who travel with the other sex are less stigmatized for it, are obvious asymmetries, tied to the asym-metries previously discussed.

Relaxed Cross-Sex Interactions

Relationships between boys and girls are not always marked by strong bound-aries, heterosexual definitions, or by interacting on the terms and turfs of the other sex. On some occasions girls and boys interact in relatively comfortable ways. Gender is not strongly salient nor explicitly invoked, and girls and boys are not organized into boundaried collectivities. These "with" occasions have been neglected by those studying gender and children's relationships, who have emphasized either the model of separate worlds (with little attention to their articulation) or heterosexual forms of contact.

Occasions where boys and girls interact without strain, where gender wanes, rather than waxes in importance, frequently have one or more of the following characteristics:

1. The situations are organized around an absorbing task, such as a group art project or creating a radio show, which encourages cooperation and lessens attention to gender. This pattern accords with other studies finding that cooper-ative activities reduce group antagonism (e.g., Sherif & Sherif, 1953, who studied divisions between boys in a summer camp; and Aronson et al., 1978, who used cooperative activities to lessen racial divisions in a classroom).

2. Gender is less prominent when children are not responsible for the forma-tion of the group. Mixed-sex play is less frequent in games like football, which

require the choosing of teams, and more frequent in games like handball or dodgeball which individuals can join simply by getting into a line or a circle. When adults organize mixed-sex encounters—which they frequently do in the classroom and in physical education periods on the playground—they legitimize cross-sex contact. This removes the risk of being teased for choosing to be with the other sex.

3. There is more extensive and relaxed cross-sex interaction when principles of grouping other than gender are explicitly invoked—for example, counting off to form teams for spelling or kickball, dividing lines by hot lunch or cold lunch, or organizing a work group on the basis of interests or reading ability.

4. Girls and boys may interact more readily in less public and crowded settings. Neighborhood play, depending on demography, is more often sex and age integrated than play at school, partly because with fewer numbers, one may have to resort to an array of social categories to find play partners or to constitute a game. And in less crowded environments there are fewer potential witnesses to "make something of it" if girls and boys play together.

Relaxed interactions between girls and boys often depend on adults to set up and legitimize the contact.[4] Perhaps because of this contingency—and the other, distancing patterns which permeate relations between girls and boys—the easeful moments of interaction rarely build to close friendship. Schofield (1981) makes a similar observation about gender and racial barriers to friendship in a junior high school.

IMPLICATIONS FOR DEVELOPMENT

I have located social relations within an essentially spatial framework, emphasizing the organization of children's play, work, and other activities within specific settings, and in one type of institution, the school. In contrast, frameworks of child development rely upon temporal metaphors, using images of growth and transformation over time. Taken alone, both spatial and temporal frameworks have shortcomings; fitted together, they may be mutually correcting.

Those interested in gender and development have relied upon conceptualizations of "sex role socialization" and "sex differences." Sexuality and gender, I have argued, are more situated and fluid than these individualist and intrinsic models imply. Sex and gender are differently organized and defined across situations, even within the same institution. This situational variation (e.g., in the extent to which an encounter heightens or lessens gender boundaries, or is infused with sexual meanings) shapes and constrains individual behavior. Fea-

---

[4]Note that in daily school life, depending on the individual and the situation, teachers and aides sometimes lessened, and at other times heightened sex segregation.

tures which a developmental perspective might attribute to individuals, and understand as relatively internal attributes unfolding over time, may, in fact, be highly dependent on context. For example, children's avoidance of cross-sex friendship may be attributed to individual gender development in middle-child-hood. But attention to varied situations may show that this avoidance is contingent on group size, activity, adult behavior, collective meanings, and the risk of being teased.

A focus on social organization and situation draws attention to children's experiences in the present. This helps correct a model like "sex role socialization" which casts the present under the shadow of the future, or presumed "endpoints" (Speier, 1976). A situated analysis of arrangements of sex and gender among those of different ages may point to crucial disjunctions in the life course. In the fourth and fifth grades, culturally defined heterosexual rituals ("goin' with") begin to suppress the presence and visibility of other types of interaction between girls and boys, such as nonsexualized and comfortable interaction, and traveling in the world of the other sex. As "boyfriend/girlfriend" definitions spread, the fifth-grade tomboy I described had to work to sustain "buddy" relationships with boys. Adult women who were tomboys often speak of early adolescence as a painful time when they were pushed away from participation in boys' activities. Other adult women speak of the loss of intense, even erotic ties with other girls when they entered puberty and the rituals of dating, that is, when they became absorbed into the institution of heterosexuality (Rich, 1980). When Lever (1976) describes best-friend relationships among fifth-grade girls as preparation for dating, she imposes heterosexual ideologies onto a present which should be understood on its own terms.

As heterosexual encounters assume more importance, they may alter relations in same-sex groups. For example, Schofield (1981) reports that for sixth- and seventh-grade children in a middle school, the popularity of girls with other girls was affected by their popularity with boys, while boys' status with other boys did not depend on their relations with girls. This is an asymmetry familiar from the adult world; men's relationships with one another are defined through varied activities (occupations, sports), while relationships among women—and their public status—are more influenced by their connections to individual men.

A full understanding of gender and social relations should encompass cross-sex as well as within-sex interactions. "Borderwork" helps maintain separate, gender-linked subcultures, which, as those interested in development have begun to suggest, may result in different milieux for learning. Daniel Maltz and Ruth Borker (1983) for example, argue that because of different interactions within girls' and boys' groups, the sexes learn different rules for creating and interpreting friendly conversation, rules which carry into adulthood and help account for miscommunication between men and women. Carol Gilligan (1982) fits research on the different worlds of girls and boys into a theory of sex differences in moral development. Girls develop a style of reasoning, she argues, which is more personal and relational; boys develop a style which is more positional, based on separateness. Eleanor Maccoby (1982), also following the insight that because of sex segregation, girls and boys grow up in different environments, suggests implications for gender differentiated prosocial and antisocial behavior.

This separate worlds approach, as I have illustrated, also has limitations. The occasions when the sexes are together should also be studied, and understood as contexts for experience and learning. For example, assymetries in cross-sex relationships convey a series of messages: that boys are more entitled to space and to the nonreciprocal right of interrupting or invading the activities of the other sex; that girls are more in need of adult protection, and are lower in status, more defined by sexuality, and may even be polluting. Different types of cross-sex interaction—relaxed, boundaried, sexualized, or taking place on the terms of the other sex—provide different contexts for development.

By mapping the array of relationships between and within the sexes, one adds complexity to the overly static and dichotomous imagery of separate worlds. Individual experiences vary, with implications for development. Some children prefer same-sex groupings; some are more likely to cross the gender boundary and participate in the world of the other sex; some children (e.g., girls and boys who frequently play "chase and kiss") invoke heterosexual meanings, while others avoid them.

Finally, after charting the terrain of relationships, one can trace their development over time. For example, age variation in the content and form of border-work, or of cross and same-sex touch, may be related to differing cognitive, social, emotional, or physical capacities, as well as to age-associated cultural forms. I earlier mentioned temporal shifts in the organization of cross-sex chasing, from mixing with fantasy play in the early grades to more elaborately ritualized and sexualized forms by the sixth grade. There also appear to be temporal changes in same and cross-sex touch. In kindergarten, girls and boys touch one another more freely than in fourth grade, when children avoid relaxed cross-sex touch and instead use pokes, pushes, and other forms of mock violence, even when the touch clearly couches affection. This touch taboo is obviously related to the risk of seeming to *like* someone of the other sex. In fourth grade, same-sex touch begins to signal sexual meanings among boys, as well as between boys and girls. Younger boys touch one another freely in cuddling (arm around shoulder) as well as mock violence ways. By fourth grade, when homophobic taunts like "fag" become more common among boys, cuddling touch begins to disappear for boys, but less so for girls.

Overall, I am calling for more complexity in our conceptualizations of gender and of children's social relationships. Our challenge is to retain the temporal sweep, looking at individual and group lives as they unfold over time, while also attending to social structure and context, and to the full variety of experiences in the present.

ACKNOWLEDGMENT

I would like to thank Jane Atkinson, Nancy Chodorow, Arlene Daniels, Peter Lyman, Zick Rubin, Malcolm Spector, Avril Thorne, and Margery Wolf for comments on an earlier version of this paper. Conversations with Zella Luria enriched this work.

REFERENCES

Aronson, E. et al. (1978). *The jigsaw classroom.* Beverly Hills, CA: Sage.

Barth, F. (Ed.). (1969). *Ethnic groups and boundaries.* Boston: Little, Brown.

Borman, K. M. (1979). Children's interactions in playgrounds. *Theory into Practice, 18,* 251–257.

Eder, D., & Hallinan, M. T. (1978). Sex differences in children's friendships. *American Sociological Review, 43,* 237–250.

Finnan, C. R. (1982). The ethnography of children's spontaneous play. In G. Spindler (Ed.), *Doing the ethnography of schooling* (pp. 358–380). New York: Holt, Rinehart & Winston.

Foot, H. C., Chapman, A. J., & Smith, J. R. (1980). Introduction. *Friendship and social relations in children* (pp. 1–14). New York: Wiley.

Gilligan, C. (1982). *In a different voice: Psychological theory and women's development.* Cambridge, MA: Harvard University Press.

Glaser, B. G., & Strauss, A. L. (1967). *The discovery of grounded theory.* Chicago: Aldine.

Goffman, E. (1977). The arrangement between the sexes. *Theory and Society, 4,* 301–336.

Goodwin, M. H. (1980). Directive-response speech sequences in girls' and boys' task activities. In S. McConnell-Ginet, R. Borker, & N. Furman (Eds.), *Women and language in literature and society* (pp. 157–173). New York: Praeger.

Greif, E. B. (1980). Sex differences in parent-child conversations. *Women's Studies International Quarterly, 3,* 253–258.

Henley, N. (1977). *Body politics: Power, sex, and nonverbal communication.* Englewood Cliffs, NJ: Prentice-Hall.

Karkau, K. (1973). *Sexism in the fourth grade.* Pittsburgh: KNOW, Inc. (pamphlet)

Katz, J. (1983). A theory of qualitative methodology: The social system of analytic fieldwork. In R. M. Emerson (Ed.), *Contemporary field research* (pp. 127–148). Boston: Little, Brown.

Knapp, M., & Knapp, H. (1976). *One potato, two potato: The secret education of American children.* New York: W. W. Norton.

Lever, J. (1976). Sex differences in the games children play. *Social Problems, 23,* 478–487.

Maccoby, E. (1982). *Social groupings in childhood: Their relationship to prosocial and antisocial behavior in boys and girls.* Paper presented at conference on The Development of Prosocial and Antisocial Behavior. Voss, Norway.

Maccoby, E., & Jacklin, C. (1974). *The psychology of sex differences.* CA: Stanford University Press.

Maltz, D. N., & Borker, R. A. (1983). A cultural approach to male-female miscommunication. In J. J. Gumperz (Ed.), *Language and social identity* (pp. 195–216). New York: Cambridge University Press.

McRobbie, A., & Garber, J. (1975). Girls and subcultures. In S. Hall and T. Jefferson (Eds.), *Resistance through rituals* (pp. 209–223). London: Hutchinson.

Ortner, S. B., & Whitehead, H. (1981). *Sexual meanings.* New York: Cambridge University Press.

Parrott, S. (1972). Games children play: Ethnography of a second-grade recess. In J. P. Spradley & D. W. McCurdy (Eds.), *The cultural experience* (pp. 206–219). Chicago: Science Research Associates.

Rich, A. (1980). Compulsory heterosexuality and lesbian existence. *Signs, 5,* 631–660.

Samuelson, S. (1980). The cooties complex. *Western Folklore, 39,* 198–210.

Savin-Williams, R. C. (1976). An ethological study of dominance formation and maintenance in a group of human adolescents. *Child Development, 47,* 972–979.

Schofield, J. W. (1981). Complementary and conflicting identities: Images and interaction in an interracial school. In S. R. Asher & J. M. Gottman (Eds.), *The development of children's friendships* (pp. 53–90). New York: Cambridge University Press.

Sherif, M., & Sherif, C. (1953). *Groups in harmony and tension.* New York: Harper.

Sluckin, A. (1981). *Growing up in the playground.* London: Routledge & Kegan Paul.

Speier, M. (1976). The adult ideological viewpoint in studies of childhood. In A. Skolnick (Ed.), *Rethinking childhood* (pp. 168–186). Boston: Little, Brown.

Sutton-Smith, B. (1971). A syntax for play and games. In R. E. Herron and B. Sutton-Smith (Eds.), *Child's Play* (pp. 298–307). New York: Wiley.

Unger, R. K. (1979). Toward a redefinition of sex and gender. *American Psychologist, 34,* 1085–1094.

Waldrop, M. F., & Halverson, C. F. (1975). Intensive and extensive peer behavior: Longitudinal and cross-sectional analysis. *Child Development, 46,* 19–26.

West, C., & Zimmerman, D. H. (1983). Small insults: A study of interruptions in cross-sex conversations between unacquainted persons. In B. Thorne, C. Kramarae, & N. Henley (Eds.), *Language, gender and society.* Rowley, MA: Newbury House.

Whitehead, H. (1981). The bow and the burden strap: A new look at institutionalized homosexuality in Native America. In S. B. Ortner & H. Whitehead (Eds.), *Sexual meanings* (pp. 80–115). New York: Cambridge University Press.

9 Implementing New Relationship Styles in American Families

Thomas S. Weisner
University of California, Los Angeles

There has never been a time in human history with more opportunity for familial and parental experimentation and innovation than now, and never a place where it is more possible than the United States. There are more available alternative models for how to structure one's family and how to be a parent than ever before. These models appear in the media, and are directly available for view in neighborhoods and among friends and relatives. The variety of ecological niches where North American families can choose to live, and the subsistence strategies they could follow, nearly reflect the range available throughout the world.

Not only are opportunities for experimentation unusually many; the risks of having made unsuccessful innovations have never been lower. Risks to children's present health or to their future survival can be corrected at a low cost and with little chance of permanent damage (assuming these are nonextreme, nonpathological experiments). Travel is relatively easy, safe, and cheap, as are other forms of communication. Food is also relatively reliably obtained, moderate in cost, and available all year. Our current cultural climate encourages open, flexible, individually generated experimentation, and has seldom if ever been as pervasive. New patterns of sexuality, parenting, and family roles are perceived as acceptable, and tolerated if not actively encouraged.

I do not mean that there are not real risks to children's health and emotional well-being in this culture. To the contrary—poverty, child abuse, neglect, or drug and alcohol abuse can be very real threats. All of these can endanger emotional and intellectual development, and even child survival (Children's Defense Fund, 1984). Barring such clearly pathological circumstances, however, it is clear that the risks to child health and mortality for most innovations in our culture are quite low. But this does not mean that parents are unconcerned about the possible consequences for other-than-life-threatening kinds of innovation and experimentation in family styles and relationships. To the contrary, the relative ease and safety with which these can be attempted makes their consequences for social, emotional, and intellectual development all the more salient.

In this paper, I explore some of the ways a sample of 150 innovative, experimenting, nonconventional American families have attempted to put their new ideals concerning family and relationship styles into practice. All these families were followed since the birth of their first or second child, in 1974–1975. It is striking that by the time these children entered first grade their tested score profiles (IQ, school readiness, and health) are indistinguishable, as a group, from a comparison group sample of 50 families. Many of these nonconventional families had problems, and their health status, emotional, and intellectual measures varied. However, there are as yet no signs of systematic pathology or troubles emerging as a direct result of the kinds of familial innovations most of these families tried.

It appears as though intentionally innovative families rarely ignored the health, safety, and other protective cultural features available to their children and themselves. And they appear not to have experimented across the full range of possible cultural scripts for child care which they might have tried. At the same time, they did selectively innovate in their relationship styles. Thus, this chapter is concerned simultaneously with two questions: How did families with young children choose to innovate in certain areas of family life and relationship styles? And, what are some of the boundaries and limits to such innovation? The first section describes one kind of innovative effort: pronaturalism. The next sections turn to a discussion of the ecocultural limits of innovation in relationship styles in our society—limits which are all the more striking in an ecological environment as open to and forgiving of experiments as ours.

THE FAMILY LIFESTYLES SAMPLE

The American family has been changing rapidly in the past 40 years, and that certainly is the popular perception as well (Tufte & Myerhoff, 1979). However, the magnitude and long-term implications of such changes are the subject of lively debate (Bane, 1976; Lasch, 1979; Masnick & Bane, 1980). Among the many kinds of changing families are those with intentionally experimental or innovative goals, such as the creation of more egalitarian family roles, shared parenting, or being more "natural" in family relationship styles. These nonconventional families have a set of definable ideals which parents are attempting to implement in their lives. The family sample described here is characterized by the attempt to implement at least some new ideals concerning relationship styles.

In addition, all the families were chosen just prior to the birth of a new baby, so all the parents are making a parenting transition as well.

One way to explore how parents attempt to change relationship styles with their mates and their children is to find families who are in the process of making such changes, and then follow them over time. The Family Lifestyles Project is such a sample. It is an ongoing longitudinal study of 200 families and children, 50 in conventional, two-parent, married, white, middle-income families, and 150 comparable families and children in a variety of nonconventional family arrangements. Many of these parents are intentionally experimenting with new family relationships and child rearing patterns (Eiduson, 1978; Eiduson, Kornfein, Zimmerman, & Weisner, 1982; Eiduson & Weisner, 1978; Weisner & Weibel, 1981; Weisner, Bausano, & Kornfein, 1983; Zimmerman, 1981).

The nonconventional family sample includes a variety of family arrangements. Some parents and children live in creedal communes or domestic living group arrangements; others are unmarried, "social contract" couples, who have decided to have children and share parenting without legal marriage; and others are single mothers of different kinds. The single mothers include some women in their early 20s who would prefer marriage but elected to keep their children and rear them independently; some are "nestbuilders," women in their 30s with higher formal education, and more stable occupational careers, who elected to have and rear their child regardless of their mate or subsequent marriage choices. Other single mothers are "adapters," women who may have preferred marriage but have adjusted to single-parenthood in various ways (Kornfein, Weisner, & Martin, 1977).

The nonconventional families were collected through a variety of snowball and network sampling techniques, including personal staff contacts, referrals from obstetricians or clinics where many such parents tended to go, advertisements in appropriate newspapers and newsletters, referrals of other parents from family participants already in the study, and so on. Even though these families are unusually mobile and change their lifestyle frequently, there has been 6% attrition in 8 years—a credit to the clinical and research skills and persistence of project staff, as well as to the commitment of many of these families themselves to the goals of the longitudinal scientific study. All the mothers were contacted during their third trimester of pregnancy, and their children and families have been followed since that point. The conventional comparison group comprise 50 two-parent, married nuclear family couples having their first or second child at the time of their inclusion in the study. Most were selected through referrals from a random sample of California obstetricians of their current patients in the third trimester, of the appropriate ages, race, etc.

The terms *conventional* and *nonconventional* have a clear meaning in describing the families in this sample. Nonconventional family lifestyles are (1) statistically infrequent and/or demographically unusual; and (2) they are not culturally normative or expectable. Children living with only one parent are not uncommon, nor are cohabiting couples. However, being single or unmarried in non-poverty, Caucasian populations, and about to have a first or second child, is still infrequent. Having young children in these circumstances for this population is also nonnormative. A good operational definition of nonnormative conduct is having to explain why one is doing something, to offer some sort of culturally acceptable account of one's lifestyle. The two-parent married, middle class Caucasian couple does not have to provide an account, a negotiated rationale, for their family relationship; it is "taken for granted," or "goes without saying." This is what is meant by normative. Thus the term nonconventional does not in any way presume that the families are necessarily deviant, bizarre, socially odd, or aberrant. Some may appear that way to some others, although the great majority do not.

These parents are typically articulate and thoughtful about their goals and plans, and what these may mean for their children's development. This does not imply that the parents are necessarily planful, highly organized, rational, or strategic about their choices of family relationship patterns; often their lives can be quite haphazard, and develop opposite to what might have been intended. But these intentionally alternative families are usually reflective about what they are doing, and are aware of the possible consequences of their ideals.

If conscious decisions to implement new family relationships do produce sustained changes in family life, they should be found in this sample. These families are making the effort. Their choices about where to live include isolated mountain retreats, collective houses, farms, exurban fringes, as well as scores of ordinary city homes and apartments. Their sexual preferences are diverse, and their ideas about marriage range from permanent monogamy, to serial monogamy, long-term commitment without formal marriage, "open" marriage relationships, and committed single parenthood. Their innovative social relationship ideals are not limited to pronaturalism, but often include ideals of sex role egalitarianism; a distrust for all authority or dominance in relationships; a fervent commitment to a particular ideology or individual leader; progressive political commitments and ideals; and others (Eiduson, Cohen, & Alexander, 1973). Additional descriptive data are available (Eiduson et al., 1982; Weisner, 1982), showing the truly unusual and innovative character of this sample.

Are Children in Nonconventional Families at Risk?

Many of the ideals and goals in these families are unusual, and culturally novel in the United States (or at least were in the early 1970s). Some of them may be related to family patterns which are potentially harmful to a child. For example, single motherhood may be more stressful for mothers and their children, whether the mother is single because she is a nestbuilder, adapter, or unwed mother. Social contract couples who do not subsequently marry may provide very tenuous, unstable parenting arrangements for the child. A mother in a commune sharing child care with other full-time community caretakers, could produce role or identity confusion in her child. High mobility, diversity, and change in family social relationships in and of itself may be potentially deleterious, quite apart from the content or reasons behind this diversity. Choices of novel foods or diets, non-Western medicines, etc., may pose health risks. Thus, the question is raised: Are these children developing *normally,* as judged by conventional tests, by independent judges, and by outside institutions such as pediatricians, or nursery and public school teachers? Quite apart from its intrinsic scientific and policy interest, this question comes prior to a consideration of pronaturalism and innovations in parent-child relationships. The effects of pronaturalism or other relationship style issues would otherwise be confounded with abnormal developmental status of the children in the sample, if pronatural families in particular, or nonconventional lifestyle families generally, are rearing children at significant risk, or in obvious difficulty because of aspects of their lifestyle.

Studies to date have not found significant differences between children in nonconventional and conventional family lifestyles on standardized psychometric assessment measures of intellectual functioning (Bayley scores at 8 months and 1 year; Stanford-Binet at 3; WISC-R at 6; and others) (Eiduson et al., 1982; Zimmerman, 1981). There also appear to be no differences in physical development or health, nor on a number of measures of socioemotional adjustment. Reading and school readiness, as well as preliminary analyses of teachers' ratings of these children in their first year of primary school also do not indicate that a child born into a family defined as nonconventional by the criteria of the Family Lifestyles Project, has measurable troubles in the first 6 years of life (Eiduson et al., 1982). These results do not at all insure that future differences might not emerge. And some subsets of the nonconventional families do face unusual stress and have chronic problems (e.g., Eiduson & Forsythe, 1983). But for the purposes of this chapter, the children in this sample are developing within the normal ranges for children in the United States, or considerably better than normal (the mean WISC-R IQ at age 6, for instance, is 113 ± 14.0).

BEING "PRONATURAL" IN FAMILY RELATIONSHIPS AND CHILD REARING

Many of the nonconventional families were committed to a "pronatural" family and child care pattern. Pronaturalism is one of the most important values parents indicated that they wanted to express in their child rearing practices and family relationships. We asked the conventional and nonconventional parents what they intended to do in order to practice more pronatural child rearing. Three distinct factors emerged in an analysis of interview and questionnaire responses concerning naturalism (see Eiduson, Cohen, & Alexander, 1973; Weisner et al., 1983).

Parents were interviewed prior to the birth of their baby on a series of family values, including sex egalitarianism, authority, pronaturalism, and others. Parents were also asked in questionnaires about things they felt were important to teach their child concerning human relationships, such as being "free," "natural," "expressive,"; developing a love for nature; openness in expressing feelings; and others. Items were included on both the degree of intensity of commitment, and the relative importance of each item. Parents also were asked about their plans for child care practices which might indicate pronaturalism, such as using only homemade toys, making one's own baby food, and others.

A series of factor analyses was done on the complete set of items, for the full population, as well as on subsamples of each major lifestyle group (e.g., single mothers, social contract couples, etc.). Varimax rotation was used to derive three final factors with high loadings, good communalities, and a substantively clear interpretation. These are labeled (1) Natural-Organic Beliefs; (2) Warmth and Emotional Expressiveness; and (3) "Laidback," Relaxed, Low Conflict. The same factors reappear when factor analyses are repeated within each lifestyle group, although the strength of eigenvalues, and order of appearance of these factors changes somewhat for each family style subgroup. The mean scores for each factor also differ significantly ($p < .01$) from the conventional comparison group factor scores.

(1) *Natural-Organic:*   Families wanted to deemphasize materialism, and to use "nonplastic" products, including making one's own foods, especially baby foods; using natural herbs and medicines; not using store-bought toys, particularly plastic ones or those with commercial logos. More generally, families did not want to be overloaded with paraphernalia and possessions.

(2) *Warm, Emotionally Expressive:*   Pronatural families emphasized the importance of teaching their children to show their feelings, and to be honest and open in their emotional expression. They emphasized the importance of warmth, intimacy, being expressive. They preferred soft, chest- or back-carry ("Snuggly"-type) devices for better mobility and closer physical contact with their child. Nudity was not to be discouraged, or negatively dealt with. Parents desired a long breastfeeding period (and no or very limited bottle feeding).

(3) *"Laidback," Relaxed, Low Conflict:*   Items loading on this factor showed families who stated that they did not want to "lay a trip" on their child, who preferred a loose, relaxed family style, emphasizing low conflict and an absence of physical punishment or aggression. This component in pronaturalism perhaps conflicts in some ways with warmth and expressiveness, which is a more directive, positive style parents hoped to encourage; but in fact, families with higher factor scores for Warmth and Natural-Organic, also were more likely to score highly on "Laidback."

Natural relationships also meant that a certain practice would produce a close fit between what a parent perceives as his or her own style for forming social relationships, and what the infant or young child *naturally* prefers. For instance, parents might mention conforming to what they perceive as a child's natural temperament. Parents would emphasize pronatural social relationship ideals because the parent believed that he or she (the parent) was already like that, and thus it was *natural* (in the sense of easier, or more appropriate) to hope for the same pattern with the child. However, this sense of natural (as a fit between parental, adult relationship desires and child care practices) was not mentioned by parents with respect to all relationship styles (e.g., moody, angry, etc.). Rather, only certain kinds of social relationships were seen as producing such a fit—warmth, low conflict, dislike of physical punishment, and so on.

Another sense of the term *natural* mentioned by some parents was that a child-care practice or social relationship style is widespread throughout our species, and thus represents a more valued pattern for parents. Such practices substitute for "over-civilized" or "false" ones. Examples of such "false" practices could include bottle feeding, or very little direct, skin-to-skin contact between caretakers and baby. A related sense of *naturalness* in relationships is that the practice insures the child's health and safety, and protects the child from the dangers of industrial society. Practices like breastfeeding and late weaning involve both the first and second senses. Feeding only *natural* foods free of artificial additives emphasizes the second.

One other sense of natural relationships is that a particular practice is culturally so desirable and expected, that "naturally" (in the sense of "of course," or "without thinking") the family does it. In general, pronatural families reported just the opposite on this matter. Pronaturalism and other valued, new relationship ideals are seen as opposed to what our culture has done and still does promote. Parents of course knew they were not entirely alone in their goals and ideals, but felt they were clearly in a minority vanguard, fighting off the tendencies of dominant, commercial, unhealthful prior cultural beliefs regarding how families should raise young children. Two contrasting results follow from this. First, our own North American cultural styles are not very natural, in these parents' views. And second, cultural features of relationship styles which parents were *not* overtly trying to change, and which were not conscious goals, are in a vague position, not clearly articulated. They were neither clearly natural, nor unnatural, nor cultural.

The Implementation of Pronatural Socialization Ideals

What did nonconventional, pronatural parents actually do with their infants and young children? Did they implement their stated socialization goals in their behavior in the family and with their child? This section summarizes these results (Weisner, 1983; Weisner et al., 1983); in the final section I attempt to derive some broader inferences regarding the general principles which may be governing the implementation of such new social relationship ideals.

Parents in the Family Lifestyles Sample completed questionnaires regarding their child rearing practices every 6 to 9 months between the birth of their child, and 6 years of age. Some instruments were mailed to parents, and some were completed during visits of the parents and children to the project offices, or during visits of observers to the families' homes. Observational data were collected on child care practices seen in the homes, such as carrying styles, feedings, toys available and used, and so forth. Where available at a given age, observational data are used (at 6 and 18 months, and 4½ years); where not available, parents' reports of their child rearing practices are used (12 months, 2 years, and up).

The central questions in analyses of the longitudinal data on pronatural parental relationship values are: How did parents put these ideals into practice in what they did with their young children? Did parents who espoused new relationship styles indeed implement them more often and longer than parents who did not have these ideals? Did the implementation of new relationship ideals include both family practices and dyadic interaction styles, or did these two levels of analysis show different patterns of results? This series of studies can best be summarized by five major findings:

1. yes, the pronatural families did alter their relationship practices on a number of relationship issues and child care patterns;
2. innovation did not extend into matters which might affect health or safety, such as medical care or putting the child into potentially dangerous situations;
3. the differences between the pronatural families and the comparison group were generally of modest magnitude; that is, the differences which were statistically significant were not of large substantive magnitude;
4. the innovative families were not nearly as innovative as they might have been, if these families' child care patterns are compared to the range of such practices around the world; and
5. innovative relationship styles did not extend from the level of patterns and practices, to the level of microinteractional differences in expression of affect, or in direct stimulation of the child.

Each of these results is now considered in more detail.

RESULTS

1. Results indicate that nonconventional, pronatural families did indeed implement their hoped-for child care practices significantly more often than did the conventional comparison group parents. For example, analyses compared mean proportion scores for the number of families reporting the use of, or those observed using, various carrying devices. Both nonconventional family groups and families high on pronatural values were significantly higher than the comparison group families by t-test. Similar analyses were run for each of the

following practices: proportion of mothers breastfeeding; age of weaning; use of homemade solid foods; age at which solid foods introduced (pronatural parents expected to introduce such foods later); use of slings vs. hard-frame carrying devices (such as a stroller); co-sleeping in the same bed with parents; beliefs regarding nudity and the body. Each of these practices is directly related to parents' pronatural goals for their children. Nonconventional families generally were more commonly found adopting the practice; and families with high pronatural ideologies were higher still.

It should also be noted that some comparison group families also did these same activities, but less frequently or for a shorter number of months than did the nonconventional groups. Pronatural families seem to have led the way in implementing relationship ideals which then continued to spread among larger segments of young United States parents. However, the nonconventional parents did these things with a more intentional, intense effort.

2. Implementation of child health and safety measures were similar throughout the propulation, regardless of pronatural beliefs or nonconventionality in lifestyle. Pediatrician-supplied data on growth and development, and reports of illness by physicians and parents alike, showed very little consistent difference between lifestyle groups (Eiduson et al., 1982).

The children nearly all had their shots; they were given well-baby checkups; and they were taken to the pediatrician about the same number of times. Knowledge of medical danger signals and parental health monitoring were similar across the sample. Pronatural parents may have used herbal medicines, or explored various novel dietary regimes in addition —but if medical problems developed with their children, they went to conventional health services. Pronaturalism did not extend to the refusal to utilize such conventional services, but rather involved the addition of some nonconventional treatments or caretaking practices. Clearly these two strategies were not seen as mutually exclusive sets of practices.

3. The *magnitude* of the percentage differences between conventional comparison groups and pronatural/nonconventional family styles were modest. *Modest* means on the order of 10 to 30% in most cases. For instance, some 18% of conventional families reported using or were observed to use a sling-type carrying device, compared to an average of 48% across all nonconventional groups. At 18 months, about 30% of nonconventional families were still breastfeeding, compared to some 10% of the comparison group families.

Two points about the magnitude or absolute amount of implemented changes are relevant. First, the fact that there are mean group differences should not blind us to an important effect: Compared to what *might* have been implemented there is still a long way for the nonconventional group to have gone. At an extreme, for instance, *all* the nonconventional and pronatural families might have been breastfeeding at 2½ years, compared to virtually none of the conventional group doing so after 12 months. Second, many nonconventional and pronatural parents did not sustain many of their initial innovative ideals for very long. Neither of these points gainsay the theoretical and substantive importance of the differences which do appear, but they do put them into perspective.

4. The next summary finding requires at least one illustrative graph (see Fig. 9.1).[1] This graph compares each of the major lifestyle groups (social contract couples, single mothers, living groups and communes, and conventionally married) on the percentage who reported breastfeeding their child from birth through 3 years. These data show that social contract parents are most likely to wean late, and that all the nonconventional family groups are higher than the comparison group until 2 years and 9 months. The top curve on the graph, however, shows cross-cultural data (Whiting, 1968, 1981) on the modal age of

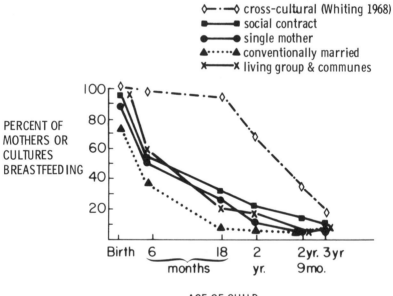

FIG. 9.1.   From Weisner, Bausano, and Kornfein (1983). Putting family ideals into practice: Pronaturalism in conventional and nonconventional California families. *Ethos, 11*(4), 1983. Reproduced by permission of the American Anthropological Association. Not for further reproduction.

---

[1]Figure 9.1 and the other cross-cultural comparisons summarized here, compares *within*-culture subgroup mean differences using the Family Lifestyles sample on the one hand, and reports of the *culturally modal* age at which weaning usually occurs, on the other. Standard deviation differences for the pooled cross-cultural data are not available for these kinds of cross-cultural studies. Thus not all the mothers in the 70% of societies which report a modal age of weaning later than age two are still breastfeeding at age two. However, without denying that there is intra-cultural variance in every society for such practices, it is safe to say that data on this variance would not change the pattern illustrated in Fig. 9.1.

weaning in a large comparative sample (Barry & Paxson, 1971, report similar data). These data show that very few societies begin weaning until after 18 months (although supplemental feeding begins early [Nerlove, 1974]). Compared to the conventional families, then, nonconventional families wean later. But compared to most cultures around the world, the United States weans very early.

Many pronatural or nonconventional mothers perceive their own weaning to be late, and see this as an important, difficult, bold, and controversial innovation in how they relate to their child. Mothers hope that children who breastfeed often, on demand, and for a long period, will be healthier, and sustain a more secure, warm empathic emotional bond with their mother and with others. But in comparative perspective, these mothers weaned relatively early. Will this relatively early weaning nonetheless influence parent-child relationships in the way parents hope? Observational data suggests not.

Put another way, it is surely "natural" (in the sense of being well within our species' behavioral range) to wean later than 18 months. Our species evolved doing just that. The pronatural or nonconventional parents moved in the direction of this cross-culturally common and species-wide practice—but did not do so in very large numbers, and weaned their children at much earlier ages than what they might have attempted to do.

The absolute amount of change in the American sample, compared to what the cross-cultural record shows is possible in implementing other practices, is nearly always very modest. For example, American parents who carried their infants and young toddlers more than 2 hours a day were rare; yet infants and young children in most cultures could easily be carried by their mothers or older siblings and cousins 6 to 8 hours a day. Even longer times would not be at all unusual. Stephens (1972) reports not a single society in his cross-cultural sample where nudity in children through age 4 or so is not expectable as a matter of course. Some 70% of societies in one sample (Barry & Paxson, 1971) co-sleep with their young children, either in the same bed or same room. This same general point holds for many of the data on early child rearing patterns where nonconventional families acted in what they perceived to be a more *natural* way. They generally did move in the direction of what the cross-cultural literature shows that most cultures do (e.g., breastfeed a long time; co-sleep with young children; use arm or sling carrying methods, etc.). However, the movement away from the modal United States pattern (measured for our purposes by the comparison group sample of conventionally married families) was rather modest for the most part. These attempts were often only partially implemented and stopped at earlier ages than is true for many of the world's cultures.

These intentional, bold changes in pronatural relationship styles and socialization patterns were often undertaken with great planning and at a real opportunity cost to parents. However, the parents were constrained in some way in the lengths they went to in changing these relationships. These constraints came from a mix of other, conflicting values; pressures of the ecocultural niche and daily routines, and implicit cultural relationship goals which contradicted the explicit pronatural ideals. I return to this theme in the conclusion.

5. Did interaction styles and actual behavior practices reflect new relationship goals? Did nonconventional or pronatural parents in fact show more warmth with their infants and young children? Were they more affectively labile, diverse, open? Did they touch and hold their children more frequently? Did they in fact show a more loose, "laid back" attitude towards their children's discipline, or respond differently to their children's crying? To anticipate the answer: interaction differences are few.

When the children in the study were 6-months-of-age, home observations were done with each family. Home observers were carefully trained, and reliability between observers was monitored. Observers used a variety of techniques during their visits, including systematic time samples of caretaker-infant or child interactions, using precoded categories; ratings of home environment and affect; event sampling procedures for standardized assessments of feeding, bathing, responses to fussing or crying, and others. The home observers came during the morning hours and stayed through at least one feeding. Family members were not required to be home, if typically they were not home during these times of the day (so if a father worked during this period, he would not have been included in the observations). In fact, however, 95% of the mothers were also primary caretakers, and were home in the morning, so mothers were usually the predominant adult observed with the child.

Pronatural parents hoped to be warm, empathic, laidback, and noncontrolling in social relationships with their children. To measure this, I summarized 15 affect-related measures of interaction styles between caretakers and the 6-month-old-child, including, for example, contingent vocalizations from caretaker to child with positive or negative affect; mutual gazing with positive affect; smiling, touching or holding with positive affect; response to fuss or cry with comfort; amount of ignoring of child-initiated, friendly interactions; and a number of others. A series of two-way analyses of variance took these interaction scores as dependent measures, and pronaturalism and nonconventional family status as independent variables. Of 15 interaction measures, three were significant at the .05 level for pronatural values, and/or nonconventional family lifestyles (amount of mother talk to child with positive affect; amount of verbal interaction with positive affect; and child smiles in response to caretaker presence). The remaining 12 measures showed no significant effects. Two of the three measures which did show differences are linked to more frequent talking and vocalizations between the child and the mother.

As for many of the child care practices, the magnitudes of the differences for the three significant measures were not large. For instance, babies in pronatural/nonconventional families had a mean of 3.8 smiles recorded for a 25-minute time sampling period, versus 3.3 for the comparison group—a statistically significant difference, but not a massive substantive difference. It appears from more detailed qualitative overview of the observational records that adults who were verbally expressive and talkative with everyone in the home, also were more so with their children, and showed more positive and less negative affect during home visits.

DISCUSSION

Close Relationships (Kelley et al., 1983) provides a recent and comprehensive effort to develop the framework for a "science of close interpersonal relationhips," and covers a host of important topics in the study of these relationships—emotion, power, gender, commitment, conflict, and others. McClintock (1983) reviews research on interaction and relationships; she emphasizes the importance of cultural scripts, and the construction of meanings by participants in ongoing relationships. To an important (but not exclusive) degree,

> . . . interaction is not a sequence of stimulus-response pairings or the automatic enactment of internalized scripts. Rather, it is the active creation of chains of causally linked events resulting from the interplay between the interactants' cognition, affect, interpretations, and behavior. (McClintock, 1983, p. 103).

It is in this creative process that most nonconventional families with pronatural ideologies put their faith and efforts. Through mutual family negotiations, parents made intentional efforts to redefine characteristics of their relationships as more natural, and tried to implement their ideology in everyday life. It is at this point that other social and cultural features of relationships intervened in parents' implementation efforts. McClintock calls some of these features "social conditions" (the larger network of relationships around the family); the "family culture," or collective myths about relationships held by parents; and environmental conditions such as household size or daily routine.

The recent resurgence of interest in Vygotsky's model (1978) for the acquisition of cognitive competencies and cultural categories is consistent with these views of how relationships are constituted. Vygotsky emphasized that learning and developmental change occur within activity units, which consist of actors with motives and goals operating under specific local contexts or conditions. The Vygotskian model stands opposed to an "individualistic" developmental perspective in which individuals are acted on by the external environment, with adaptive consequences for each actor (Wertsch et al., 1984). As applied to parental efforts to implement new relationship goals and styles, this social developmental view suggests that parents' relationship goals can never be freed from implicit cultural theories about children, about the person, and about the consequences of social action, all of which have been acquired through the parents' participation in American culture. Ecocultural constraints on pronatural relationship changes influence parental motives, goals, and the contextual circumstances within which implementation of new relationship styles occurs. By cultural default, parents chose relationship styles which perpetuate standard American cultural ideals regarding relationships.

Wertsch et al. argue that the theory of activity

> . . . suggests that independent of characteristics of the individual, the organization of systems of activity at the societal level establishes important parameters that determine the manner in which an individual or group of individuals carries out and masters a particular type of goal-directed action. (Wertsch et al., 1984, p. 171)

American parents learned about relationships and development in American activity units. Parents attempt relationship change within an implicit framework of these same units. It is not merely that "it is hard to make changes in this culture," or that "goals and motives are inevitably inconsistent," although both of these complaints are true (and are frequently made by innovating parents themselves). The larger issue is that change is constrained even if the niche is relatively easy to change, and forgiving of change, and even when pronatural or other goals are relatively consistent, and parental motives are clear.

The reasons for this lie in the social-environmental conditions surrounding activity units. These constraints are much more powerful in shaping close relationships than can be revealed through exclusive attention to dyadic interaction. The analysis of nonconventional family efforts at change and innovation in close family relationships suggests the particular importance of two such effects: ecocultural constraints; and implicit cultural assumptions about parent-child relationships.

Ecocultural Constraints on Relationship Changes

Ecocultural constraints include proximal home environment measures (such as stimulation available, or personnel in the home, or immediate social supports) but are broader. The ecocultural model tries to understand how the local, proximal home environment came to be in the first place—what wider features of society and ecology around the family make a difference in what relationships occur and how they develop (Bronfenbrenner, 1979; Super & Harkness, 1980).

A useful way to describe ecocultural niche effects is by their functions in family and community adaptation (Whiting, 1980). One group of niche influences affects health and mortality (variables such as community safety, health risks, population size, and family size). Another cluster of niche variables affects subsistence, which in our culture involves work roles, the provision of food and shelter, and the division of labor for the household and wider economy. A third class of niche features relates to the child and child care more specifically: who does child care; who shares child care responsibilities and obligations; children's play groups, supports for caretakers, especially women. A final cluster of niche dimensions relates to the knowledge of and availability of permissible alternatives for family and child roles—diversity and heterogeneity. Each of these features of the American niche (health, demographics; subsistence and work; personnel and child care; and complexity) influenced how, how much, or whether, new family relationship goals and ideals were put into practice.

For example, it is striking that pronatural ideals were rarely allowed to interfere with normal medical supervision or illness. Adults might have experimented with unusual diets and medical treatments on themselves without physician intervention, but this did not extend to their children. LeVine (1977) has proposed that child care patterns linked to issues of child or parent health, safety, danger, or risk, would be more resistant to rapid change, and more sheltered from experimentation. This was by and large true of the ways parents implemented pronatural ideas in the Family Lifestyle sample with respect to health.

Similarly, pronatural ideals motivating efforts to change relationships which involve all the family personnel (siblings, fathers, etc.), and/or many different elements of the niche (personnel, play groups, work, etc.) are less easily implemented in the child's schedule than those that can be directly tried out by adults, without wider niche involvement. Thus, many pronatural parents wanted highly involved, warm caretakers around their children in addition to them—fathers, grandparents, friends, older siblings. But to implement such a highly shared caretaking system is difficult (though possible) in our niche. As a result, some 95% of mothers were the primary caretakers of the 6-month-old children, and about 86% at 18 months. *Supplemental* care supporting and helping mothers, however, did increase in nonconventional families; this was easier to implement than substitute or truly shared and co-equal care.

The cultural niche also shapes the family's conception of *possible* plans and scripts for change. For instance, not a single family involved older siblings or other children in regular, responsible child care, even where this would have been available. Yet this form of care is among the most common in societies around the world, and in some American subcultures as well (Stack, 1975; Weisner & Gallimore, 1977). Not a single parent used their sling or carrying device to carry their baby around 6 to 10 hours a day. Very few conceived of breastfeeding past 18 months. No family in our sample loaned their baby out to another household for even a limited period of time. Only a few ever asked for an older child or young adult to be "loaned" to them from another household, to live with them and help care for their child (Goody, 1982). Yet every one of these practices is widespread elsewhere in the world, in other ecocultural niches. And they all *could* have been attempted by pronatural families. Each one would have aided families to be more pronatural in some respects, as parents themselves conceived of this ideal. Implementation of new relationship goals and ideals is thus subtly, surreptitiously shaped by our niche, insofar as the niche sets boundaries on what is "thinkable" as well as doable. The niche thus defines what families are likely to even consider as possible scripts for implementation.

A pattern similar to that found for pronaturalism occurs in parents' efforts to be looser and more "laid back" in their compliance and discipline patterns with their children at 18 months of age. Lambert (Lambert, Hamers, & Frasure-Smith, 1979), suggests that American parents are already unusually "lenient" compared to nine other national samples in verbal reports about how they would handle typical child training and compliance situations. Individualistic and economically expansionist white working and middle class Americans appear to be relatively mild, reasonable and negotiation-prone disciplinarians, compared to other cultures (see also Ellis, Lee, & Peterson, 1978). Home observations focused on compliance training techniques in the Family Lifestyles sample showed a pattern of verbal negotiation, acceptance of deferred compliance to adult requests, and presentation to children by adults of alternatives for conduct. Children were then encouraged to select between these alternatives. Although nonconventional and pronatural families used reason and verbalization of alternatives more often than the comparison group families, differences were small in magnitude (Weisner, 1982). The nonconventional families appear not to have strayed too far from American cultural conventions.

Cultural Assumptions about Relationship Styles

Environmental constraints shade into and are influenced by cultural ideas about the person, the child, and about the character of relationships themselves. Cultural presumptions are both explicit, and also implicit and unarticulated. They are harder to measure directly, and often require qualitative and comparative data to define them, but they are no less powerful for that. Examples include the parental assumption that the young child is an independent decision-maker, whose opinions and wishes need to be elicited and understood by others. Or the idea that parental control of the child, and responsibility for one's own child, is nearly absolute. Or the idea that family relationships are indeed available for experimentation, and that entrepreneurialism in restructuring relationships will be rewarded with good outcomes.

Ochs (1982) and Ochs and Schieffelin (1984) provide examples of differences in implicit cultural beliefs about language training which shows the role of ideas about parent-child relationships in shaping what children learn about relationships. Mothers and other caregivers in their Samoan and Kaluli (New Guinea) samples did not do what Western mothers routinely do with infants and young children during language acquisition (and what the Family Lifestyle sample mothers did with their children). The Western mother will simplify the register used with the child, and vary the pattern of her response to the child and elicitation of speech from the child, to match the child's developing levels. Samoans and Kaluli, in contrast, do not simplify speech or contingently respond at a child's speech level; rather, they model speech which the child should have used to another third party. Yet all these children become competent speakers of their language. The cultural expectation of the Western mother is that the situation should adapt to the child, particularly situations involving speech and skill training. The mother should coregulate the child's speech and social rela-relationships. The contrasting expectation regarding social relationships is that the child should adapt to the situation around him or her. The situation should provide a scaffold for children to use. Training efforts in this approach focus not on dyadic, empathic helping done by adults at the young child's level, but rather on establishing through modeling what the child should be attending to in the situation surrounding him or her which will help in learning.

The implicit American cultural model for parent-child relationships identified by Ochs and Schieffelin was also followed by the Family Lifestyles innovators. Their strategy in relationship change was to alter their own practices, and styles of interaction with their child and mates. Being warmer, more intimate, and even more "laid back," implied making direct active efforts at new styles of behavioral coregulation in social relationships. To be more natural did not imply reducing such direct efforts at control and intervention, or lessening attempts to respond directly to the child. Such a strategy, even if articulated and considered by parents, would have been thought "unnatural."

There seem to be other culturally implicit relationship expectations in Western societies which also appear in the Family Lifestyles sample: an expectation of taking the child's point of view; reflexivity in parent-child relationships; granting a child some control over adults' behavior; the importance of individuation and separation of a child from adults and others in one's family; an implicit permission for children to negotiate over family resources; the inference that there is a private world or self within the child; allowing privacy to the child within the family circle—privacy in possessions, space, and in having one's "own business." These implicit cultural beliefs about parent-child relationships were seldom directly questioned. For the most part, American parents consider them to be *natural* in a sense suggested earlier: they are culturally comfortable and expectable; they "go without saying."[2]

---

[2]There is one group of innovative families which did directly challenge these cultural assumptions about parent-child and family relationships: certain creedal communes. These groups were most likely to share parental controls of important decisions regarding their child with their group. These parents often did place their roles within the collective community ahead of their child's "own needs." These parents did not always provide privacy and choice for their children, and were unwilling to negotiate over issues such as food choice, the daily routine, discipline, or sex role training, as other families did. Such matters were more often predetermined by the ecocultural niche and explicit cultural/religious assumptions of their collective communities. It is striking that it is in just such areas that these parents are most severely criticized by nonmembers. My discussion here excludes this subset of families and their niches and cultural assumptions. (See Werner & Martin, 1979.)

Another largely unquestioned script for interaction with infants and young children is the belief that major responsibility for changing the family and the child rests on the parent—the American cultural theme of individualism and personal responsibility. Many innovative parents created and relied on social networks of friends, kin, and like-minded souls for aid, but these other persons are intended to support and complement parental decisions rather than competing for or coopting parental control. Parents saw such expanded networks as extending their control and decision-making authority, not as reducing it. Few innovative American parents had a passive view of their individual roles and influence.

Another cultural assumption is related to a kind of American entrepreneurialism and pragmatism regarding relationships—try a variety of things, and stay with those that seem successful in the short term. The criterion of success is what works for the parents or children, rather than what is conventional or accepted by the community or by the state. Relationships have this same character—the parent believes that these are manageable, that they can be analyzed, intentionally manipulated, and changed by the parent, with recognizable, immediate outcomes.

American parents also implicitly assume that their relationships with their children are reflexive—that the child has some choice and autonomy in family activities. The parent must at least take the child's point of view into account. The child's feelings and needs are assumed to be worthy of at least some serious attention by parents. The child is asked what food he or she would like to eat, and when and where to go out or play with someone, or which toy or playsuit to wear. Parents take the child's schedule, needs, and likes into account when planning the day. This presumption of a child's autonomy and power in sharing decision-making starts in infancy, and continues throughout childhood. This is clearly visible in the high rates of questioning, negotiations and deferral of compliance recorded at the 18 month and 4½ year periods in the home observations.

But along with granting of an autonomous, private, and sometimes powerful self to the child, the parents establish another requirement: The child must negotiate and collaborate with others' personal business as well. The relationship styles in virtually all the American families in the Family Lifestyle sample—whether relatively more or less innovative and experimental—in large part continued and even intensified this pattern. The parent grants control, autonomy and some decision-making power to the child, but immediately requires that this individuation and separation be combined with emotional dependency of the child on the parents or other adult caretakers. Beatrice Whiting (1977) has called this American dilemma the "dependency hang-up."

A contrasting message about cultural relationships is a predominant one in much of the non-Western world, but was only rarely to be found in the ideology or practices of these American families. In this contrasting view, parents do not grant the child her or his own business and personal autonomy. The presumption of this view is that the child's needs and wishes are not continually taken into account, and that the child does not have control of adult behaviors during bouts of interactions or in the determination of the family's daily routine. But in return for this lessened imputation of power to the child, the child is provided with a very secure sense of group or community attachment. The child can count on interdependence with the larger family group, siblings, and peers. The American child does not experience this kind of confidence and security in *non*parental relationships during the first 6 years of life. The American relationship model presumes that the world outside the family is uncertain, unreliable, dangerous, not to be trusted, and will be very *different* from parental and family relationships. Attachment is to parents and siblings and close relatives and friends, not to the larger community outside the home. The alternative view of relationships is that parental ties are balanced by, even overshadowed by, a child's obligations to others in the family or to other kin in the community, or to work in order to help in family survival. Attachment objects include peers, siblings, and wider extended family, who are often more powerful than the parent. The child sees the parent enmeshed in relationships where the parent relates in just this way him or herself with the wider community. The community and wider circle of kin and companions are powerful and will provide—not only or necessarily the parent. Power and control of the child, and resources important to the child, are openly acknowledged to exist outside the parent and the domestic group altogether.

Pronatural and egalitarian families did try to encourage a wide circle of social support, and they fought against the encapsulation of the nuclear family and the placing of exclusive responsibility for care on the parents. Thus many of the nonconventional families had as an important goal the formation of ''community,'' by reaching out for new networks and nonexclusive marital, economic, and familial and social attachments. But this involvement had a very different implication for basic relationship styles than the non-Western alternatives. These adult ideals about relationships seldom extended very far into the child's daily routine of activities. Parents still made final decisions, and remained in charge of subsistence, discipline and major decisions concerning safety, schooling, health, etc. Parents rarely disengaged themselves from primary responsibility for their children for very long. Such parents made a real effort to extend the caretaking network, and ''share out'' the child to some extent with a circle of friends and like-spirited kin and mates, yet retained American ideals of intense parental bonding.

CONCLUSION

Dyadic and family-level interaction occurs within the context of ecocultural constraints which are not always recognized by actors, even among those who are intentionally striving to analyze and change relationship styles. The two constraints I have illustrated in this essay—the environmental niche, and cultural assumptions about relationships—influence relationship styles both by making some kinds of change structurally difficult (e.g., balancing time-bound work schedules with child care), and by shaping through a kind of cultural preselection, the choices made in forming relationships (e.g., ideas about the individuality of children, or about their power to negotiate relationships). Pronatural changes in parent–child relationships illustrate both these kinds of influences.

The degree of conscious recognition of these influences on relationships varies. Parents were very conscious about changing some aspects of their niche (such as help with child care, or flexible working hours) and perhaps not very aware of others (high American public health standards). Pronatural parents were conscious cultural analysts of sex roles and the medical establishment, but probably not aware of many of their implicit cultural expectations in parent-child relationships.

In spite of the constraining features of the niche and cultural scripts, pronatural families have changed their relationship styles with their mates, friends, and children. They emphasize equality between the sexes as both a political and a relationship goal. They practice their politics and religious beliefs with fervor. They have a view of the environment and ecology which is conserving and appreciative, and is being transmitted to their children. In their construction of and interpretation of family roles and the world around them, such families are innovating. They are teaching their children a different view of their world. Just because implementation of these ideals at the level of interaction has only been modest and selective should not at all suggest that these families are "not different," for they certainly are. Indeed, the transmission of these new cultural *ideals* may be among the most innovative steps parents have taken in changing their children's future relationship styles.

Similarly, the fact that many innovations and experiments cannot be sustained for a long period of time, does not mean that there will not be larger societal changes coming from them. Many of the new ideals of pronatural families have already been widely imitated by large sectors of the population (witness breast-feeding, or natural childbirth, or concern for nutrition). Those beliefs and practices that do spread in this way will finally themselves become encoded in cultural scripts, and become useful, widely shared patterns of American child care and relationship styles. They will then cease to be viewed as innovative experiments, and become one among the accepted alternatives for family lifestyles. Those that will spread in this way will be those that can be implemented and sustained in our ecocultural niche. This process of family innovation and experimentation; followed by partially successful implementation; followed by diffusion through imitation; followed by transformation into more widely shared, stable scripts for use in establishing family relationship styles and child rearing patterns—is precisely the process of cultural evolution at work.

ACKNOWLEDGMENTS

This research is supported by the National Institute of Mental Health Grant No. 1-R04 MH 24947, and Carnegie Corporation Grant B3694-06, Bernice T. Eiduson, Principal Investigator. The work has also been supported by the Department of Psychiatry and Biobehavioral Sciences, UCLA. Portions of this paper are based on Weisner, Bausano, and Kornfein, 1983. Figure 9.1 is reproduced from that paper.

REFERENCES

Bane, M. J. (1976). *Here to stay: American families in the twentieth century.* New York: Basic Books.

Barry, H., & Paxson, L. (1971). Infancy and early childhood: Cross-cultural codes 2. *Ethnology, 10*(4), 466–508.

Bronfenbrenner, U. (1979). *The ecology of human development: Experiments by nature and design.* Cambridge, MA: Harvard University Press.

Children's Defense Fund. (1984). *A Children's Defense Budget. An Analysis of the President's FY 1985 Budget and Children.* Washington, D.C.: Children's Defense Fund, Inc.

Eiduson, B. (1978). Child development in emergent family styles: A research update. *Children Today,' 7,* 24–31.

Eiduson, B., Cohen, J., & Alexander, J. (1973). Alternatives in child rearing in the 1970s. *American Journal of Orthopsychiatry, 43,* 720–731.

Eiduson, B. T., & Forsythe, A. (1983). Life change events in alternative family styles. In E. J. Callahan & K. A. McClusky (Eds.), *Life-span developmental psychology: Non-normative life events.* New York: Academic Press.

Eiduson, B. T., Kornfein, M., Zimmerman, I. L., & Weisner, T. S. (1982). Comparative socialization practices in traditional and alternative families. In M. Lamb (Ed.), *Nontraditional families: Parenting and child development* (pp. 315–346). Hillsdale, NJ: Lawrence Erlbaum Associates.

Eiduson, B., & Weisner, T. S. (1978). Alternative family styles: Effects on young children. In J. Stevens & M. Mathews (Eds.), *Mother/child, father/child relationships* (pp. 197–221). Washington, D.C.: National Association for the Education of Young Children.

Ellis, G., Lee, G., & Peterson, L. (1978). Supervision and conformity: A cross-cultural analysis. *American Journal of Sociology, 84,* 386–403.

Goody, E. (1982). *Parenthood and social reproduction: Fostering and occupational roles in West Africa.* Cambridge: Cambridge University Press.

Kelley, H. H., Berscheid, E., Christensen, A., Harvey, J. H., Huston, T. L., Levinger, G., McClintock, E., Peplau, L. A., & Peterson, D. R. (1983). *Close relationships.* San Francisco: W. H. Freeman.

Kornfein, M., Weisner, T., & Martin, J. (1977). Women into mothers: Experimental family lifestyles. In J. R. Chapman & M. Gates (Eds.), *Women into wives: The legal and economic impact of marriage* (pp. 259–291). Beverly Hills: Sage Publications.

Lambert, W., Hamers, J., & Frasure-Smith, N. (1979). *Child-rearing values: A cross-cultural study.* New York: Praeger.

Lasch, C. (1979). *Haven in a heartless world: The family besieged.* New York: Basic Books.

LeVine, R. (1977). Child rearing as cultural adaptation. In P. H. Leiderman, S. Tulkin, & A. Rosenfeld (Eds.), *Culture and infancy. Variations in the human experience* (pp. 15–27). New York: Academic Press.

Masnick, G., & Bane, M. J. (1980). *The nation's families: 1960–1990.* Cambridge, MA: Joint Center for Urban Studies of MIT and Harvard University.

McClintock, E. (1983). Interaction. In H. Kelley, E. Berscheid, A. Christensen, J. Harvey, T. Huston, G. Levinger, E. McClintock, L. Peplau, & D. Peterson (Eds.), *Close relationships* (pp. 68–109). San Francisco: W. H. Freeman.

Nerlove, S. (1974). Women's workload and infant feeding practices: A relationship with demographic implications. *Ethnology, 13,* 207–214.

Ochs, E. (1982). Talking to children in Western Samoa. *Language in Society, 11,* 77–104.

Ochs, E., & Schieffelin, B. (1984). Language acquisition and socialization: Three developmental stories and their implications. In R. Shweder & R. LeVine (Eds.), *Culture and its acquisition.* New York: Academic Press.

Stack, C. (1975). Who raises black children? Transactions of child givers and child receivers. In T. Williams (Ed.), *Socialization and communication in primary groups* (pp. 183–205). The Hague: Mouton.

Stephens, W. (1972). A cross-cultural study of modesty. *Behavior Science Notes, 7,* 1–28.

Super, C., & Harkness, S. (Eds.). (1980). *Anthropological perspectives on child development. New directions for child development, No. 8.* San Francisco: Jossey-Bass.

Tufte, V., & Myerhoff, B. (Eds.). (1979). *Changing images of the family.* New Haven: Yale University Press.

Vygotsky, L. S. (1978). *Mind in society.* Cambridge, MA: Harvard University Press.

Weisner, T. (1982). As we choose: Family life styles, social class and compliance. In J. G. Kennedy & R. B. Edgerton (Eds.), *Culture and ecology: Eclectic perspective.* Washington, D.C.: American Anthropological Association.

Weisner, T., Bausano, M., & Kornfein, M. (1983). Putting family ideals into practice: Pronaturalism in conventional and nonconventional California families. *Ethos, 11*(4), 278–304.

Weisner, T., & Gallimore, R. (1977). My brother's keeper: Child and sibling caretaking. *Current Anthropology, 18*(2), 169–191.

Weisner, T., & Martin, J. (1979). Learning environments for infants: Communes and conventionally married families in California. *Alternative Lifestyles, 2,* 201–242.

Weisner, T., & Weibel, J. C. (1981). Home environments and family lifestyles in California. *Environment and Behavior, 13,* 417–460.

Wertsch, J. V., Minick, N., & Arms, F. J. (1984). The creation of context in joint problem-solving. In B. Rogoff & J. Lave (Eds.), *Everyday cognition: Its development in social context.* Cambridge, MA: Harvard University Press.

Whiting, B. (1977, Sept.). *The dependency hang-up and experiments in alternative life styles.* Paper presented at the American Sociological Association, Chicago.

Whiting, B. (1980). Culture and social behavior: A model for the development of social behavior. *Ethos, 8* (2), 95–116.

Whiting, J. (1968). Methods and problems in cross-cultural research. In G. Lindzey & E. Aronson (Eds.), *The handbook of social psychology* (Vol. 2, 2nd ed.). (pp. 693–728). Reading, MA: Addison-Wesley.

Whiting, J. (1981). Environmental constraints on infant care practices. In R. H. Munroe, R. L. Munroe, & B. Whiting (Eds.), *Handbook of cross-cultural human development* (pp. 155–180). New York: Garland Press.

Zimmerman, I. L. (1981, April). *Intellectual competence in three year olds reared in alternative lifestyles.* Paper presented at the meeting of the Society for Research in Child Development, Boston, MA.

Author Index

Subject Index

213